GOOD COOKING
MADE·EASY

GOOD COOKING
MADE·EASY

Compiled by Bridget Jones

HAMLYN

This edition published in 1986 by
Hamlyn Publishing
Bridge House, London Road, Twickenham, Middlesex, England

© Copyright Hamlyn Publishing 1986
a division of The Hamlyn Publishing Group Ltd

First published as a collection under the title
Les Bonnes Recettes de France
© 1984 La Nouvelle Librairie

ISBN 0 600 32507 5

Set in 10 and 11pt Monophoto Plantin 110
by Tameside Filmsetting Ltd, Lancashire, England

Printed in Czechoslovakia

CONTENTS

Measuring accurately

Correct measuring of ingredients is essential to ensure consistent results. All measurements given in this book are level unless otherwise stated.

Choosing measuring cups: When purchasing measuring cups you should choose one set for dry ingredients and another for liquids.

For dry ingredients: Buy a set of four graduated measuring cups consisting of a $\frac{1}{4}$-cup, $\frac{1}{3}$-cup, $\frac{1}{2}$-cup and 1-cup measure. Always level off with the edge of a spatula or knife.

For liquid ingredients: Buy a 1-cup measuring cup, the rim of which is above the 1-cup line to avoid spillage. 2-cup and 1-quart size measuring cups are also very useful. Set the cup on a level surface. Lower your head so that the measuring line will be at eye level and fill the cup to the correct mark.

Choosing measuring spoons: A good set of measuring spoons will give you accurate small measurements. It should include $\frac{1}{8}$-teaspoon, $\frac{1}{4}$-teaspoon, $\frac{1}{2}$-teaspoon, 1-teaspoon, $\frac{1}{2}$-tablespoon and 1-tablespoon measurements. 16 tablespoons equal 1 cup.

Equivalent measures

Pinch	As much as can be held between the tip of the finger and the thumb
3 teaspoons	1 tablespoon
2 tablespoons	$\frac{1}{8}$ cup
4 tablespoons	$\frac{1}{4}$ cup
5 tablespoons + 1 teaspoon	$\frac{1}{3}$ cup
8 tablespoons	$\frac{1}{2}$ cup
10 tablespoons + 2 teaspoons	$\frac{2}{3}$ cup
12 tablespoons	$\frac{3}{4}$ cup
16 tablespoons	1 cup
2 cups	1 pint
2 pints	1 quart
1 quart	4 cups
4 quarts	1 gallon
16 oz (dry measure)	1 lb

Can sizes: We have tried to utilize whole cans of ingredients whenever possible.

Flour: Unless specified, either all-purpose or self-rising flour may be used in the recipes. If using self-rising flour, omit baking powder and salt if called for. For fine-textured cakes, you may substitute $1\frac{1}{8}$ cups cake flour for each cup of all-purpose flour. Seasoned flour is flour mixed with salt and freshly ground pepper.

Butter or margarine: One ($\frac{1}{4}$-lb) stick of butter or margarine equals $\frac{1}{2}$ cup or 8 tablespoons. If a recipe calls for melted butter, it doesn't matter if you measure it before or after melting – the result will be the same.

Equivalents

Eggs

5 eggs	about 1 cup
8–10 egg whites	1 cup
12–15 egg yolks	1 cup

Butter or margarine

2 tablespoons	1 oz
$\frac{1}{2}$ cup	$\frac{1}{4}$ lb (1 stick)
2 cups	1 lb

Dairy products

1 cup milk	$\frac{1}{2}$ cup evaporated milk + $\frac{1}{2}$ cup water
1 cup milk	$\frac{1}{4}$ cup powdered whole milk + 1 cup water
1 cup cream	2 cups whipped cream
1 cup cottage cheese	8 oz
$\frac{1}{4}$ lb Cheddar or American cheese	1 cup shredded

Flour: Flour is sifted before measuring

4 cups all-purpose flour	1 lb
1 cup cake flour	1 cup all-purpose flour, minus 2 tablespoons
2 tablespoons flour	1 tablespoon cornstarch for thickening
5 teaspoons flour	2 teaspoons arrowroot for thickening

Sugar: Confectioner's sugar is measured before sifting
Brown sugar is measured firmly packed

2 cups sugar	1 lb
$3\frac{1}{4}$–4 cups confectioner's sugar	1 lb
$2\frac{1}{4}$ cups brown sugar	1 lb

Key to symbols

easy	moderately easy	difficult

cheap	moderately cheap	expensive

time guide

INTRODUCTION

Whether you are looking for a dish to serve for a family meal or something special to present at a company dinner, there are lots of ideas to choose from in the chapters which follow. All the recipes have symbols which indicate whether they are likely to be cheap or expensive, easy or difficult, or quick or time-consuming to prepare. This is a useful guide if you are unfamiliar with the dish or any particular cooking technique which it employs: however, it is difficult to estimate the preparation time for any dish because, of course, people work at different speeds and the more experienced the cook the quicker he or she will be. The advantage which the experienced cook often has in addition to speed and well-polished culinary skills is a knowledge of all the short-cuts which save on time without resulting in any loss of quality.

Many kitchens are equipped with a selection of time-saving electrical appliances and gadgets which perform an incredible range of tasks from opening cans to making ravioli. No matter how well equipped the kitchen, if the modern technology sits idle in a corner then it is of no practical help, but if these appliances are put to full use, then they can save the cook a great deal of time.

Kitchen efficiency does not depend on gadgetry alone: being well-organized about the utensils required, the order in which the ingredients are prepared and the clearing up are all more important. The notes which follow may be of some help when it comes to planning your kitchen time.

Planning the menu
No matter how informal the meal, there has to be a certain amount of decision-making in advance about what to serve. If you are planning a company dinner, then it is important to plan the menu so that it is well balanced in texture, color and flavor. When you are thinking about the dishes you should also bear in mind the time you can set aside to prepare them and your ability; it is not a good idea to aim to serve several complicated courses, all requiring attention right at the end of cooking.

The chapter introductions give some advice on selecting dishes but there are a few points to remember whatever the course. If you are entertaining, then it is best to get as much of the cooking completed in advance so that you are free to be with your guests. Try to keep the last-minute preparation to the minimum – a salad, the vegetables or the gravy, for example. Once you have decided what to cook, try to work out a rough time-scale for the cooking, taking into account any dishes which can be frozen, chilled or marinated well in advance. Decide which items really do need attention just before they are served and be prepared as far as possible for this.

Cutting down on preparation time
Organization is the key to success when it comes to cooking. Disaster can result from an overcrowded work surface leaving little or no space for transferring hot pots from the stove, no room to roll out the pastry, or worse, meaning that the bowl or dish near the edge is knocked on to the floor scattering the contents everywhere. So, try to keep the kitchen tidy – keep the dish-washing to a minimum or stack it in the dishwasher as you work, put all the scraps and unwanted peelings or wrappers in the disposal or garbage can and keep the food preparation as

neat as possible. This may seem obvious and unwanted advice but it does make sense.

There are a few practical hints which can often help with the most basic preparation. Chopping onions, for example, can be quicker if the onion is cut in half, laid flat on the board, then cut into slices in one direction. Holding the slices firmly together cut across them to give small pieces. If the onion should be finely chopped, then make the slices thin; for chunky pieces make the slices thicker. A quick way of chopping parsley is to put the washed and trimmed herb into a coffee mug, then snip at it with a pair of scissors – the pieces will not be evenly tiny but usually good enough for a quick garnish or to flavor casseroles, soups and sauces. This way of chopping parsley is ideal if you don't want to employ a chopping board or if you don't have a very sharp knife.

Kitchen scissors are a useful accessory which are often forgotten – they can be invaluable for trimming the edges off pastry, for cutting out pastry leaves for decoration (if you are confident enough to make them freehand) and for trimming excess fat from meat. They are also ideal for snipping chives and scallions, for cutting fish fillets and bacon into strips and for lots of similar tasks.

If you do have the additional help of electrical appliances, then be sure you make the most of them. Remember to read the manufacturer's instructions and always follow their guidelines. Food mixers and blenders are very commonplace pieces of equipment. Remember to use the mixer for preparing creamed mixtures of all types, for beating egg whites, for whipping cream, for making batters and mayonnaise. You can also turn to the food mixer if you are creaming savory butters, rubbing the fat into flour to make pastry or similar mixtures and preparing a range of frostings. If you have a large food mixer then it will probably cope with bread dough, fruit cakes and even mashed potatoes.

The blender is invaluable when it comes to making sauces, soups and purées. This piece of equipment can also be used for making bread crumbs, for crushing ice cubes, and for chopping or mincing dry ingredients like nuts and herbs. Mayonnaise prepared in the blender is less likely to curdle than that made by hand

and lumpy sauces can be rescued by processing them in a blender until smooth. For pâtés, dips and other similar creamy mixtures, turn to the blender – you will find life much easier than if you spend hours battling with a grinder, sieve or food masher.

A more recent addition to the range of time-saving equipment is the food processor. This compact piece of equipment will carry out most of the tasks which a food mixer can fulfill and many of those which a blender will perform. In addition, a food processor can be used for lots of the simple yet time-consuming tasks, like chopping onions, slicing vegetables and grating cheese. For making cakes and pastry, even bread dough, and for puréeing, blending and grinding, there is no better utensil in the kitchen. Many of the models available are also designed to be easy to assemble and simple to clean.

When it comes to the cooking time which the dish requires, there are often ways in which even this can be reduced. Microwave ovens offer a speedy solution to many cooking processes. For example vegetables and rice can be cooked quite successfully in the microwave along with fish dishes and some chicken dishes. The important point to remember is that microwave cooking requires a whole new approach and it is a good idea to take careful note of the manufacturer's suggested recipes. By experimenting with different foods and dishes you will establish which are successful and which you choose to cook in the microwave oven.

Pressure cookers have been around for years but they still play an important part when it comes to cooking the tougher cuts of meat quickly and successfully. For steaming vegetables, making steamed puddings and for a broad range of other recipes you can use the pressure cooker with confidence.

Slow cookers work on a completely different principle – these employ a very low temperature to cook food slowly over a period of many hours. Successful for meat casseroles and dried legume dishes, these cookers have fairly limited use and require a fair amount of forethought. However, if you do want to prepare a full-flavored, tender casserole and think far enough ahead to prepare all the ingredients and set the dish cooking then you will find this sort of appliance very helpful.

First Courses

The menu centers on the main course of the meal but it is the opening dish which is the one to tempt the appetite and offer a sample of the quality of the food to follow. If this course is lacking in flavor it will dampen the diners' enthusiasm and if it is too rich or filling there will be no room for the main dish. A little forethought and some careful planning will ensure that this opening recipe is a good one to serve.

The food should be chosen to complement the main dish, offering a contrast in texture and flavor. The portions should be small and attractively presented. If the main course is a cold dish, then a hot appetizer may be welcome. In warmer weather, or if the main dish is a heart-warming hotpot, for example, it may be preferable to offer a light, cool savory cocktail or a splendid platter of mixed hors d'oeuvre.

In this chapter you will find a wide variety of recipes ranging from classic Shrimp Cocktails and Eggs in Aspic to a selection of quiches, pies and pastry dishes as well as interesting Eggplant Fritters, stuffed tomatoes and savory crêpes. Select a recipe which differs from the main food of the meal – a seafood specialty before meat or an unusual vegetable dish if the main course vegetables are fairly ordinary. If the main dish is a fish one, then why not serve a meaty quiche, Beef in Aspic or Ham Cornets for the first course?

Offer some hot crisp toast, warm crusty bread or nutty whole wheat rolls with the appetizer (depending on the texture of the dish and whether it is a light or filling creation). It is also important when planning a dinner party to make sure that you have chosen dishes which you feel confident enough to make. Usually it is best to select an appetizer which can be prepared in advance, ready for serving or for putting in the oven at the last minute. This way you will be free to relax with your guests instead of performing cooking chores in the kitchen.

Lastly, remember to prepare the garnishes, butter dish and bread basket in advance. If you really do not want to prepare an appetizer, or if the main part of the meal is quite substantial, then why not offer a simple selection of colorful crudités instead?

Beef in Aspic with Four Sauces

Serves 8

½ lb carrots, thinly sliced
4 lb flank steak, cut into pieces
½ lb onions, thinly sliced
3 sprigs thyme
1 bay leaf
salt and pepper
1 quart dry white wine
½ cup butter
2 envelopes unflavored gelatin
1 celery stalk, sliced
3 sprigs tarragon
1 small bunch chives

Set aside about 30 carrot slices for garnish. Put the beef into a deep dish with the rest of the carrots, the onions, thyme, bay leaf, salt and pepper. Add the white wine and marinate for 12 hours in a cool place, turning the meat from time to time.

Drain the pieces of beef, reserving the marinade. Melt the butter in a flameproof casserole and brown the meat. Add the marinade, cover and cook for 2 hours over a medium heat, then a further 2 hours over a low heat.

Remove the meat and carrots from the casserole. Set aside. Add the gelatin to the broth and stir to dissolve. Strain and leave to cool.

Cook the celery for 10 minutes in boiling salted water. Cut the reserved carrot slices into flower shapes.

Coat a terrine with the aspic. Garnish the sides with tarragon leaves and the carrot shapes, so that they look like flowers. Remember to put the carrots in first so that the "flowers" will be the right way up when the terrine is unmolded. On the bottom of the terrine make a lattice shape with individual chives. Put the carrots around the edge and pieces of celery in the lattice work. Pour over a little aspic and leave to set in a cool place.

Arrange the meat and the cooked carrots in the dish. Press down well, taking care not to damage the edges. Then pour over the rest of the aspic. Refrigerate for at least 5 hours.

Prepare the tray of sauces: horseradish sauce with a little cream added, tomato chutney, Garlic Mayonnaise (see page 399) and sour cream with chopped chives and capers.

To unmold the terrine: plunge it into hot water for 30 seconds. Arrange on a serving dish and return to the refrigerator for 5 minutes. Serve with the sauces and toast.

Meat Pastries

Serves 4

½ lb ground beef
1 onion, finely chopped
1 shallot, finely chopped
2–3 teaspoons chopped parsley
1 tablespoon strong mustard
salt and pepper
1 (14-oz) package frozen puff
   pastry, thawed
2 slices cooked ham, halved
1 egg, beaten
lettuce for serving

Put the ground beef into a mixing bowl and add the onion, shallot, parsley and mustard. Sprinkle with salt and pepper and mix thoroughly.

On a lightly floured board, roll out the pastry to a thickness of ½ inch and cut out eight rectangles. Reserve the pastry trimmings. Divide the filling into four balls and put one on each of four pastry rectangles. Cover each with half a slice of ham then with the remaining pastry rectangles. Moisten the pastry edges and press together to seal. Decorate with strips made from the pastry trimmings. Brush with egg and bake in a preheated 400° oven for 20 minutes. Serve hot, on a bed of lettuce.

Mussel Quiche

Serves 6

1 quart fresh mussels, well
  scrubbed
1 bouquet garni
1 onion, thinly sliced
6 tablespoons white wine
a few black peppercorns
pinch of cayenne
$\frac{1}{4}$ cup butter
2 cups thinly sliced mushrooms
2 tablespoons flour
1 cup milk
salt and pepper
pinch of grated nutmeg
$\frac{1}{2}$ cup grated Gruyère cheese
1 (14-oz) package frozen puff
  pastry, thawed

If any of the mussels are open, tap them and discard if they do not close. Put them in a large kettle with the bouquet garni, onion, white wine, a few peppercorns and the cayenne. Bring to a boil. Simmer for 5 to 6 minutes until the shells open. Discard any mussels that do not open. Keep the mussels hot. Melt 2 tablespoons butter in a skillet and brown the mushrooms. Set aside.

Make a white sauce: melt the rest of the butter in a small saucepan, over a low heat. Add the flour and stir for 1 to 2 minutes. Remove from the heat and gradually add the milk. Season with salt and pepper and add the nutmeg. Return to the heat and stir for about 5 minutes until the sauce thickens. Remove from the heat and add the grated Gruyère.

On a lightly floured board, roll out the puff pastry to a thickness of $\frac{1}{4}$ inch and line a dampened quiche dish. Shell the mussels and arrange them in the pastry case. Add the mushrooms and pour the sauce on top. Bake in a preheated 425° oven for 20 minutes.

Potato Nests

Serves 6

2½ cups Potato Purée (below)
2 tablespoons butter
2 cups thinly sliced mushrooms
3 cups skinless boneless chicken
   meat, cut into strips
salt and pepper
few parsley sprigs

Spoon the potato purée into a pastry bag and pipe six purée nests on a buttered baking sheet. Bake in a preheated 400° oven for 10 minutes or until golden.

Meanwhile, melt the butter in a pan and brown the mushrooms. Add the chicken strips and heat through. Season with salt and pepper.

Fill the purée nests with the chicken mixture and serve immediately, garnished with parsley sprigs.

Potato Purée

Cook 1 lb potatoes in boiling salted water for 20 minutes. Drain thoroughly and mash until smooth. Beat in 2 tablespoons of butter and 2 tablespoons milk. Beat with a wooden spoon or press the potato through a sieve.

Snails with Garlic Butter

Serves 4

1 lb (4 sticks) butter, softened
2 tablespoons coarsely chopped
  parsley
2 tablespoons chopped garlic
2 tablespoons dried mixed
  herbs
3 shallots, finely sliced
juice of 1 lemon
salt and pepper
24 canned snails, drained, with
  shells separate
coarse salt for serving (optional)

Mix the butter with the parsley, garlic, herbs and shallots. Gradually blend in the lemon juice and season with salt and pepper. Mix thoroughly and place a little of the mixture at the bottom of each snail shell. Add a snail and finish filling the shells with the seasoned butter. Place the shells in an ovenproof dish and bake in a preheated 375° oven for 10 minutes, taking care not to boil the butter. Serve immediately, arranged on a bed of coarse salt, if desired.

Shrimp Cocktails

Serves 4

½ lb cooked shrimp in shell
2 avocados
3 tomatoes, quartered
1 head Bibb or Boston lettuce
¼ cup Vinaigrette Dressing
   (page 410)
¼ cup Mayonnaise (page 409)

Reserve a few shrimp in shell for decoration and shell the others. Halve the avocados, discard the seed and peel carefully. Cut the flesh into large dice. Put the avocado flesh, the tomatoes and shrimp into a salad bowl and mix.

Line four individual serving glasses with lettuce leaves, then fill with the shrimp mixture. Sprinkle each serving with 1 tablespoon Vinaigrette dressing. Decorate with Mayonnaise and the reserved shrimp in shell.

Crudités

Serves 6

1 green pepper
1 small bunch radishes
1 cucumber, peeled and diced
1 lb carrots, grated
½ head white cabbage, shredded
½ head red cabbage, shredded
4 tomatoes, quartered
1 teaspoon chopped parsley
¾ cup Vinaigrette Dressing
   (page 410)

Remove stalk and cut the green pepper in half; remove seeds and pith. Chop the pepper. Make two cross-shaped cuts lengthwise in each radish, without cutting right through.

Put the cucumber into the center of a large round serving dish. Arrange the other vegetables attractively around them. Sprinkle with parsley and serve with the Vinaigrette dressing.

Carrot and Zucchini Quiche

Serves 4

½ lb carrots, thinly sliced
½ lb zucchini, thinly sliced
1¼ quantities Basic Pie Pastry
   (page 431)
1 cup Potato Purée (page 14)
1 cup grated Gruyère cheese
1 teaspoon dried chervil
salt and pepper

Cook the carrots in boiling salted water for about 5 minutes. Plunge the zucchini into the boiling water and leave carrots and zucchini to cook for a further 5 minutes. Drain well.

On a lightly floured board, roll out the pastry to a thickness of ½ inch and use to line a quiche or flan dish. Arrange the carrots and zucchini in the pastry case and cover with a layer of potato purée. Sprinkle with Gruyère and chervil and season with salt and pepper. Bake in a preheated 400° oven for 30 minutes. Serve warm.

Stuffed Artichoke Hearts

Serves 6

6 globe artichokes
3 tablespoons butter
½ lb cooked ham, diced
6 tablespoons Tomato sauce
   (page 391)
1 (8-oz) can peas, drained
salt and pepper
1 tablespoon peanut oil
few sprigs parsley or chervil

Break the stems off the artichokes and remove the driest of the outside leaves. Cut off the top of the leaves, leaving about two-thirds of the vegetable. Cook the artichokes for 10 minutes in boiling salted water.

Melt 1 tablespoon butter in a skillet and brown the ham. Add the tomato sauce and peas. Season to taste and leave to simmer.

Meanwhile drain the artichokes thoroughly and remove their chokes. To do this remove the inner leaves and pull out the fine leaves which are attached to the hairy choke; this should lift out in one piece but remove any remaining hairs. Heat the oil and the rest of the butter in another skillet and add the artichokes. When golden, arrange them on a serving dish and fill with the hot stuffing. Serve garnished with a few sprigs of parsley or chervil.

Toasted Cheese and Ham Sandwiches with Tomato

Serves 4

2 slices cooked ham, halved
8 slices white bread
¼ cup Béchamel sauce (page 384)
4 slices Gruyère cheese
3 tomatoes, sliced
¼ cup grated Gruyère cheese

Fold the ham slices in half. Spread four slices of bread with a little béchamel and place a slice of folded ham and a slice of Gruyère on top. Cover each with another slice of bread, then with one or two slices of tomato. Sprinkle each sandwich with grated Gruyère. Bake in a preheated 425° oven for about 20 minutes or until the cheese is melted and golden. Garnish with leftover tomato slices and serve at once.

Potted Meat (Rillettes)

Makes about 2 lb potted meat

1 lb lard, diced
1½ lb lean boneless pork, diced
pinch of ground allspice
pinch of grated nutmeg
1 teaspoon chopped fresh thyme
    or ½ teaspoon dried thyme
salt and pepper

Melt the lard over a gentle heat and add the pork, spices, thyme, about 2 tablespoons salt and a few pinches of pepper. Mix well and leave to cook gently in a covered pan for 4 or 5 hours, stirring occasionally.

At the end of cooking, grind the meat and press it down well with a fork. Taste and adjust the seasoning. Return to the heat for a few minutes, then pack into storage jars with airtight lids. Pack the meat in well, pressing it down. Allow to cool before sealing the jars and store for at least 4 or 5 days before eating.

Surprise Croquettes

Serves 6

2 lb potatoes
3 eggs, beaten
2 tablespoons butter
salt and pepper
¼ cup dry white bread crumbs
1 quart peanut oil
2 (5-oz) cans or jars almond-
   stuffed green olives, drained

Cook the potatoes in boiling salted water for 20 minutes. Drain and mash them. Blend in two-thirds of the eggs and the butter and season with salt and pepper to taste. Leave to cool.

Put the remaining egg into a shallow dish and put the bread crumbs into another one.

Heat the oil for deep frying to 375°, or until a bread cube browns in 50 seconds.

Form the potato mixture into balls and enclose a stuffed olive in each. Roll each ball in the beaten egg, then coat in the bread crumbs.

Deep fry the potato balls in small batches so they do not stick to each other. When golden, remove with a slotted spoon and drain on paper towels. Serve hot.

Eggplant Fritters

Serves 4

1¼ cups flour
1 egg, beaten
1¼–1½ cups beer
salt and pepper
4 eggplants
2 egg whites
1 quart peanut oil

Make the batter: put the flour, egg and beer into a bowl. Add a pinch of salt and beat with a whisk until thick. Leave to stand for 1 hour in a cool place.

Meanwhile, peel the eggplants. Cut into round slices ¼ inch thick and put into a bowl. Sprinkle with salt to draw out their bitter juices and leave for 20 minutes.

Just before making the fritters, rinse, drain and dry the eggplant slices. Flour them lightly. Beat the egg whites with a pinch of salt until standing in stiff peaks and add to the batter, cutting them in with a metal spoon.

Heat the oil for deep frying to 375° or until a bread cube browns in 50 seconds. Dip the eggplant slices in the batter and fry in the oil until golden. Drain thoroughly on paper towels, sprinkle with salt and pepper and serve very hot.

Carrot Mold

Serves 6

2 lb carrots
1 cup milk, warmed
salt and pepper
3 eggs, beaten
parsley sprigs for garnish

Cut four medium-sized carrots in half lengthwise. Cut two of them into slices and set aside. Chop the rest of the carrots and cook in a pan of boiling salted water for 25 minutes.

Meanwhile, cook the carrot slices and carrot strips in another saucepan of boiling salted water for 10 minutes. Drain thoroughly and set aside.

Drain the chopped carrots and purée in a blender or food processor, gradually adding the milk. Add salt and pepper to the eggs and mix with the carrot purée.

Butter a 1½-quart charlotte mold. Line the bottom and sides with carrot strips and slices and fill with the purée. Cover with strips of carrots and bake in a preheated 350° oven for 20 minutes. Remove from the oven and leave to cool a little before unmolding. Garnish with parsley.

Mushroom Pie

Serves 4

1 (14-oz) package frozen puff
    pastry, thawed
2 tablespoons butter
2 tablespoons flour
$2\frac{1}{2}$ cups milk
salt and pepper
pinch of grated nutmeg
$\frac{1}{2}$ lb skinless, boneless cooked
    chicken meat, sliced
$\frac{1}{2}$ lb flat mushrooms, chopped

On a lightly floured board, roll out the pastry to a thickness of $\frac{3}{4}$ inch and use to line a shallow 8-inch square baking pan. Prick the bottom, line with parchment paper and weight down with baking beans. Bake blind in a preheated 400° oven for 10 minutes.

Meanwhile, make a white sauce: melt the butter over a low heat. Add the flour and stir for 1 to 2 minutes. Remove from the heat and gradually add the milk. Season and return to the heat. Sprinkle with grated nutmeg and stir for about 5 minutes until the sauce thickens. Add the chicken and the mushrooms.

Discard the beans and parchment paper from the pastry case and fill with the sauce mixture. Bake in a preheated 400° oven for about 15 minutes. Serve at once.

Mixed Hors d'Oeuvre

Serves 6

$\frac{3}{4}$ lb potatoes, cubed
6 slices salami
$\frac{3}{4}$ cup capers
few lettuce leaves
2 tomatoes, quartered
1 small bunch radishes, sliced
1 (8-oz) can button mushrooms,
   drained and halved
few gherkins, chopped
4 shallots, thinly sliced
1 cup pimiento-stuffed olives,
   sliced

Cook the potatoes for 20 minutes in boiling salted water. Drain.

Roll the slices of salami into cornets and fill them with the capers.

Line a large serving platter with the lettuce leaves and arrange all the ingredients on it.

Ham Cornets with Asparagus

Serves 4

2 lb asparagus, trimmed
$\frac{2}{3}$ cup Mayonnaise (page 409)
$\frac{1}{2}$ (16-oz) can mixed diced
    vegetables, drained
4 slices smoked ham
salt
2 tomatoes, quartered
1 cup black olives
2 hard-cooked eggs
few sprigs fennel
few sprigs chervil or parsley
    (optional)

Tie the asparagus in a bundle, stand it in a deep saucepan of boiling salted water and simmer for about 10 minutes.

Meanwhile, stir the Mayonnaise into the mixed vegetables. Roll the slices of ham into cornets, fill them with the mayonnaise mixture and arrange them on a serving dish.

Drain the asparagus, season lightly with salt and arrange between the ham cornets. Garnish with the tomato quarters, black olives and one hard-cooked egg, quartered.

Chop the yolk of the second egg and sprinkle in the center of the dish. Garnish with sprigs of fennel and chervil if wished.

Leek Quiche

Serves 4

2 lb leeks
$\frac{1}{4}$ cup butter
$1\frac{1}{4}$ quantities Basic Pie Pastry
  (page 431)
1 egg, beaten
$\frac{2}{3}$ cup Crème Fraîche (page 398)
salt and pepper

Cook the leeks for 10 minutes in boiling water. Drain and chop them. Melt the butter in a skillet and fry the leeks for about 5 minutes.

On a lightly floured board, roll out the pastry to a thickness of $\frac{1}{4}$ inch and use to line a quiche or flan dish. Mix the egg with the Crème fraîche and season well with salt and pepper.

Fill the pastry case with the leeks and pour over the crème fraîche mixture. Bake in a preheated 400° oven for about 35 minutes. Serve warm or cold.

Veal Quiche with Red Wine Sauce

Serves 4

$1\frac{1}{2}$ cups diced cooked veal
$\frac{1}{4}$ cup flour
$2\frac{1}{2}$ cups milk
4 eggs, beaten
salt and pepper
2 shallots, thinly sliced
1 bouquet garni
$2\frac{1}{2}$ cups red wine
2 tablespoons butter

Put the meat into a buttered quiche or flan dish. Sift 3 tablespoons flour into a bowl and gradually add the milk, then the eggs. Season with salt and pepper. Pour into the dish and bake in a preheated 400° oven for 25 minutes.

Meanwhile, put the shallots into a small saucepan with the bouquet garni and cover with the red wine. Bring to a boil and continue boiling until the liquid has reduced by half. Strain and pour back into the rinsed-out pan. Set aside.

Blend the butter with the rest of the flour and season with salt and pepper. Gradually stir into the sauce, then return to the heat and simmer gently, stirring constantly, for 3 to 4 minutes until the sauce thickens.

Remove the quiche from the oven and unmold it at once. Serve with the sauce.

Ham and Goat's Cheese Loaf

Serves 5

¼ lb goat's milk cheese, rind
    scraped off
1 lb cream cheese
pepper
1½ teaspoons dried chervil
1 cup crushed walnuts
8 fairly large slices cooked ham
few lettuce leaves, shredded
1 tablespoon paprika
4–5 tablespoons strong mustard

Mash the goat's milk cheese and mix it throughly with the cream cheese. Season with pepper and add the chervil and walnuts.

Using a palette knife, spread a ½ inch thick layer of the cheese mixture over a slice of ham. Top with another slice of ham and spread it with the cheese mixture. Continue layering the ingredients, finishing with a slice of ham. Refrigerate the ham "loaf" for about 30 minutes.

To serve, arrange a bed of shredded lettuce on a serving dish. Cut the ham loaf into five portions and place on the lettuce. Mix the paprika and mustard and use to garnish each ham portion. Add sprigs of chervil or parsley, if desired, and serve very cool.

Rosemary Sausage Puffs

Serves 6

1 cup black olives, pitted and
  chopped
1 teaspoon dried rosemary
$\frac{1}{2}$ lb bulk pork sausage meat
salt and pepper
1 (14-oz) package frozen puff
  pastry, thawed
1 egg, beaten

Mix the olives and rosemary with the sausage meat and
season with salt and pepper.

On a lightly floured board roll out the puff pastry to a
thickness of $\frac{1}{4}$ inch and cut out 12 ovals or rounds.

Divide the sausage meat mixture into six portions and
put one in the middle of each of six of the pastry rounds.
Cover with the remaining six pieces of pastry. Moisten
the pastry edges and press together to seal. With the tip
of a knife, draw decorative patterns on the top of the
puffs. Brush with egg and bake in a preheated 425° oven
for 30 minutes. Serve warm, with a green salad.

Asparagus Pie

Serves 6

$\frac{3}{4}$ lb asparagus tips
3 tablespoons butter
3 tablespoons flour
$2\frac{1}{2}$ cups milk
salt and pepper
pinch of grated nutmeg
1 tablespoon Crème Fraîche
   (page 398)
4 eggs
$1\frac{1}{4}$ quantities Basic Pie Pastry
   (page 431)

Blanch the asparagus tips for 3 minutes in boiling salted water. Drain thoroughly.

Melt the butter over a low heat. Add the flour and stir for 1 to 2 minutes. Remove from the heat and gradually add the milk. Season with salt, pepper and nutmeg and return to the heat to cook for about 10 minutes, stirring. Stir in the crème fraîche.

Meanwhile, cook three eggs for 7 minutes in boiling water: they must remain soft.

On a lightly floured board, roll out half the pastry to a thickness of $\frac{1}{4}$ inch and use to line a pie pan. Arrange the asparagus on the bottom and cover with the sauce.

Shell the eggs, carefully halve them and arrange on top of the sauce.

Roll out the rest of the pastry and use to cover the pie. Moisten the pastry edges and press together to seal. Make a hole in the center of the lid. Beat the remaining egg and brush over the top of the pie. Bake in a preheated $425°$ oven for 20 minutes.

Chicken and Vegetable Cake

Serves 6

1 lb carrots, sliced
1 celeriac, sliced
1½ lb potatoes, cubed
2 tablespoons Crème Fraîche
  (page 398)
2 eggs, beaten
salt and pepper
2 cups cubed skinless boneless
  chicken

Cook the carrots and the celeriac for 5 minutes in just enough boiling salted water to cover them. Add the potatoes and continue cooking for a further 10 minutes.

Meanwhile, mix the Crème fraîche with the eggs and season with salt and pepper.

Drain the vegetables thoroughly. Butter an ovenproof dish and add the potatoes and celeriac then the carrots and chicken. Pour in the egg mixture. Bake in a preheated 375° oven for 20 minutes. When golden, remove from the oven and leave to cool slightly before unmolding.

Ham and Cheese Puffs

Serves 6

2 tablespoons butter
2 tablepoons flour
1¼ cups milk
salt and pepper
1 cup grated Gruyère cheese
1 cup chopped cooked ham
24 small unsweetened hot
   Cream Puffs (page 436)

Make a white sauce: melt the butter over a low heat. Add the flour and stir for 1 to 2 minutes. Remove from the heat and gradually add the milk. Season, return to the heat and stir for about 5 minutes until the sauce thickens. Add the Gruyère and stir until it melts. Remove the saucepan from the heat and mix in the ham.

Make a slit on the top of the little choux, and pipe or spoon the filling into them. Serve immediately.

Ham Soufflé

Serves 6

6 tablespoons butter
¼ cup flour
1 cup milk
salt and pepper
pinch of grated nutmetg
6 eggs, separated
1 cup ground cooked ham
1¼ cups grated Gruyère cheese

Melt the butter over a low heat. Add the flour and stir for 1 to 2 minutes. Remove from the heat and gradually add the milk. Season with salt, pepper and nutmeg. Return to the heat and stir for about 5 minutes until the sauce thickens. Remove from the heat and add the egg yolks, one at a time. Mix well, then blend in the ham and the cheese, stirring constantly.

Add a pinch of salt to the egg whites and beat into stiff peaks. Add to the sauce mixture, cutting them in well with a metal spoon. Pour into a buttered soufflé dish and bake in a preheated 375° oven for about 40 minutes. Serve immediately.

Tomato Quiche

Serves 4

5 tomatoes, peeled and sliced
salt and pepper
1 cup milk
2 tablespoons Crème Fraîche
  (page 398)
2 eggs, beaten
1¼ quantities Basic Pie Pastry
  (page 431)

Put the tomatoes into a bowl, sprinkle with salt and leave for 30 minutes to extract their juices.

Add the milk and the Crème fraîche to the eggs. Season with pepper and beat well to mix.

On a lightly floured board, roll out the pastry to a thickness of ½ inch and use to line a quiche or flan dish.

Drain, rinse and dry the tomatoes and arrange in the pastry case, in several layers if necessary. Pour over the milk mixture. Bake in a preheated 400° oven for about 20 minutes. If the filling has not quite set, turn off the oven and leave the quiche inside for a few minutes longer.

Ham and Potato Skillet Cake

Serves 4

1½ lb potatoes, coarsely grated
2 onions, thinly sliced
3 garlic cloves, chopped
4 thick slices cooked smoked
   ham, cut into strips
2 teaspoons chopped parsley
salt
¼ cup butter

Rinse the grated potatoes well in cold water, to wash off their starch, and dry on a dish towel.

In a bowl, mix the potatoes, onions, garlic, ham and parsley. Season with salt and shape the mixture into a large flat cake.

Melt the butter in a large skillet and cook the cake until lightly browned on each side.

Scallion Quiche

Serves 4

½ cup butter
2 lb scallions or shallots, thinly
    sliced
1 tablespoon flour
1 cup milk
salt and pepper
1¼ quantities Basic Pie Pastry
    (page 431)

Melt half the butter in a skillet and brown the scallions or onions. Set aside.

Melt the rest of the butter in a saucepan over a low heat. Add the flour and stir for 1 to 2 minutes. Remove from the heat and gradually add the milk. Season with salt and pepper and return to the heat. Stir for about 5 minutes until the sauce thickens.

On a lightly floured board, roll out the pastry to a thickness of ½ inch and use to line a quiche or flan dish. Put the scallions into the pastry case and pour the sauce over them. Bake in a preheated 375° oven for 30 minutes, and serve warm.

Stuffed Onions

Serves 4

8 large onions
2 cups chopped cooked beef
1 egg, beaten
½ teaspoon dried thyme
salt and pepper
1 cup white wine
1 tablespoon Calvados or
    applejack
2 tablespoons butter

Blanch the onions for 5 minutes in boiling water. Rinse in cold water and drain. Cut off the onion tops, hollow out the onions carefully and chop the removed pulp.

Mix the chopped onion, beef, egg and thyme. Season with salt and pepper and use the mixture to stuff the onions.

Arrange the stuffed onions in a buttered ovenproof dish. Sprinkle with the white wine and Calvados and dot the onions with the butter. Pour a little water into the bottom of the dish. Bake in a preheated 375° oven for about 45 minutes or until the tops of the onions are well browned, sprinkling occasionally with the pan juices. Serve very hot.

Mushroom Crêpes

Serves 4

1 cup + 2 tablespoons flour
salt and pepper
2 eggs
1 quart milk
$\frac{1}{4}$ cup butter
2 cups thinly sliced mushrooms
$\frac{1}{4}$ lb Canadian bacon, cut into
  strips
oil, for frying the crêpes
1 cup canned tomato sauce,
  heated
1 tablespoon chopped parsley

Sift 1 cup flour and a pinch of salt into a bowl. Gradually beat in the eggs and add $1\frac{1}{2}$ cups milk. Set aside.

Melt half the butter in a skillet and brown the mushrooms. Stir in the rest of the flour and pour in the rest of the milk. Season and cover the pan. Simmer for 10 minutes. In another skillet, melt the rest of the butter and lightly fry the bacon strips. Mix in the mushrooms.

To cook the crêpes: lightly grease a heavy-based 7-inch crêpe pan with oil and heat it thoroughly. Whisk the batter and pour about $1\frac{1}{2}$ tablespoons into the center of the pan, then tilt it so that the batter forms a thin even covering. Cook for about 1 minute or until the underside is golden. Turn and cook the other side until golden. Remove from the pan. Continue making crêpes, interleaving each with wax paper. Keep them warm.

Put a little filling on each crêpe and roll up. Arrange in a dish. Pour the tomato sauce over and serve sprinkled with parsley.

Eggs in Aspic

Serves 6

6 eggs
1½ envelopes unflavored gelatin
2½ cups boiling chicken broth
¼ cup Madeira
salt and pepper
1 carrot
few radishes
1 tomato
2 sprigs chervil
2 sprigs tarragon
sprigs of parsley
lettuce leaves

Cook the eggs in boiling water for about 7 minutes: they must remain soft. Drain and shell the eggs.

Prepare the aspic: dissolve the gelatin in the boiling broth and flavor with the Madeira. Add salt and pepper if wished. Pour a ¼ inch layer of aspic into the bottom of six small molds and leave it to set.

Cut decorative shapes of carrot and radishes and small pieces of tomato. Dip these and the herbs into the aspic mixture and arrange them on the bottom of the molds. Pour over a little aspic to hold them in place. Put a soft-cooked egg in each mold and cover with aspic. Leave to set for 2 hours in the refrigerator.

To serve, unmold the aspic eggs onto a serving dish and decorate the dish with lettuce leaves, radishes and parsley sprigs.

Little Cheese and Spinach Pies

Serves 6

1 lb fresh bulk spinach
½ lb (2 cups) ricotta cheese
1 cup grated Gruyère cheese
1 bunch chives, coarsely
   chopped
2 eggs, beaten
salt and pepper
1 (14-oz) package frozen puff
   pastry, thawed

Cook the spinach for 10 minutes in boiling salted water. Drain, chop and put into a mixing bowl. Add the ricotta cheese, the Gruyère, chives and eggs. Season with salt and pepper and mix thoroughly.

On a lightly floured board, roll out the pastry to ½ inch thickness. Cut out 12 rounds. Divide the cheese mixture between six of them and cover each with another pastry round. Moisten the pastry edges and press together to seal. Place on a baking sheet and bake in a preheated 425° oven for 40 minutes. Serve warm.

Anchovy Pies

Serves 6

1¼ quantities Basic Pie Pastry
   (page 431)
1 cup milk
2 tablespoons Crème Fraîche
   (page 398)
2 eggs, beaten
pepper
1 (2-oz) can anchovy fillets in
   oil, drained
1 cup mixed green and black
   olives, pitted and chopped

On a lightly floured board, roll out the pastry to a thickness of ¼ inch. Using a fluted pastry cutter, cut out six rounds and use to line tartlet molds.

Add the milk and Crème fraîche to the eggs. Season with pepper, mix thoroughly and divide between the tartlet cases. Place two anchovy fillets and a few pieces of green olives and black olives on each one. Bake in a preheated 425° oven for 15 minutes. Serve warm.

Avocado Mousse with Green Peppercorns

Serves 4

4 fresh scallops
salt
juice of $\frac{1}{2}$ lemon
$\frac{1}{4}$ cup green peppercorns
2 avocados
2 tablespoons chopped chives

Cut the scallops in half lengthwise, if using sea scallops. Leave bay scallops whole. Poach the scallops in simmering salted water for 5 minutes. Drain and sprinkle with the lemon juice. Cool.

Coarsely crush 2 tablespoons peppercorns. Halve the avocados lengthwise and remove the seeds. Scoop out the flesh, using a small spoon, and taking care not to damage the skins. Purée the flesh with the crushed peppercorns in a blender or food processor and use to fill the avocado skins. Arrange the scallops on top.

Reserve a few peppercorns and crush the rest. Sprinkle whole and crushed peppercorns and the chives over the avocados.

Eggplant Purée

Serves 6

6 eggplants
2 garlic cloves, crushed
1 cup olive oil
salt and pepper

Broil the eggplants for 10–15 minutes, turning occasionally, until the skins will peel off easily. Halve the eggplants and scoop out the pulp. Tip into a bowl or a mortar. Add the garlic. Gradually, pour in the olive oil, stirring with a wooden spoon, or with a pestle, to form an emulsion. Season with salt and pepper to taste. (Alternatively, purée in a blender or food processor.)

Serve the eggplant purée with slices of toast and black olives, or accompanied by tomatoes.

Tomatoes Stuffed with Tuna Fish

Serves 6

6 large tomatoes
¾ cup rice
1 sweet red pepper
few lettuce leaves, shredded
1 (7-oz) can tuna in brine or oil,
    drained
1 tablespoon coarsely chopped
    parsley
4–6 tablespoons Vinaigrette
    Dressing (page 410)
salt and pepper
6 black olives

Cut a slice from the top of each tomato and hollow the tomatoes out with a small spoon. Salt the tomato shells lightly and leave upside-down to drain for a few minutes. Cook the rice in boiling salted water for about 15 minutes until just tender. Meanwhile, cut off the stalk end from the sweet pepper and remove the seeds and pith. Chop the pepper.

Drain the rice and rinse in cold water. Put into a bowl with the red pepper, lettuce, tuna fish, parsley and the vinaigrette dressing. Season with salt and pepper. Use to fill the tomatoes and garnish each with a black olive.

Eggplant Timbale

Serves 6

2 lb eggplants (long rather than
  round), peeled
2 cups milk
2 eggs, beaten
2 garlic cloves, chopped
salt and pepper

Cut three eggplants into slices lengthwise. Cut the others into fairly thin crosswise slices. Cook all the eggplant slices for 10 minutes in boiling salted water, then drain and leave to cool.

Whisk the milk and the eggs together and set aside. Butter a round 8-inch diameter cake pan and line the bottom and sides with the long eggplant slices.

Chop the small eggplant slices coarsely and mix with the garlic and the egg and milk mixture. Season with salt and pepper, then pour into the lined cake pan. Bake in a preheated 375° oven for about 30 minutes. Unmold from the pan while still hot and serve warm.

Oyster Vol-au-Vents

Serves 4

4 large frozen vol-au-vent
  cases (patty shells), thawed
3 dozen fresh oysters
¼ cup butter
2 tablespoons flour
2 cups milk
salt and pepper
pinch of grated nutmetg
1 (8-oz) can mushrooms,
  drained
8 small Pike Dumplings, halved
  (below)

Warm the vol-au-vent cases for 15 minutes in a preheated 400° oven.

Meanwhile, shuck the oysters over a container in order to collect the liquor which they contain: slip a knife between the shells and twist until the hinge of the shell breaks. Loosen the oyster with the knife and put into a pan. Strain the reserved liquor and add to the pan. Over a gentle heat, bring to simmering point then remove from the heat. Drain the oysters and set aside.

Melt the butter in a small saucepan over a low heat. Add the flour and stir for 1 to 2 minutes. Remove from the heat and gradually add the milk. Season with salt, pepper and nutmeg. Return to the heat and stir for about 5 minutes until the sauce thickens. Add the mushrooms and quenelles and heat through. Add the oysters and reheat briefly.

Use to fill the hot vol-au-vent cases and serve immediately.

Pike Dumplings

Serves 6

¾ cup flour
2 eggs, beaten
¼ cup butter, diced
salt and pepper
pinch of grated nutmeg
⅔ cup milk, warmed
½ lb pike fillet, chopped
½ cup margarine or lard,
  chopped

Put the flour into a heavy saucepan, add the eggs and mix to a firm paste. Work in the butter gradually and season with salt, pepper and nutmeg. Add the milk. Cook over a low heat, stirring constantly, for 6 minutes. Do not boil. Butter a plate and pour the panada onto it to cool.

Meanwhile, mix the pike and margarine together. Add the cooled panada and work together with a fork, then sieve the mixture so it is completely smooth.

Cut the mixture into 12 equal portions and roll into sausage shapes. Poach the dumplings for about 8 minutes in a large saucepan of salted water until they swell. Remove and drain on a clean cloth.

Leek and Ham Quiche

Serves 4

1 (14-oz) package frozen puff
   pastry, thawed
8 small leeks, chopped
1 cup Crème Fraîche (page 398)
1 egg, beaten
salt and pepper
2 slices cooked ham, trimmed
   and roughly chopped

On a lightly floured board, roll out the puff pastry to a thickness of $\frac{1}{4}$ inch and use to line a quiche or flan dish. Cook the leeks for 5 minutes in boiling salted water and drain thoroughly. Beat the crème fraîche into the egg. Season with salt and pepper.

Put the leeks into the pastry case, add the ham and pour over the cream mixture. Bake in a preheated 400° oven for 20 minutes. Serve hot or warm.

Ham Puff

Serves 4

$\frac{1}{4}$ cup butter
1 tablespoon flour
1 cup milk
salt and pepper
1 (14-oz) package frozen puff
    pastry, thawed
4 slices cooked ham

Melt the butter over a low heat. Add the flour and stir for 1 to 2 minutes. Remove from the heat and gradually add the milk. Season with salt and pepper. Return to the heat and cook, stirring, for about 5 minutes until the sauce thickens.

On a lightly floured board, roll out half the pastry to a thickness of $\frac{1}{2}$ inch and use to line a dampened layer cake pan, or lay the pastry on a baking sheet. Arrange a slice of ham on the pastry and cover it with sauce. Repeat the layers until the ham and sauce are used up, leaving a pastry border all around the edge if the pastry is on a baking sheet.

Roll out the rest of the pastry and use to cover the filling. Moisten the pastry edges and press together to seal. Make several cuts with a knife on the top and bake in a preheated 400° oven for 40 minutes. Serve hot or warm.

Zucchini Bake

Serves 6

4½ lb zucchini, thickly sliced
1¼ cups Crème Fraîche (page 398)
3 eggs, beaten
salt and pepper
pinch of grated nutmeg
1 cup grated Gruyère cheese

Blanch the zucchini for about 3 minutes in boiling salted water. Drain carefully and put into a buttered ovenproof dish.

Beat the Crème fraîche into the eggs. Season with salt and pepper and sprinkle with nutmeg. Pour over the zucchini. Sprinkle with Gruyère and bake in a preheated 425° oven for about 15 minutes.

PÂTÉS, TERRINES AND PIES

At the very mention of homemade pâtés or pies many people shrink back in horror because they think these items are far too difficult to prepare. Admittedly, some highly decorative pies are not quick and simple to make, but there are lots of pâtés and terrines which require time more than culinary skill when it comes to their preparation.

Here you will find a complete mixture of recipes for fish, meat, variety meats, poultry, game and vegetables in traditional pies, rich pâtés and light vegetable-based terrines. Some are encased in pastry and you can decide whether to make the dough yourself or to use frozen pastry. A food processor or blender are invaluable when you are preparing the ingredients, otherwise a good sharp knife and large chopping board are quite adequate. Once all the ingredients are prepared and mixed, most terrines and pâtés need fairly lengthy cooking. Depending on the texture, the pâté may need weighting down and chilling for several hours before it is served. The finished dish can be an elaborate creation with lots of additional garnishing ingredients set in aspic or it can be served very simply, scooped out of the cooking container.

These recipes are incredibly versatile – they can be served for the first course, for the main course or as a light lunch or supper dish. For picnics, buffet meals or as a filling snack, pâtés, terrines and pies are all excellent foods to offer. The accompaniments you serve depend upon the occasion: for a light snack some crisp crackers, celery and tomatoes would complement a simple pâté. Hot toast or rolls with pâté make a substantial appetizer, or hot crusty bread, pâté and salad go to make a tasty lunch. Pies and terrines can be served with salads, bread and baked potatoes to make substantial meals.

The real advantage of preparing your own pâtés and terrines lies in quality – these items, when homemade, can be outstandingly delicious compared to the purchased alternatives. The cooked items can be frozen for several months – up to 6 months if they are not too fatty. If you like, individual portions can be wrapped and frozen, ready for a hasty weekend lunch break.

Vegetable Terrine

Serves 6 to 8

3 lb carrots
14 oz leeks
1¼ lb fresh peas, shelled
2 envelopes unflavored gelatin
salt and pepper
1¼ cups Crème fraîche (page 398)

Cut six carrots into 3-inch sticks. Cut the remaining carrots into slices. Cook all the carrots in boiling salted water. Drain and set aside. Cut the white parts of 2 leeks into slices, and the rest into 3-inch chunks and cook in boiling salted water in the rinsed-out pan. Drain and set aside. Rinse the pan again and cook the peas. Leave the vegetables to cool.

Dissolve the gelatin in ¼ cup hot water. Purée most of the cooked carrot slices in a blender or food processor. Add 6 tablespoons of the purée to the gelatin mixture, then stir this into the rest of the carrot purée. Season with salt and pepper and stir in the crème fraîche.

Line a 14 × 5 × 3 inch loaf pan with buttered parchment or wax paper. Arrange a row of carrot slices around the edge of the bottom, and then a row of leek slices inside the carrots. Decorate the sides with the chunks of leek alternated with the carrot sticks. Then add the peas between the carrots and pour over the carrot purée. Smooth the surface, lay a board on top, weight down, and refrigerate until the next day.

Remove the pâté from the pan, peel off the parchment paper and smooth the surface with a spatula so that it is perfectly flat.

Serve cold on a bed of shredded lettuce with slices of toast.

Variations
The pâté can be made with artichoke hearts, leeks, spinach, salsify or zucchini.

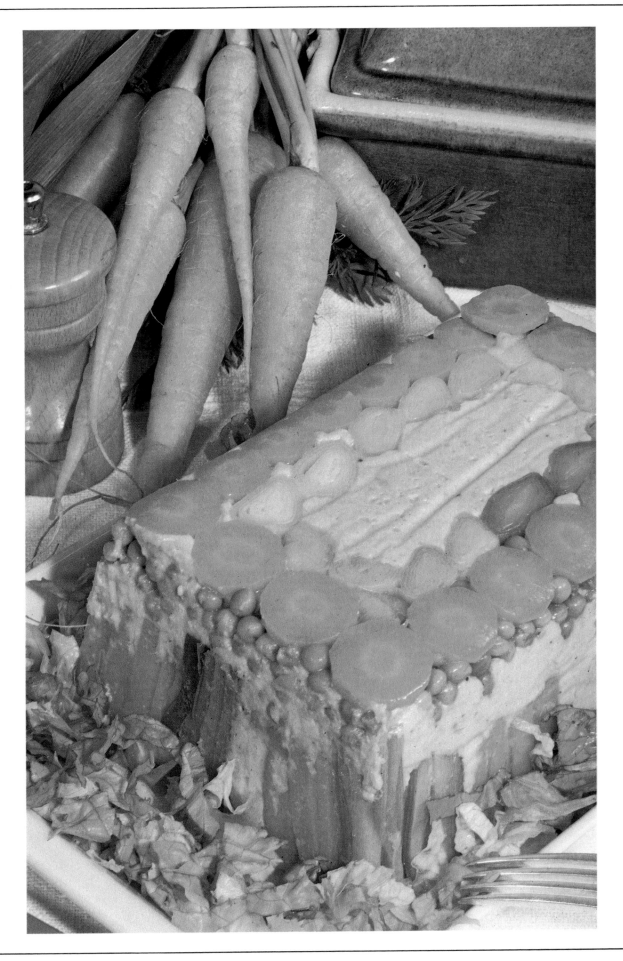

Rainbow Vegetable Terrine

Serves 4

1 lb carrots
1 lb white turnips
3 lb bulk spinach
3 eggs
1 cup Crème Fraîche (page 398)
salt and pepper
carrot flowers, lemon slices and
  lemon baskets for garnish
  (optional)

Cook the carrots and the turnips separately for about 20 minutes in boiling salted water. Cook the spinach for 5 minutes in boiling water. Drain the carrots and purée in a blender or food processor. Add an egg and one-third of Crème fraîche to the carrot purée. Season with salt and pepper. Repeat this puréeing and mixing with the turnips and the spinach, keeping the three vegetables separate.

Put half the spinach purée into a 9 × 5 × 3 inch loaf pan or an ovenproof dish, pressing down well in a very firm layer. Add the turnip purée, then the carrot purée and then spread the rest of the spinach purée on top. Place the terrine in a roasting pan. Pour in water to come halfway up the sides of the loaf pan. Bake in a preheated 400° oven for 20 minutes.

Prepare the garnishing ingredients at this stage, making them simple or elaborate. Unmold the terrine onto a warmed serving dish and add the garnish.

Country Pie

Serves 6

2 cups finely ground cooked
   pork
2 cups finely ground cooked
   veal
4 slices bread, crusts removed,
   crumbled
1 cup white wine
4 onions, thinly sliced
3 tablespoons chopped parsley
salt and pepper
1¼ quantities Basic Pie Pastry
   (page 431)
1 egg, beaten

Put the ground meats into a bowl and add the bread, wine and the onions. Mix well and marinate for 2 hours. Add the parsley to the meat mixture and season with salt and pepper.

On a lightly floured board, roll out three-quarters of the pastry and use to line a deep 8-inch loose-bottomed cake pan. Allow the pastry to overhang by 1 inch.

Spoon in the filling. Roll out the remaining pastry and use to cover the filling. Reserve the pastry trimmings. Moisten the pastry edges and press together to seal. Make a hole in the center and decorate with pastry trimmings. Brush the pie with egg and bake in a preheated 375° oven for 1½ hours.

Remove the pie from the oven and remove from the pan. Serve piping hot with Tomato Sauce (see page 383), cold ratatouille, fried zucchini sprinkled with parsley, or a salad of young spinach.

Terrine of Veal in Aspic

Serves 6

½ lb pork rind, chopped
1 lb veal bones
1 (3½-lb) veal shank
2 carrots, sliced
2 onions, thinly sliced
1 bouquet garni
2 cloves
1 cup white wine
salt and pepper
2½ cups water
1 cup olives, pitted and sliced
2 oranges, sliced
1 sprig tarragon

Put the pork rind and the veal bones into a large kettle of cold water. Bring to a boil, cover and simmer for 30 minutes. Drain and rinse the rind and bones. Put the rind back into the rinsed-out pan, place the veal shank on top and add the carrots, onions, bones, bouquet garni and cloves. Pour over the wine, season with salt and pepper and bring to a boil.

Add the water, return to a boil, cover and simmer for 2 hours.

Drain the veal shank. Remove the meat and chop it. Mix with the olives. Strain the stock and reserve 1½ cups.

Arrange the orange slices in a shallow dish and add a few tarragon leaves. Spoon over a little of the stock. Chill until set. Place the veal and olive mixture on the orange slices and cover with the rest of the stock. Refrigerate until set.

Country Paté

Serves 10

2 lb Canadian bacon
1 lb lard, diced
3½ lb pork liver, chopped
2 tablespoons flour
4 teaspoons salt
2 teaspoons pepper
2 eggs, beaten
1 pork caul, soaked and rinsed
   (optional)
2 strips pork fat

Cut one-quarter of the bacon into small pieces and grind the rest. Mix all the bacon with the lard, liver and flour and add the salt and pepper. Blend in the eggs.

Spread the caul (if used) over the bottom and sides of an ovenproof dish, stretching it out evenly. Fill it with the bacon mixture and place the strips of pork fat on top. Cover the dish and place in a roasting pan. Pour in water to come halfway up the dish. Bake in a preheated 425° oven for 1¾ hours. Set aside to cool, and store in a cool place for at least 24 hours before serving.

Lamb and Mint Terrine

Serves 6 to 8

4 slices bread, crusts removed
$\frac{2}{3}$ cup milk
2 lb boneless lamb from the
    shoulder, half cut into strips
    and half ground
2 sprigs mint, leaves chopped
2 eggs, beaten
3 onions, thinly sliced
2 pinches ground cumin
salt and pepper
about 10 bacon slices

Soak the bread in the milk. Put the ground lamb into a bowl. Squeeze the bread and add to the meat with the mint leaves, eggs, onions and cumin. Season with salt and pepper and mix together well.

Fill a 3-pound terrine or 12 × 5 × 3 inch loaf pan with alternate layers of the ground lamb mixture and lamb strips, then add the bacon. Cover the terrine and seal the lid with a flour and water paste. Cook in a preheated 375° oven for $1\frac{1}{2}$ hours.

Remove the terrine from the oven and leave to rest for 25 minutes. Serve warm with puréed tomatoes, a dish of zucchini and eggplant, and fried button mushrooms.

Three-Meat Terrine

Serves 6 to 8

1 (5½-lb) duck, skinned and
  boned (page 83), skin
  reserved
¾ lb pork tenderloin, cut into
  strips
¾ lb boneless veal, cut into
  strips
⅔ cup port wine
salt and pepper
2 tablespoons butter
½ lb chicken livers, sliced
10 bacon slices
1 bay leaf

Cut the best bits of duck meat into strips and grind the rest with the skin, the pork and the veal. Mix the ground meats with the wine and season with salt and pepper. Generously butter a 2-pound terrine or 9 × 5 × 3 inch loaf pan. Spoon in a layer of the ground meat. Add layers of duck strips and liver and finish with the remaining ground meats.

Lay the slices of bacon on top. Add the bay leaf, cover the terrine and seal the lid with a flour and water paste. Put into a baking pan and pour in water to come halfway up the terrine. Cook in a preheated 350° oven for 2 hours.

Remove the terrine from the oven and break the seal. Remove the lid and place a small board on top with a weight to press the meat down. Cool, then refrigerate for 24 hours. Serve well chilled with a salad.

Chicken and Herb Terrine

Serves 6

1 ($3\frac{1}{2}$-lb) chicken, boned (page 83)
$\frac{3}{4}$ lb bacon slices
$\frac{1}{2}$ lb cooked ham
$\frac{1}{4}$ lb boneless veal
2 eggs
2 tablespoons brandy
2 tablespoons chopped parsley
1 tablespoon chopped chervil
1 tablespoon chopped tarragon
salt and pepper
$\frac{1}{2}$ tablespoon unflavored gelatin
1 cup chicken broth
tarragon leaves for garnish (optional)

Cut the best pieces of chicken into strips and set aside.

Grind half the bacon with the remaining chicken meat, the ham and the veal. Put the ground meat into a large bowl and add the eggs, brandy and herbs. Season with salt and pepper, and mix together well.

Grease a 4-pound terrine or 14 × 5 × 3 inch loaf pan and fill it with alternating layers of ground meats and strips of chicken. Finish with a layer of ground meats and cover with the remaining bacon slices. Cover the terrine and seal with a flour and water paste. Cook in a preheated 350° oven for $1\frac{1}{2}$ hours.

Remove the terrine from the oven and leave to rest for 15 minutes. Remove the lid, weight down and cool.

Dissolve the gelatin in the broth. Leave until tepid. Remove the weight and board from the terrine and garnish the top with tarragon leaves. Pour the cooled aspic around the edges and on top. Set before serving.

Rabbit and Artichoke Terrine

Serves 6 to 8

6 frozen or canned artichoke
   hearts
juice of 1 lemon
1 lb pork tenderloin
3 shallots
salt and pepper
3 lb rabbit pieces, boned and
   cut into strips
6 chicken livers, coarsely
   chopped
1 bay leaf
1 envelope unflavored gelatin
2 cups chicken broth
coriander leaves

Cook the frozen artichoke hearts (if used) in boiling water with the lemon juice for 15 minutes. Drain.

Purée the pork, 2 artichoke hearts and the shallots in a blender or food processor and season with salt and pepper.

Generously grease a 2-pound terrine or 9 × 5 × 3 inch loaf pan and spoon in a layer of the pork mixture. Add layers of rabbit meat, liver and the whole artichoke hearts and finish with the remaining pork mixture. Lay a bay leaf on top and bake in a preheated 350° oven for 2 hours. Dissolve the gelatin in the broth and leave to cool.

When the pâté is cooked, remove from the oven and leave to cool slightly then garnish with coriander leaves. Pour over the aspic. Leave to set in a cool place for 24 hours and serve well chilled.

Salmon Koulibiac

Serves 8 to 10

¾ cup long-grain rice
6 tablespoons butter
1½ lb fresh salmon fillet, cut into
    crosswise slices
1 (1-lb) package frozen chopped
    spinach
¾ lb button mushrooms, thinly
    sliced
½ lb onions, thinly sliced
double quantity Basic Pie
    Pastry (page 431)
4 hard-cooked eggs, sliced
2 tablespoons each of chopped
    parsley and chives
salt and pepper
1 egg, beaten

Cook the rice in boiling salted water until just tender. Meanwhile, melt 3 tablespoons butter and fry the salmon slices for 2 minutes. Leave to cool. Thaw the spinach in a saucepan with a little water and a pat of butter, and drain. Cook the mushrooms in the rinsed-out pan in a pat of butter, until soft. Set aside. Cook the onions in the remaining butter, until soft.

On a lightly floured board, roll out the pastry fairly thinly to give a rectangle and lay it on a baking sheet. Reserve the pastry trimmings. On the center one-third of the pastry, arrange the filling in layers, in the following order: rice, spinach, salmon, eggs, mushrooms and herbs. Season lightly.

Close the pie by folding over the rest of the pastry and sealing the edges. Make a hole in the center and decorate with pastry trimmings. Brush with egg. Bake in a preheated 375° oven for 30 minutes, then lower the temperature to 325° and bake for a further 15 minutes. Serve hot or cold.

Duck and Olive Terrine

Serves 6 to 8

1 (3½-lb) duck, boned (page 83)
¾ lb pork tenderloin
¾ lb boneless veal
1 egg, beaten
⅔ cup port wine
3 bay leaves
salt and pepper
2 cups green olives, pitted
1 envelope unflavored gelatin
2 cups chicken broth

Cut the best pieces of duck meat into strips. Grind the rest with the pork and veal.

Put the ground meats into a bowl, add the egg, port wine and 1 bay leaf, crumbled, and season with salt and pepper. Mix together well, then add the strips of duck meat and the olives, reserving about 12.

Grease a 2¼-quart capacity terrine and spoon in the mixture. Press down well and cover, sealing the lid with a flour and water paste. Bake in a preheated 350° oven for 2 hours. Remove the terrine from the oven, remove the lid and set aside for 30 minutes. Meanwhile, dissolve the gelatin in the broth and leave to cool.

Pour off any surplus fat from the terrine. Pour in the aspic and refrigerate to set.

Cut the reserved olives into slices, and arrange them around the edge of the terrine and in the center. Garnish with the remaining bay leaves. Glaze the top of the dish with the rest of the aspic. Keep in a cold place for 24 hours. Serve well chilled with crusty bread.

Fish and Smoked Salmon Terrine

Serves 8

1 lb whiting fillets
1 cup Crème Fraîche (page 398)
2 egg yolks
salt and pepper
pinch of cayenne
3 tablespoons butter
$\frac{1}{2}$ lb fresh sorrel or spinach
   leaves
$\frac{3}{4}$ lb smoked salmon, sliced
2 lb monkfish, skinned and cut
   into $\frac{1}{2}$-inch pieces

Purée the whiting fillets in a blender or food processor. Beat the cream with the egg yolks and add to the puréed fish. Season with salt and pepper and add the cayenne.

Generously butter a 14 × 5 × 3 inch loaf pan. Arrange a few sorrel leaves in the bottom of the pan, where the sides join the bottom, and a few slices of smoked salmon along the sides. Arrange the filling in the following order: monkfish, whiting purée, sorrel leaves and salmon. Continue layering until the ingredients are used up, sprinkling with pepper and a little salt between each layer.

Cover the pâté with foil and put the loaf pan into a roasting pan. Pour in water to come halfway up the loaf pan. Bake in a preheated 400° oven for 1 hour.

Remove the pan from the oven and leave to rest for a few minutes. Carefully unmold and serve hot or cold with Lemon-flavored melted butter (see below).

To serve hot, accompany with spinach cooked in butter. If served cold, accompany with a salad of spinach or chicory mixed with a few pieces of smoked salmon.

Lemon-flavored melted butter
In a heavy-based saucepan, heat $\frac{2}{3}$ cup butter (cut into small pieces) over a very low heat. When it has melted, pour off the clear butter and discard the sediment. Season with salt and pepper and add the juice of a lemon. Serve in a heated sauceboat.

Melba Toast
Crisp pieces of melba toast would complement the texture of the fish terrine. Take medium-thick slices of bread and cut off the crusts. Lightly toast the slices on both sides then, working quickly while the bread is still hot, slice horizontally through each piece to make very fine slices. Lightly toast the uncooked side of the bread. Cooled melba toast can be stored in an airtight tin for several weeks.

Fillet of Sole Timbale

Serves 8 to 10

2 lb carrots
4 potatoes
1 (1-lb) package frozen leaf
   spinach
3 tablespoons butter
$\frac{1}{4}$ cup Crème Fraîche (page 398)
salt and pepper
$8\frac{1}{2}$ cups fish broth
7 sole fillets
3 envelopes unflavored gelatin

Cook the carrots and potatoes for 30 minutes in simmering salted water. In another saucepan, heat a little water and thaw the spinach over a low heat.

Drain the carrots and potatoes. Reserve one carrot for garnish, then purée the remaining carrots and 2 potatoes in a blender or food processor. Add a pat of butter and 2 tablespoons of crème fraîche. Season with pepper. Leave to cool in a bowl. Drain the spinach, squeeze well and purée in the blender or food processor with the rest of the potatoes. Season with salt and pepper and pour the purée into a large bowl. Add a pat of butter and remaining crème fraîche. Leave to cool.

Heat $2\frac{1}{2}$ cups of the fish broth, then poach the fillets of sole in it, a few at a time, and leave to cool. Dissolve the gelatin in the remaining fish broth and leave to cool.

Cut each fillet of sole in half lengthwise. Cover half the strips of fish with a thin layer of carrot purée and roll them up carefully. Repeat with the remaining strips of fish and spinach purée.

Coat a large deep cake pan (about 10 inches in diameter) with a little aspic and leave to set in a cool place. Arrange the fish rolls in the pan, alternating the colors, then cover with more aspic. Leave in a cold place to set for at least 5 hours. Cut attractive shapes from pieces of the reserved carrot.

Coat a small cake pan (about 6 inches in diameter) with aspic, set the carrot shapes in the aspic and leave to set in a cool place. Add $\frac{1}{4}$ cup aspic to the remaining carrot purée and 2 tablespoons aspic to the spinach purée. Mix well. Pour the carrot purée into the small pan to within 2 inches of the top. Carefully pour the spinach purée on top of the carrot purée, and leave to set in a cold place. Pour the rest of the aspic into a shallow dish and put in a cold place to set.

Plunge the two molds into hot water and turn the aspics out. Place the vegetable aspic on top of the fish aspic. Chop the rest of the aspic and arrange it around the base. Serve well chilled.

Fish and Bacon Terrine

Serves 6 to 8

1 lb whiting fillets
salt and pepper
3 tablespoons butter
1 cup thinly sliced button
   mushrooms
2 shallots, thinly sliced
2 eggs
1 cup Crème Fraîche (page 398)
sprigs of tarragon
$\frac{1}{8}$ teaspoon grated nutmeg
$\frac{3}{4}$ lb smoked salmon, thinly
   sliced
10 thin slices bacon

Slice and season two whiting fillets. Melt the butter in a skillet and cook the mushrooms and shallots until all the mushroom liquid has evaporated.

Purée the remaining whiting fillets, the eggs, mushroom and shallot mixture, Crème fraîche, tarragon (reserving a few leaves) and the nutmeg in a blender or food processor. Season with salt and pepper.

Generously grease a 9 × 5 × 3 inch loaf pan or terrine and spoon in a layer of the blended mixture. Cover with layers of the reserved whiting fillets, the smoked salmon and bacon. Continue layering until all the ingredients are used. Garnish with the reserved tarragon and stand the terrine in a baking pan. Pour in water to come halfway up the terrine. Bake in a preheated 350° oven for 1 hour. Remove the terrine from the oven. Cool, then serve well chilled.

Pork Pie

Serves 4 to 5

1 lb pork tenderloin, diced
1 onion, thinly sliced
2 garlic cloves, crushed
1¼ cups dry white wine
salt and pepper
1½ quantities Basic Pie Pastry
   (page 431)
1 egg, beaten

Put the pork, onion, garlic and white wine into a large bowl and season with salt and pepper. Mix together and marinate for 3 hours in a cool place, but not the refrigerator.

On a lightly floured board, roll out half the pastry and use to line a charlotte mold or deep 6-inch cake pan, letting the pastry overlap by about 1 inch. Put the meat into the lined mold with as much wine as possible.

Roll out the rest of the pastry and use to cover the mold. Reserve the pastry trimmings. Moisten the pastry edges and press together to seal.

Make a hole in the center of the pie and decorate with pastry trimmings. Brush with egg and bake in a preheated 350° oven for 20 minutes. Lower the heat to 325° and bake for a further 50 to 60 minutes.

Remove the pie from the oven and allow to cool in the mold. Turn out when cooled and serve with salad.

Duck and Pork Pâté in Pastry

Serves 6 to 8

1 (3½-lb) duck, boned (page 83)
¾ lb pork tenderloin, cut into pieces
¼ lb slab bacon, cut into pieces
2 onions
2 shallots
¼ cup brandy
2 eggs, beaten
salt and pepper
1½ (14-oz) packages frozen puff pastry, thawed
¾ lb duck livers, cut into pieces

Cut the best bits of duck meat into strips. Grind the rest with the pork, bacon, onions and shallots in a food processor or meat grinder. Pour into a bowl, add the brandy and half the egg, and season with salt and pepper. Mix together well.

On a lightly floured board, roll out three-quarters of the pastry and use to line a dampened 2¼-quart capacity terrine, allowing it to overhang by 1 inch. Fill with layers of the ground meat mixture, strips of duck meat and duck livers, finishing with a layer of ground meat.

Roll out the rest of the pastry and use to cover the filling. Reserve the pastry trimmings. Moisten the pastry edges and press together to seal. Make a hole in the center and decorate with pastry trimmings. Brush the pie with egg and bake in a preheated 350° oven for 1½ hours.

Serve warm or cold with salad.

Veal and Pistachio Pie

Serves 6 to 8

1 lb boneless veal
¼ lb slab bacon
1 lb cooked ham, diced
5 shallots, thinly sliced
½ cup shelled pistachio nuts
4 egg yolks
salt and pepper
1¼ quantities Basic Pie Pastry
   (page 431)
1 egg, beaten

Grind the veal and bacon together and mix in a bowl with the ham, shallots, pistachios and egg yolks. Season with a little salt and a lot of pepper. Mix thoroughly.

On a lightly floured board, roll out two-thirds of the pastry and use to line a 9 × 5 × 3 inch loaf pan, allowing the pastry to overhang.

Spoon in the filling. Roll out the rest of the pastry and use to cover the filling. Reserve the pastry trimmings. Moisten the pastry edges and press together to seal. Make a hole in the center, and decorate with pastry trimmings. Brush with egg and bake in a preheated 350° oven for 2 hours.

Remove the pie from the oven and leave to rest for 20 minutes, then remove from the tin. Serve warm or cold with a chicory or tossed green salad.

Easter Pie

Serves 6

1 lb bulk pork sausage meat
1 lb ground veal
1 tablespoon chopped chives
1 tablespoon chopped parsley
pinch of ground allspice
2 tablespoons brandy
salt and pepper
2 (14-oz) packages frozen puff
   pastry, thawed
6 hard-cooked eggs
1 egg, beaten

Mix the sausage meat, veal, herbs, allspice and brandy together thoroughly and season with salt and pepper.

On a lightly floured board, roll out half the pastry fairly thinly to give an oblong shape. Lay on a dampened baking sheet. Cover with half the filling, leaving a margin of 1 inch all around.

Make six hollows in the filling and lay the eggs in them, lengthwise. Cover with the rest of the filling.

Roll out the rest of the pastry and use to cover the filling. Moisten the pastry edges and press together to seal. Brush with egg and bake in a preheated 350° oven for 1 hour 20 minutes.

Remove the pie from the oven. Serve hot or cold with a salad.

Berrichon Pie

Serves 6

1 smoked ham hock, boned and
    cut into strips
14 oz boneless veal, roughly
    chopped
¼ lb slab bacon, roughly
    chopped
4 shallots, thinly sliced
3 eggs, beaten
3 pinches ground allspice
salt and pepper
1¼ quantities Basic Pie Pastry
    (page 431)

Put the ham, veal and bacon into a bowl and add the shallots, 2 of the eggs and the allspice. Season with salt and pepper and mix together well.

On a lightly floured board, roll out three-quarters of the pastry and use to line a deep 8-inch round cake pan, allowing the edges of the pastry to overhang. Spoon in the meat mixture and press down well. Roll out the rest of the pastry and use to cover the filling. Reserve the pastry trimmings. Pinch the edges of the pastry together to seal. Make a hole in the center of the pie and decorate with pastry trimmings. Brush with the remaining egg and bake in a preheated 350° oven for 1¾ hours.

Remove the pie from the oven, unmold from the pan, and leave to rest. Serve hot or cold with a chicory salad.

Meat Turnovers

Serves 6 to 8

3 cups roughly chopped meat
   (pork, chicken or veal)
2 onions, sliced
4 garlic cloves
1 bunch parsley
1 bunch chives
3 eggs, beaten
3 tablespoons heavy cream
$\frac{1}{8}$ teaspoon cayenne
salt and pepper
$1\frac{1}{4}$ quantities Basic Pie Pastry
   (page 431)

Grind the meat, onions, garlic, parsley and chives finely. Add 2 of the eggs, the cream and the cayenne, and season with salt and pepper. Mix together well.

On a lightly floured board, roll out the pastry to $\frac{1}{4}$ inch thickness and cut out six to eight 6-inch rounds. Put 2 heaped tablespoons of filling on half of each round. Moisten the edges of the pastry, fold over and pinch together to seal.

Brush the turnovers with the remaining egg. Place them on a baking sheet and bake in a preheated 350° oven for 30 minutes.

Remove the turnovers from the oven. Serve hot or cold with Tomato sauce (see page 383) or serve with a dish of raw vegetables such as celery.

Turkey and Chestnut Pie

Serves 6

¼ cup butter
1 lb onions, thinly sliced
1¼ quantities Basic Pie Pastry
   (page 431)
1¼ lb turkey breast meat, thinly
   sliced
3 apples, peeled, quartered and
   cored
½ (1-lb) can unsweetened whole
   chestnuts, drained and rinsed
   in hot water
salt and pepper
1 egg, beaten

Melt the butter in a pan and gently fry the onions for 15 minutes until soft.

On a lightly floured board, roll out half the pastry and use to line a round 2-quart capacity baking dish, allowing the pastry to overhang by at least ½ inch.

Put the meat, onions, apples and chestnuts into a large bowl. Season well, mix together thoroughly and spoon into the pastry-lined dish.

Roll out the rest of the pastry and use to cover the filling. Moisten the pastry edges and press together to seal. Make a hole in the center. Brush the pastry with egg and bake in a preheated 350° oven for 1 hour 10 minutes. Serve very hot with a green salad.

Alsace Pie

Serves 8

1 veal tongue
$\frac{2}{3}$ cup vinegar
1 carrot, cut into 4 sticks
2 bay leaves
3 sprigs thyme
1 lb boneless rabbit, cubed
$\frac{3}{4}$ lb pork tenderloin, cubed
2 onions
2 shallots
1 garlic clove
salt and pepper
$2\frac{1}{2}$ cups dry white wine
2 tablespoons brandy
double quantity Basic Pie
    Pastry (page 431)
1 egg, beaten

Cover the tongue with cold water, add the vinegar and leave to soak for 6 hours. Drain.

Put the carrot, 1 bay leaf and a sprig of thyme into a large pan of boiling salted water and boil for 5 minutes. Add the tongue and cook for 30 minutes. Drain the tongue, rinse under cold water and remove the skin using the tip of a pointed knife – it should come off very easily. Leave to cool.

Put the cooled tongue into a large saucepan with the rabbit, pork, onions, shallots, garlic, and the remaining thyme and bay leaf. Season with salt and pepper. Pour over the white wine and brandy and marinate for 24 hours in a cool place, but not the refrigerator. Drain the meat. Slice the tongue then set it aside. Grind half the rabbit and pork in a food processor.

On a lightly floured board, roll out three-quarters of the pastry and use to line a 2-pound raised pie mold or 9 × 5 × 3 inch loaf pan, letting it overlap by about 1 inch.

Spoon in a layer of the ground meat, then a layer of cubed rabbit and pork, another layer of ground meat and then the tongue. Finish with a layer of ground meat.

Roll out the rest of the pastry and use to cover the pie. Reserve the pastry trimmings. Moisten the pastry edges and press together to seal. Make a hole in the center of the pie and decorate with the pastry trimmings. Brush with egg and bake in a preheated 350° oven for $1\frac{1}{2}$ hours.

Remove the pie from the oven. Leave to rest for a few minutes before unmolding.

Serve with a salad in season or cold ratatouille.

Spiced Pigeon and Almond Pie

Serves 8

5 oven-ready squab pigeons,
  thawed if frozen
6 tablespoons oil
1½ lb onions, thinly sliced
6 tablespoons chopped parsley
  or coriander
1 tablespoon ground ginger
pinch of saffron powder
salt and pepper
3 tablespoons ground cinnamon
2 tablespoons sugar
7 eggs
1 (14-oz) package frozen puff
  pastry, thawed
1¾ cups roughly chopped
  blanched almonds

Seal the pigeons in the oil without browning. Add the next five ingredients, a tablespoon cinnamon and enough water to come halfway up the pigeons. Cook, covered, for 10 minutes, then uncovered for 20 minutes.

Remove the pigeons. Boil fast to reduce the cooking liquid to a paste. Lower the heat, add the sugar, 2 tablespoons cinnamon and eggs, one by one. Stir briskly for 5 minutes and set aside. Slice the pigeon flesh into bite-sized pieces. Roll the pastry out into a 12 × 10 inch rectangle; cut in half lengthwise. Spread half the almonds on one piece of pastry leaving a border, then top with the egg, pigeon meat and remaining almonds. Brush the pastry edge with water. Lay the remaining pastry on top and seal the edges. Make two holes in the top, decorate with the trimmings and glaze. Bake in a preheated 400° oven for 30–40 minutes.

Cold Spinach, Veal and Egg Pie

Serves 6

3 tablespoons butter
2 (1-lb) packages frozen leaf
   spinach
3 tablespoons Crème Fraîche
   (page 398)
4 shallots, thinly sliced
double quantity Basic Pie
   Pastry (page 431)
6 hard-cooked eggs
2 veal cutlets, cut into thin
   strips
salt and pepper
1 egg, beaten

Heat a little water and the butter in a saucepan and thaw the spinach over a low heat. Drain and squeeze the spinach well, then add the Crème fraîche and shallots.

On a lightly floured board, roll out half the pastry and place on a baking sheet. Lay half the spinach down the center. Make six hollows, in two parallel rows and lay an egg in each one. Cover with the rest of the spinach and then lay the strips of veal on top. Season with salt and pepper.

Roll out the remaining pastry and use to cover the filling. Reserve the pastry trimmings. Moisten the pastry edges and press together to seal. Make a hole in the top of the pie and decorate with pastry trimmings. Brush the pie with egg and bake in a preheated 350° oven for 40 minutes.

Remove the pie from the oven and leave on a rack to cool. Serve cold with lemon wedges.

Turkey Pie

Serves 6 to 8

3 tablespoons butter
14 oz onions, thinly sliced
½ lb ground lean pork
few sage leaves, chopped
salt and pepper
1¼ quantities Basic Pie Pastry
   (page 431)
2½ lb turkey meat, cut into
   strips
1 egg, beaten

Melt the butter in a skillet and cook the onions until soft. Moisten with a little water and allow to reduce on a low heat.

Put the ground pork, the onions and sage into a bowl. Season with salt and pepper and leave for 15 minutes.

On a lightly floured board, roll out the pastry to a rectangle ½ inch thick. Place on a baking sheet and lay half the pork filling along the center. Arrange the strips of turkey meat on top and cover with the remaining pork mixture.

Fold over the edges of the pastry to make an envelope and seal with a little beaten egg. Slash the top of the pastry with the point of a small knife. Brush the pie with egg and bake in a preheated 375° oven for 2 hours. Serve hot or cold. If hot, accompany with braised endive, or puréed vegetables: carrots or celeriac mixed half and half with potatoes. To serve cold, accompany with a mixture of salad vegetables in season.

Variations
Substitute tarragon, dill or chives for the sage. Or try adding 5 or 6 chopped shallots, a little grated nutmeg and a little vodka to the pork, instead of onions and sage.

To bone whole poultry
Use a sharp pointed knife. Turn the bird so that the breast is downwards, then make a cut along the length of the back. Cut the meat off the bones, working on one side at a time as far as the breast bone. Carefully cut the meat off the breast bone, taking the merest sliver of bone with it.

Burgundy Pie

2h 40m

Serves 6

1 lb cooked pork tenderloin,
  coarsely chopped
1 lb cooked shoulder of veal,
  coarsely chopped
1 cup dry red wine
¼ cup brandy
3 tablespoons chopped parsley
salt and pepper
1½ quantities Basic Pie Pastry
  (page 431)
1 egg, beaten

Put the pork and veal into a bowl. Add the wine, brandy and parsley and season with salt and pepper. Mix together thoroughly and leave to marinate for several hours, overnight if possible.

On a lightly floured board, roll out two-thirds of the pastry and use to line a 2½-lb capacity terrine or a deep 8-inch cake pan. Spoon in the meat mixture and press down well. Roll out the remaining pastry and use to cover the meat mixture. Reserve the pastry trimmings. Moisten the pastry edges and press together to seal. Make a hole in the center of the pie and decorate with the pastry trimmings. Brush with egg and bake in a preheated 350° oven for 2 hours.

Remove the terrine from the oven and leave to rest for a few minutes, then unmold onto a serving dish. Serve hot or cold.

FISH AND SEAFOOD

Seafood is particularly versatile – it can be used to make hot or cold dishes for all occasions, from inexpensive meals to the most elaborate dinner party dishes. You will find a broad selection of ideas in this chapter, from simple dishes like poached cod with tomato sauce to special recipes like Mussel Vol au Vent. Well-known specialties are also included: Bouillabaisse, Sole Vallée d'Auge, Skate au Beurre Noir and Lobster Thermidor for example.

There is often a tendency to shy away from cooking fish because of the preparation involved – cleaning, filletting and skinning – but the fish merchant will do this when asked. Alternatively the common varieties of fish are available frozen in the most convenient forms. To add interest to seafood cooking lots of unusual types of fish are available and they sometimes compare favorably price-wise with many cuts of meat.

Broiled, baked, poached or fried, fish and shellfish can be turned into any number of light or satisfying meals. To poach fish, white wine or cider can be used in some recipes or a court bouillon or fish stock can be used in others. Fish bouillon cubes are available, but if you would prefer, prepare your own stock. To do this boil fish trimmings – heads, tails, skin and bones – in plenty of water with a roughly chopped onion, parsley sprigs, bay leaf and a few peppercorns for about 30–40 minutes. Strain and reduce as necessary. Alternatively use a cheap white fish to flavor the stock.

For anyone who is diet conscious, whether simply counting the calories or trying to reduce the fat content of daily meals, then fish is an excellent standby. Poached very simply with the minimum of fish stock or broiled with just a little lemon juice, white fish is a low-calorie food. For extra flavor fresh herbs and vegetables can also be used.

Special occasions offer an opportunity to prepare some shellfish specialties using crab, lobster, shrimp or scallops. If you are not buying frozen shellfish, select the freshest ingredients from a reputable supplier and the flavor will be at its best. If you decide not to offer these seafood in the simplest way – poached and dressed, with a mayonnaise and lemon – then try some of the tempting recipe ideas in this chapter.

Scallops of Cold Hake

Serves 4

2 quarts Court Bouillon (below)
4 fresh hake or cod steaks
   (about 1½ lb)
10 lettuce leaves
2 small tomatoes, quartered
1 lemon, sliced
1 tablespoon capers
salt and pepper
1 cup Mayonnaise (page 409)

Bring the court bouillon to a boil and poach the fish steaks over a low heat for 15 minutes. Remove from the pan with a slotted spoon, taking care not to break the slices. Leave to cool.

Line four scallop shells or small ovenproof dishes with the lettuce leaves and arrange the cold fish in them with the tomatoes, lemon and capers. Season with salt and pepper. Garnish with a spoonful of the mayonnaise and serve the rest separately.

Court Bouillon
Pour 2¼ quarts of water into a saucepan. Add 1 bay leaf, 1 onion, sliced, 2 large carrots, quartered, a handful of parsley and a sprig of thyme. Pour in ⅔ cup dry white wine and add 6 black peppercorns. Bring to a boil, then simmer for 30 minutes and strain before use.

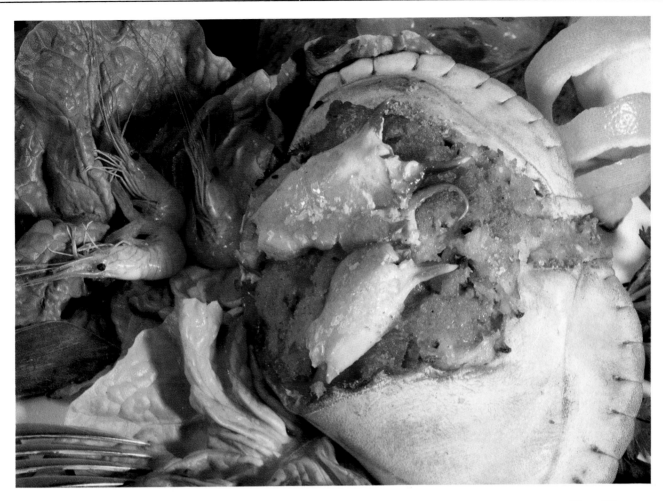

Stuffed Crab

Serves 2

2 quarts Court Bouillon (left)
1 large live crab
2 tablespoons butter
3 shallots, finely chopped
1 slice bacon, chopped
1 teaspoon chopped garlic
1½ cups soft bread crumbs
⅔ cup milk
salt and pepper
juice of 1 lemon
1 tablespoon dried white bread
  crumbs

Bring the court bouillon to a boil over a high heat and cook the crab for about 15 minutes.

Meanwhile, melt half the butter in a skillet and gently fry the shallots. Add the bacon and garlic and continue cooking for 5 minutes. Soak the soft bread crumbs in the milk, then squeeze out excess liquid. Remove the shallot mixture from the heat and mix in the soaked bread.

Drain the crab and take the meat from the shell carefully, discarding all the unedible parts. Reserve the shell and add both the brown and white meat to the shallot mixture. Season to taste.

Pour the lemon juice into the crab shell. Add the stuffing and sprinkle with the bread crumbs. Top with the remaining butter and brown in a preheated 475° oven for 2 minutes. Serve immediately.

Oven-Baked Herrings

Serves 6

3 large potatoes, unpeeled
1 tablespoon peanut oil
1 cup bay leaves
6 medium-sized smoked
   herrings
pepper
1 tablespoon grated Gruyère
   cheese

Cook the potatoes in a pan of boiling salted water for 20 minutes. Drain and leave to cool for a few minutes. Cut the potatoes in half lengthwise, but do not peel.

Pour the oil into an ovenproof dish and cover the bottom with the bay leaves. Arrange the potatoes on the bay leaves, cut side up, and place the herrings on top.

Season with pepper and sprinkle with the grated Gruyère. Brown in a preheated 425° oven for about 15 minutes, and serve from the same dish.

Cod with Ratatouille

Serves 4

2 eggplants, sliced
$\frac{1}{4}$ cup peanut oil
2 onions, finely chopped
2 tablespoons chopped garlic
3 tomatoes, peeled and chopped
4 zucchini, chopped
salt and pepper
4 fresh cod steaks (about $1\frac{1}{2}$ lb)
1 tablespoon chopped parsley
$\frac{1}{2}$ lemon, sliced

Sprinkle the eggplants with salt to draw out the bitter juices. Leave for 20 minutes. Rinse and drain.

Pour 1 tablespoon oil into a large saucepan and add the onions. When they begin to brown, add the garlic, tomatoes, eggplants and zucchini. Season and simmer for about 20 minutes.

Heat the remaining oil in a large skillet, add the cod steaks and cook for about 10 minutes over a medium heat until golden brown, turning the fish steaks once halfway through cooking time.

Pour the ratatouille into a deep serving dish and arrange the cod steaks on top. Sprinkle with parsley and garnish with slices of lemon.

Cod in Tomato Sauce

Serves 6

2 quarts Court Bouillon (page 86)
2 lb skinless, boneless cod, cut into slices
¾ cup ripe olives for garnish
TOMATO SAUCE
1 tablespoon peanut oil
1 onion, chopped
3 garlic cloves, chopped
1 (2-lb) can tomatoes
1 tablespoon chopped thyme
1 bay leaf
salt and pepper

Bring the court bouillon to a boil in a large pan, add the fish and poach over a medium heat for 20 minutes.

Meanwhile, prepare the tomato sauce: heat the oil and fry the onion and garlic. Add the tomatoes, stir and add the thyme, bay leaf and a few pinches of salt and pepper. Cover and leave to simmer for 10 minutes.

Remove the fish from the pan with a slotted spatula and drain thoroughly. Arrange on a serving dish, cover with the sauce and garnish with black olives.

Pike with Piquant Sauce

Serves 4

2 canned anchovy fillets
¼ cup dried mushrooms
1 carrot, diced
3 garlic cloves, finely chopped
1 onion, finely chopped
1 bunch of celery, finely chopped
3 fresh sage leaves, chopped, or ½ teaspoon dried sage
2 tablespoons chopped parsley
1 small sweet red pepper
2 lb pike, scaled, cleaned and cut into slices
¼ cup peanut oil
¾ cup pine nuts
1 tablespoon capers
1 bay leaf
⅔ cup white wine
⅔ cup water
salt and pepper

Soak the anchovies in water for 20 minutes to remove the salt. Drain and chop. Soak the dried mushrooms for 20 minutes in very hot water and then drain. Mix the carrot, garlic, onion, celery, sage and parsley. Set aside.

Remove the stalk of the sweet pepper, cut the pepper in half and remove the seeds and pith. Chop the pepper. Set aside.

Bring a large pan of water to a boil and poach the fish over a gentle heat for 30 minutes. Meanwhile, heat the oil and fry the herb and vegetable mixture. Add the anchovies, pine nuts, capers, bay leaf, red pepper and soaked dried mushrooms. Simmer for 5 minutes, stirring occasionally. Add the white wine and the water. Bring to a boil and simmer for 30 minutes.

Remove the fish from the pan with a slotted spatula. Arrange in a serving dish and season. Either serve the sauce separately or pour it over the fish just before serving.

Sole Vallée d'Auge

Serves 6

6 small (or 3 large) sole fillets,
  skinned
2 tablespoons flour
2 tablespoons butter
salt and pepper
$\frac{2}{3}$ cup hard cider
4 shallots, finely chopped
$\frac{1}{2}$ cup Creme Fraîche (page 398)
1 tablespoon chopped parsley

Coat the fish in the flour. Melt the butter in a large skillet and cook the sole for about 4 minutes each side. Season during cooking.

Meanwhile, pour the cider into a large saucepan and add the shallots. Season and bring to a boil. Boil for a few minutes, then remove from the heat and stir in the Crème fraîche.

When the fish is golden brown, arrange on a serving dish and cover with the sauce. Sprinkle with chopped parsley.

Fried Sole

Serves 6

¼ cup milk
3 tablespoons flour
salt
6 small sole fillets
2 tablespoons butter
1 tablespoon chopped parsley
lemon slices for garnish

Put the milk and the flour into separate shallow dishes and season the milk with salt. Coat the sole first in the milk and then in the flour.

Melt the butter in a large skillet and cook the sole for 5 minutes each side, turning it carefully.

When the sole is golden brown, place on a serving dish. Sprinkle with chopped parsley and garnish with lemon slices.

Monkfish Stew

Serves 6

¼ cup olive oil
2½ lb monkfish fillet, cut into
    pieces
2 tablespoons tomato paste
3 shallots, chopped
1 bouquet garni
⅔ cup dry white wine
⅔ cup Madeira
salt and pepper
cayenne

Heat the oil in a large saucepan and add the pieces of fish. Cook over a medium heat, turning occasionally so that the fish does not stick to the pan.

When the fish begins to brown, add the tomato paste, shallots, bouquet garni, white wine and Madeira.

Season to taste with salt, pepper and cayenne and leave to simmer over a gentle heat for 20 minutes. Remove the bouqUet garni before serving.

Fluke Fillets with Spinach

Serves 4

6 fluke fillets (about 1½ lb)
2 cloves
4 sprigs mint
salt and pepper
⅔ cup white wine
⅔ cup water
½ lb fresh bulk spinach
1 tablespoon peanut oil
2 onions, finely chopped
2 tablespoons butter
2 tablespoons flour
1 cup Crème Fraîche (page 398)
pinch of grated nutmeg
pinch of sweet paprika
1 lemon, sliced

Put the fish into a saucepan and add the cloves and the mint. Season and add the white wine and water. Cover and cook for 20 minutes over a gentle heat.

Meanwhile, cook the spinach in a pan of salted water over a high heat for 6 minutes. Drain thoroughly and chop.

Heat the oil in a pan and brown the onions. Add the chopped spinach, mix and set aside.

Melt the butter in a pan, add the flour and then the Crème fraîche. Season with salt and nutmeg and cook over a very low heat for 6 minutes, stirring constantly.

Remove from the heat and mix in the spinach and onions. Spoon three-quarters of the mixture into a serving dish.

Drain the fish. Cool a little then roll up the fillets and arrange on the bed of spinach. Spoon the remaining spinach mixture on the fish rolls. Sprinkle with paprika and garnish with the lemon.

Monkfish with Spinach

Serves 4

2 lb fresh bulk spinach
1¼ lb monkfish, cut into slices
salt and pepper
1 tablespoon chopped parsley
 for garnish (optional)

Put the spinach into a large saucepan with just a little water and cook for about 5 minutes.

Meanwhile, put the fish on a rack in a roasting pan and bake in a preheated 425° oven for 10 minutes.

Drain and finely chop the spinach. Spoon into a serving dish. Arrange the fish on the spinach and season with salt and pepper. Sprinkle with parsley if desired and serve hot.

Mackerel Baked in Paper

Serves 6

6 medium-sized mackerel,
  scaled and cleaned
1 tablespoon peanut oil
salt and pepper
3 slices cooked ham, halved
  lengthwise
3 small tomatoes, sliced
1 tablespoon chopped parsley

Brush the fish with oil and season with salt and pepper. Cut out six pieces of parchment paper or foil the length of the mackerel and twice their width.

Wrap two strips of ham around each fish and place them on the paper. Garnish with two or three tomato slices and sprinkle with the parsley. Fold over the paper to make packages and place in an ovenproof dish. Bake in a preheated 425° oven for 20 minutes.

Serve the fish in the paper packages, which are opened just before serving.

Skate with Almonds

Serves 6

½ cup butter
4 onions, chopped
3 lb tomatoes, peeled
salt and pepper
6 small skate *or* 3 wings of skate
2 quarts Court Bouillon (page 86)
2 tablespoons chopped almonds
juice of 1 lemon

Melt three-quarters of the butter in a skillet and fry the onions until they begin to brown. Add the tomatoes and cook for about 10 minutes. Season with salt and pepper.

Meanwhile, put the skate in the court bouillon, bring to a boil and simmer without boiling (to prevent the fish disintegrating) for 4 minutes. Drain and skin the fish. Keep it warm.

Melt the remaining butter in a small pan and brown the almonds. Pour the tomato mixture into a large serving dish and arrange the skate on top. Sprinkle the whole dish with the lemon juice and the fish with the browned almonds. Serve hot.

Skate with Black Butter Sauce

Serves 6

2½ lb skate, cut into 6 pieces
2 quarts Court Bouillon (page 86)
½ cup butter
⅓ cup capers
3 tablespoons chopped parsley
3 tablespoons vinegar
salt and pepper

Soak the skate in cold water for 30 minutes. Drain and put into the Court bouillon. Bring to a boil and simmer without boiling (to prevent the fish disintegrating) for 4 minutes. Drain and skin the fish on each side.

Melt the butter in a large skillet and brown the fish. Add the capers and cook for 5 minutes until the butter has turned a light brown. Sprinkle the pieces of skate with the parsley and turn off the heat. Pour the vinegar quickly over the fish in the pan, diluting the juices.

Adjust the seasoning. Transfer the skate to a warmed serving dish, pour the butter sauce over it, and serve immediately.

Salt Cod Paste with Cheese

Serves 6

1 lb potatoes
1 lb salt cod, soaked overnight
1 bay leaf
1 cup olive oil
1 garlic clove, chopped
$\frac{2}{3}$ cup milk, at room
    temperature
salt and pepper
1 tablespoon chopped parsley
$\frac{3}{4}$ cup grated Gruyère cheese

Cook the potatoes in boiling salted water for 20 minutes until tender. Drain, cool a little and slice. Set aside.

Drain and rinse the cod and put into a saucepan with just enough fresh water to cover. Add the bay leaf and bring just to a boil, then remove from the heat and leave the cod to poach in the pan for about 10 minutes. Drain and separate into small pieces.

Heat 3 tablespoons oil in a flameproof dish and add the chunks of cod. Over a low heat, work into a paste with a wooden spoon. Add the garlic, and continue to mix the ingredients, gradually adding the remaining oil and the milk alternately until both ingredients are incorporated. Adjust the seasoning.

Cover the cod paste with the potato slices and sprinkle with the parsley and Gruyère. Brown in a preheated 475° oven for about 6 minutes. Serve at once.

Salt Cod Provençal

Serves 4

1¼ lb salt cod, soaked overnight
3 tablespoons peanut oil
1 cup finely chopped onions
3 garlic cloves, finely chopped
1 lb tomatoes, peeled and chopped
¾ cup ripe olives
1 tablespoon capers
salt and pepper

Drain and rinse the cod and put into a saucepan of fresh water, making sure that the fish is completely covered. Bring just to a boil, then remove from the heat and leave the cod to poach in the pan for about 10 minutes. Drain, separate into chunks and put into a flameproof dish.

Heat the oil in a skillet and fry the onions and garlic. When they begin to brown, add the tomatoes, olives and capers. Season and leave to simmer for 10 minutes.

Pour the tomato mixture over the cod and simmer over a low heat for 10 minutes. Remove from the heat and serve immediately.

Bouillabaisse

Serves 6

$\frac{2}{3}$ cup olive or peanut oil
2 onions, chopped
6 garlic cloves, halved
1 tablespoon chopped parsley
3 quarts water
1 bouquet garni
$\frac{1}{8}$ teaspoon saffron powder
salt and pepper
3 lb assorted fish, scaled,
  cleaned and cut up, with
  heads left on
18 slices French bread

Heat 4 tablespoons oil in a large saucepan and fry the onions. Add half the garlic and the parsley and cook 2–3 minutes longer, stirring occasionally.

Add the water to the pan and bring to a boil over a high heat. Simmer for 5 minutes. Add the bouquet garni, saffron and salt and pepper to taste.

Add the fish pieces to the stock and cook over a low heat for 20 minutes. Drain the fish and remove the heads. Keep hot. Strain the stock and set aside.

Heat the remaining oil in a skillet and fry the bread slices until golden on both sides. Rub them with the rest of the garlic and put into a deep dish. Add the pieces of fish to the dish and pour over the strained stock. Serve accompanied by spicy sauces (Provençal or Garlic Mayonnaise, see page 390), or serve the stock as a soup to start the meal followed by the fish as a main course.

Seafood Soup

Serves 5

⅔ cup olive oil
1 onion, chopped
2 tomatoes, peeled and chopped
¾ lb squid, cut into thin strips
⅔ cup white wine
1 lb fresh cod fillet, cut into
  chunks
½ lb raw shrimp in shell
1 quart mussels, scrubbed
15 clams, scrubbed
1 garlic clove
1 tablespoon chopped parsley
1 teaspoon saffron powder
salt and pepper
5 slices bread, crusts removed

Heat three-quarters of the oil in a flameproof casserole and fry the onion with the tomatoes and squid. Add the white wine and cook over a low heat for 15 minutes.

Meanwhile, poach the cod and shrimp in a large pan of boiling salted water for 10 minutes.

If any of the mussels or clams are open, tap them and discard if they do not close. Put them into a large pan of water and bring to a boil. Simmer for 5 to 6 minutes until the shells open. Discard any that do not open. Remove the mussels and clams from their shells and set aside.

Drain the cod and shrimp, reserving the cooking liquid. Crush the garlic in a mortar. Add the parsley, the rest of the oil and the saffron and mix well. Season with salt and pepper.

Toast the bread and cut into small squares. Add the garlic mixture to the casserole, then stir in the reserved cooking liquid. Bring to a boil. Add the cod, shrimp, mussels and clams. Serve with the croûtons.

Mussel Vol-au-Vent

Serves 4

2 quarts mussels, scrubbed
⅔ cup dry white wine
3 tablespoons butter
4 scallops
¼ lb cod fillet
2 cups Béchamel sauce (page 384)
5 oz cooked shrimp, peeled
1 (8-oz) can mushrooms, drained and sliced
1 cup grated Gruyère cheese
3 tablespoons Crème Fraîche (page 398)
1 hard-cooked egg, mashed
1 large frozen vol-au-vent case (patty shell) for 4 servings *or* 4 individual vol-au-vent cases, thawed

If any of the mussels are open, tap them and discard if they do not close. Put them into a large pan with water to cover. Add the wine and bring to a boil. Simmer for 5 to 6 minutes until the shells open. Discard any that do not open. Remove the mussels from their shells and set aside.

Melt 2 tablespoons butter in a skillet and cook the scallops and cod.

Add the mussels to the Béchamel sauce together with the shrimp, cod, scallops and the mushrooms. Add the Gruyère, Crème fraîche and hard-cooked egg. Cook over a gentle heat for 10 minutes.

Pour into the vol-au-vent case, or cases and top with the remaining butter. Bake in a preheated 425° oven for 5 minutes.

Fisherman's Brochettes

Serves 6

1 pint mussels, scrubbed
6 clams, scrubbed
6 scallops
12 slices bacon, cut into strips
½ lb raw shrimp, peeled
1 tablespoon peanut oil
¼ cup butter
2 tablespoons flour
1½ cups fish broth or bottled clam juice
salt
1 tablespoon curry powder

If any of the mussels or clams are open, tap them and discard if they do not close. Put them into a large pan of water and bring to a boil. Simmer for 5 to 6 minutes until the shells open. Discard any that do not open. Remove the clams and mussels from the shells.

If using sea scallops, cut them in half or into quarters. Thread with the bacon, mussels, clams and shrimp onto six metal skewers. Brush the skewers with oil and cook under a preheated broiler for 5 minutes on each side.

Meanwhile, melt the butter in a small pan over a low heat. Add the flour and stir for 1 to 2 minutes. Remove from the heat and gradually add the fish broth or clam juice. Season with salt and add the curry powder. Return to the heat and cook, stirring, for about 5 minutes.

Serve the kabobs with the sauce.

Stuffed Mussels

Serves 4

1 quart large mussels, scrubbed
3 tablespoons soft bread crumbs
⅔ cup milk, warmed
½ lb bulk pork sausage meat
¼ lb slab bacon, diced
1 tablespoon chopped parsley
2 tablespoons chopped garlic
1 onion, finely chopped
pinch of grated nutmeg
1 egg, beaten
salt and pepper
½ cup sea salt

If any of the mussels are open, tap them and discard if they do not close. Put them into a large pan of water and bring to a boil. Simmer for 5 to 6 minutes until the shells open. Discard any that do not open, and the empty top shells.

Soak the bread in the milk. Put the sausage meat, bacon and soaked bread into a bowl. Add half the parsley, the garlic, onion, nutmeg and the egg. Add salt and pepper to taste and mix together with a fork.

Cover the bottom of an ovenproof dish with the sea salt. Cover the mussels in their shells with the stuffing and place them in the dish. The salt will keep the mussels upright during cooking. Bake in a preheated 475° oven for 20 minutes. Serve from the dish, garnished with the rest of the parsley.

Gulf Shrimp in Court Bouillon

Serves 3

2 quarts Court Bouillon (page 86)
15 raw Gulf shrimp in shell
salt
juice of 1 lemon
1 cup Mayonnaise (page 409)

Bring the court bouillon to a boil in a large saucepan. Immerse the shrimp, add salt and cook for 10 minutes over a low heat. Drain thoroughly, then peel and devein.

Add the lemon juice to the mayonnaise. Serve the shrimp cold, accompanied by the Mayonnaise.

Crêpes with Mussels

Serves 6

1½ quarts mussels, scrubbed
3 tablespoons butter
1 tablespoon flour
2 cups milk
salt and pepper
pinch of grated nutmeg
1 tablespoon chopped parsley
CRÊPES
1 cup flour
pinch of salt
2 eggs
1½ cups milk

Make the crêpe batter: sift the flour and salt into a bowl. Beat in the eggs and gradually add the milk. Leave to stand while preparing the mussels.

If any of the mussels are open, tap them and discard if they do not close. Put them into a large pan of water and bring to a boil. Simmer for 5 to 6 minutes until the shells open. Discard any that do not open. Remove the mussels from their shells and set aside. Strain the liquid contained in the shells and reserve.

Make a white sauce: melt 2 tablespoons butter over a low heat. Add the flour and stir for 1 to 2 minutes. Remove from the heat and gradually add the milk. Season with salt, pepper and nutmeg and return to the heat. Stir for about 5 minutes until the sauce thickens. Stir in 1 to 2 tablespoons of the reserved mussel liquid; the sauce must remain smooth and thick.

Add the mussels to the sauce and mix together to heat through. Keep warm.

Briefly whisk the crêpe batter. Pour about 1½ tablespoons into the center of a heavy-based crêpe pan or skillet and tilt the pan to spread the batter evenly. Cook for about 1 minute until the underside is golden. Turn and cook the other side for about 30 seconds until golden. Continue making crêpes, interleaving each with wax paper. Keep them warm.

Divide the mussel sauce between the crêpes, sprinkle with half the parsley and roll them up. Arrange in an ovenproof dish.

Dot the crêpes with the remaining butter and sprinkle over the remaining parsley. Bake in a preheated 425° oven for 3 minutes to reheat.

Trout with Bacon

Serves 2

¼ lb slab bacon, cut into small
    strips
¼ cup butter
2 medium-sized trout, scaled
    and cleaned
salt and pepper
1 tablespoon chopped parsley

Cook the bacon in a skillet until it is beginning to brown.

Meanwhile, heat the butter in another skillet and cook the trout over a low heat for 6 minutes on each side. Season with salt and pepper.

Add the bacon and rendered fat to the trout. Continue cooking over a low heat until the trout is cooked.

Arrange the trout on a serving dish with the fried bacon. Sprinkle with chopped parsley.

Mussels in White Wine

Serves 4

1½ quarts mussels, scrubbed
⅔ cup butter
1 tablespoon chopped chervil
3 onions, chopped
3 tablespoons chopped parsley
2 cups white wine
pepper
½ cup Crème Fraîche (page 398)

If any of the mussels are open, tap them and discard if they do not close. Soak in cold water to cover for 2 to 3 hours, changing the water several times.

Melt the butter in a saucepan and add the chervil, onions and half the parsley. Cook over a low heat for 5 minutes, stirring occasionally.

Add the white wine, and season with pepper, then add the mussels. Cover, bring to a boil and cook over a low heat for 6 minutes until the shells open. Discard any that do not open.

Remove from the heat. Transfer the mussels with a slotted spoon to a soup tureen. Strain the cooking juices and mix with the Crème fraîche. Pour over the mussels and sprinkle with the remaining parsley. Serve immediately.

Rock Lobster with Avocados

Serves 6

2 quarts Court Bouillon (page 86)
3 live, medium-sized rock or spiny lobsters or crawfish
2 avocados
½ cup Crème Fraîche (page 398)
juice of 1 lemon
salt and pepper
2 tablespoons butter
2 tablespoons grated Gruyère cheese

Bring the court bouillon to a boil and immerse the lobsters head first. Poach for 20 minutes over a medium heat, making sure the water simmers but does not boil. Drain in a colander and shell the lobsters using a sharp knife or scissors: split the shells along the stomach so that they are not damaged. Arrange the shells in a baking dish.

Discard the black thread and dice the lobster meat. Halve the avocados, discard the seed, peel and slice the flesh. Mix the avocados and lobster meat in a bowl and add the crème fraîche, lemon juice and seasoning to taste. Mix thoroughly.

Fill the lobster shells generously with this mixture and garnish the dish with any that remains.

Dot with the butter, sprinkle with the Gruyère and brown in a preheated 450° oven for 10 minutes. Serve at once.

Scallops au Gratin

Serves 6

6 scallops
½ cup butter
1 shallot, chopped
½ lb mushrooms, sliced
2 tablespoons flour
⅔ cup milk
⅔ cup white wine
salt and pepper
¾ cup grated Gruyère cheese

Cook the scallops in a saucepan of simmering salted water for about 3 minutes. Drain and chop the scallops. Set aside.

Melt 3 tablespoons butter in a skillet and fry the shallot and mushrooms for 10 minutes.

Meanwhile, melt 2 tablespoons butter in a saucepan over a low heat. Add the flour and stir for 1 to 2 minutes. Remove from the heat and gradually add the milk and wine. Season and return to the heat. Stir for about 5 minutes until the sauce thickens.

Add the scallops to the sauce with the mushrooms and shallot. Stir in the grated cheese.

Fill 6 scallop shells with this mixture and dot each with the remaining butter. Brown in a preheated 475° oven for 10 minutes. Serve immediately.

Scallop Brochettes

Serves 6

18 sea scallops
1 tablespoon peanut oil
1 tablespoon sea salt

Thread the scallops onto metal skewers Brush the skewers with oil, salt lightly and place on a rack in a roasting pan. Bake in a preheated 475° oven for 10 minutes, turning occasionally.

Fish Loaf

Serves 4

2½ cups soft bread crumbs
⅔ cup milk, warmed
¾ lb skinless boneless white fish, cooked
salt and pepper
1 cup Béchamel Sauce (page 384)
3 egg whites
Tomato sauce (page 391)

Soak the bread crumbs in the milk, then squeeze dry. Put the cooked fish into a bowl and flake with a fork. Add the soaked bread, mix well and season with salt and pepper. Add the Béchamel sauce.

Beat the egg whites until stiff and fold into the fish mixture.

Butter a 5 × 4 × 3 inch loaf pan and pour in the mixture. Bake in a preheated 425° oven for about 20 minutes. Unmold and serve immediately with Tomato sauce.

To serve cold, garnish the loaf with hard-cooked egg, anchovies, ripe olives and Mayonnaise (see page 401).

Squid Stuffed with Sorrel

Serves 4

2 lb sorrel
2 lb squid, cleaned
¼ lb slab bacon, diced
½ lb small onions, chopped
4 eggs
salt and pepper
⅛ teaspoon saffron powder
¼ cup peanut oil
3 slices bread, each cut into 4
   triangles

Cook the sorrel in a pan of salted water, over a high heat, for 6 minutes. Drain thoroughly and purée in a blender or food processor. Cut off and finely chop the tentacles of the squid. Mix with the bacon, onions, sorrel and one egg. Season with salt, pepper and saffron and use the mixture to stuff the squid bodies.

Heat 2 tablespoons oil in a skillet and cook the stuffed squid over a very low heat for 1 hour.

Meanwhile, hard-cook the remaining eggs. Shell and slice. Heat the remaining oil and fry the bread until golden brown.

Arrange the squid in a serving dish and garnish with the egg slices and the croûtons.

Clams au Gratin

Serves 6

36 large clams
2 tablespoons chopped garlic
2 tablespoons chopped parsley
salt and pepper
2 tablespoons dried white bread
   crumbs
1 cup grated Gruyère cheese
2 tablespoons butter
flat-leaved parsley and lemon
   slices for garnish

If any of the clams are open, tap them and discard if they do not close. Put them into a large pan of water and bring to a boil. Simmer for 5 to 6 minutes, until the shells open. Discard any that do not open. Remove the clams from the shells. Discard the black-tipped tube and rinse the clams under running water to get rid of any sand. Reserve the bottom shells.

Mix the clams with the garlic and parsley and fill the bottom shells with the mixture. Season with salt and pepper and sprinkle over the bread crumbs and grated cheese. Place a pat of butter on each.

Arrange the shells in a large ovenproof dish and brown in a preheated 475° oven. Remove from the oven and arrange on a serving dish garnished with parsley and lemon slices. Serve very hot.

Lobster Thermidor

Serves 4

2 quarts Court Bouillon (page 86)
2 live, medium-sized lobsters
1 tablespoon flour
$\frac{1}{2}$ cup butter
$\frac{2}{3}$ cup Crème Fraîche (page 398)
$\frac{2}{3}$ cup Madeira
$\frac{2}{3}$ cup champagne
salt and pepper
2 cups grated Gruyère cheese

Bring the Court bouillon to a boil and immerse the lobsters head first. Poach for 10 minutes over a medium heat, making sure the water simmers but does not boil. Drain in a colander. Split the lobsters in half lengthwise using a sharp knife, and carefully remove the flesh. Reserve the shells.

Cut the lobster meat into pieces, discarding all inedible parts, and coat in the flour. Melt the butter and brown the lobster pieces for 2 minutes. Pour in the crème fraîche then the Madeira and champagne. Season with a few pinches of salt and pepper, mix thoroughly and use to fill the lobster shells. Sprinkle with grated cheese and brown in a preheated 450° oven for 15 minutes. Serve at once.

Tuna with Tomatoes

Serves 4

1 green pepper
¼ cup peanut oil
1 onion, chopped
2 lb tomatoes, peeled
salt and pepper
1 bay leaf
1 tablespoon chopped thyme
1 tablespoon chopped garlic
1¼ lb fresh tuna steaks

Cut off the stalk end from the green pepper. Remove seeds and pith and slice the pepper. Heat 3 tablespoons oil in a large skillet and add the onion and pepper. Fry for about 10 minutes and then add the tomatoes. Season with salt and pepper. Add the bay leaf, thyme and garlic. Cover and simmer over a low heat for 30 minutes.

Meanwhile, brush the tuna steaks with the rest of the oil and cook under a preheated broiler for about 15 minutes on each side.

Spoon the tomato sauce into a serving dish and arrange the fish on it.

— POULTRY AND GAME —

Poultry was once thought of as an expensive delicacy, set aside for special occasion cooking. Nowadays, chicken and turkey are among the cheapest of main-meal ingredients and they are no longer available only in the form of whole birds. As pieces, boneless breasts, breast fillets or in the shape of boneless rolls of meat, these poultry require little preparation before cooking.

Game on the other hand is both seasonal and more expensive. You will find recipes for guinea hen, pheasant, hare and partridge in this chapter. In fact, guinea hen, as well as squab (small pigeon) is domesticated and therefore is not seasonal. The short hunting season for wild pheasant and other game birds is in the fall. Some of these – pheasant in particular – are now reared on game farms.

Recipes for duck are also included in this chapter. Frozen ducks are sold in most supermarkets and duck pieces or duck breast are also available in some stores. Goose is not as widely available but can be purchased from good specialty butchers where it is expensive compared to other poultry. This is the traditional bird to roast for the Christmas meal, but turkey is now more popular and has virtually replaced the goose.

This chapter offers a broad range of dishes, suitable for all occasions, from economical chicken dishes to a selection of special recipes for game birds. Some are quick and easy, others will take longer cooking and a few require more attention to the preparation: a complete mixture of dishes for all occasions.

Chicken in the Pot

Serves 6 to 8

½ lb salt pork
5 quarts water
3 carrots
3 turnips
1 onion
3 leeks
1 bouquet garni
5 tablespoons long-grain rice
1¼ cups chopped mushrooms
½ cup diced smoked ham
1 (4½-lb) chicken, heart and
    liver reserved
salt and pepper
1 teaspoon dried tarragon
¼ cup butter
2 tablespoons flour
1 egg yolk
juice of 1 lemon

Put the pork into a large kettle, cover with the water and bring to a boil. Add the carrots, turnips, onion, leeks and the bouquet garni and simmer for 30 minutes.

Meanwhile, cook the rice in a pan of boiling salted water for 15 minutes until just tender. Drain, transfer to a bowl and add the mushrooms and ham. Grind the chicken liver and heart and add to the rice. Season with salt and pepper, add the tarragon and mix together thoroughly. Use to stuff the chicken. Truss the chicken, tying the opening securely. Strain the vegetables from the stock and set them aside, then plunge the stuffed chicken into the stock. Simmer gently for 1½ hours.

When the chicken is cooked, prepare the sauce: melt the butter over a low heat. Add the flour and stir for 1 to 2 minutes. Gradually add 1½ cups of the chicken stock and stir until the sauce thickens. Blend the egg yolk with the lemon juice and add to the sauce, stirring constantly until heated through. Reheat the vegetables briefly in a little stock.

Drain the chicken and serve on a large warmed dish, surrounded by the vegetables and the pork. Serve the sauce separately, in a sauceboat.

Chicken Soup
Boiled chickens yield large quantities of excellent stock which can be used to make delicious soups. Boil the stock until it is reduced to approximately 1 quart in quantity. Finely chop a large onion and a potato, then cook both in a pat of butter until the onion is soft but not brown. Add 1 tablespoon of flour, cook for 1 minute, then pour in the stock and bring to a boil. Simmer for 30 minutes, then blend the soup in a blender or food processor until smooth. Reheat and season to taste. Add some chopped, cooked chicken meat, a handful of chopped parsley and ½ cup light cream. Heat without boiling then serve.

Basque Chicken

Serves 4 to 6

5 tomatoes
1 green pepper
1 sweet red pepper
3 tablespoons peanut oil
3 onions, thinly sliced
2 tablespoons olive oil
1 (3½-lb) chicken
3 garlic cloves, chopped
salt and pepper
YELLOW RICE
2 tablespoons olive oil
1½ cups long-grain rice
1 teaspoon ground turmeric
3 cups chicken broth

Leave one tomato whole; peel and quarter the others. Remove stalks from the peppers; cut one ring from the green pepper and set aside. Cut the peppers in half and remove seeds and pith. Chop the peppers.

Heat the peanut oil and fry the onions until golden. Heat the olive oil in a flameproof casserole and brown the chicken well all over. Add the onions, quartered tomatoes, chopped peppers, garlic, and the whole tomato. Season, cover and cook gently for 1 hour.

Prepare the yellow rice: heat the oil in a heavy-based pan, add the rice and stir for 2 minutes. Add the turmeric and cook, stirring over low heat for a further 1 to 2 minutes. Pour in the broth gradually, stirring. Bring to a boil, lower the heat and cover with a tight-fitting lid. Cook over a very low heat for about 15 minutes or until the liquid has been absorbed and the rice is tender.

Cut the chicken into portions and serve on the rice. Garnish with the vegetables from the casserole, the green pepper ring and the whole tomato.

Chicken with Crawfish

Serves 4 to 6

1 (3½-lb) chicken, liver reserved
5 oz bacon slices
1 (8-oz) can mushrooms, drained
1 tablespoon chopped chives
1 tablespoon chopped parsley
salt and pepper
2 eggs, beaten
1 large piece pork fat, for barding
15 raw crawfish or Gulf shrimp in shell
3 sprigs thyme
1 bay leaf
¼ cup butter
juice of 1 lemon

Grind together the chicken liver, bacon and mushrooms. Mix in the herbs and seasoning. Bind with the eggs. Use to stuff the chicken. Cover with the barding pork fat and roast in a preheated 425° oven for 1 hour.

Cook the crawfish or shrimp for 5 minutes in simmering salted water with plenty of pepper, the thyme and bay leaf. Drain. Reserve the six nicest shellfish whole for decoration. Peel the remaining ones, reserving the roe if there is any. Purée the shellfish in a blender or food processor. Melt the butter on a low heat, add the shellfish purée and cook for 7 minutes, then push through a fine sieve to make crawfish or shrimp butter.

Just before serving, mash any reserved roe and add to the crawfish or shrimp butter. Reheat gently – the mixture must not boil – and blend in the lemon juice. Adjust the seasoning, if necessary.

Remove the barding fat from the chicken and place the chicken on a serving dish. Garnish the dish with the reserved shellfish and serve the sauce separately.

Chicken with Almonds

Serves 4 to 6

3 tablespoons olive oil
1¾ cups flaked almonds
1 (3½-lb) chicken, cut up
3 sweet red peppers
3 large onions, thinly sliced
2 tomatoes, peeled and
  quartered
¼ teaspoon saffron powder
salt and pepper
2 cups hot chicken broth
⅓ cup raisins
1 teaspoon whole coriander
  seeds, crushed
a few cloves
⅔ cup ripe olives
1 cup pine nuts
3 cups fine or medium grain
  couscous

Heat the olive oil in a flameproof casserole and fry the almonds until golden brown. Remove and set aside. In the same dish, brown the chicken pieces. Set aside.

Remove the stalk from the red peppers. Cut the peppers in half and remove seeds and pith. Chop the peppers. Add the peppers, onions and tomatoes to the casserole and cook them for 5 minutes, stirring occasionally. Return the chicken pieces to the casserole, sprinkle with saffron and season with salt and pepper.

Pour over the broth and add the raisins, coriander seeds and cloves. Cover and cook over a moderate heat for 40 minutes.

Add the olives, the pine nuts and the almonds and cook for a further 10 minutes. Meanwhile, cook the couscous, following the package instructions.

Arrange the chicken on a warmed serving dish and coat with the pan juices. Serve accompanied with the couscous.

Chicken in Rosé Wine

Serves 4

5 oz slab bacon, chopped
10 small onions, thinly sliced
1 garlic clove, crushed
1 (4½-lb) chicken, cut up
2 tablespoons flour
2 cups dry rosé wine
salt and pepper
1 bouquet garni
2 tablespoons butter

Cook the bacon in a flameproof casserole until browned and rendered of fat, then add the onions and garlic. Soften them. Remove the onions and bacon and set aside.

Put the chicken pieces into the casserole and brown thoroughly. Pour off any excess fat and sprinkle the chicken with the flour. Add the wine and season with salt and pepper. Stir well. Add the bouquet garni together with the onions and bacon. Cover and simmer for 45 minutes.

Just before serving, remove the chicken pieces and arrange them on a heated serving dish. Discard the bouquet garni and melt the butter in the cooking liquid, stirring until the sauce is smooth. Pour over the chicken pieces and serve at once.

Duck Pâté in a Pastry Case

Serves 12

1 (2½-lb) duck, boned, with liver
   reserved (page 83)
¾ lb bulk pork sausage meat
2 egg yolks, beaten
salt and pepper
1 teaspoon ground allspice
2½ quantities Basic Pie Pastry
   (page 431)
½ lb pork tenderloin, cut into
   strips
3 tablespoons brandy

Cut the duck meat into strips, carefully removing the skin and fat. Grind the liver. Mix the sausage meat with half the egg yolk and add the liver. Season with salt and pepper and add the allspice.

On a lightly floured board, roll out the pastry and use to line a 2¼-quart capacity terrine. Put in half the duck, then a layer of the sausage meat mixture, a layer of pork strips, and finish with the remaining duck. Pour over the brandy. Roll out the rest of the pastry and use to cover the filling. Reserve the pastry trimmings. Moisten the pastry edges and press together to seal. Make a hole in the center of the pie lid and decorate with pastry trimmings. Brush with the remaining egg yolk and bake in a preheated 425° oven for 1 hour. Cover with foil, make a hole in the center and bake for a further 30 minutes.

The pâté is cooked when the pastry is really golden and when the point of a knife pushed into the filling comes out clean.

Remove the pâté from the oven and leave to cool a little before unmolding. Cool completely before eating.

Variations
Crushed garlic cloves can be added to the pâté with the seasoning and allspice. Grated orange rind makes an excellent addition – use the grated rind of 1 large orange and add it to the pâté with the seasoning. Drained canned peach slices can also be included in the pie; buy fruit canned in natural juice and drain the slices thoroughly, then layer them with the sausage meat, pork and duck in the pie.

Duck with Tarragon

Serves 4

1 (4½-lb) duck
salt and pepper
3 tablespoons chopped fresh
   tarragon *or* 1½ tablespoons
   dried tarragon
2 tablespoons peanut oil
1 tablespoon flour
⅔ cup hot water
⅔ cup dry white wine, warmed
double quantity Potato Purée
   (page 14)
20 tarragon leaves

Sprinkle the inside of the duck with salt and pepper and insert 2 tablespoons chopped tarragon.

Heat the oil in a flameproof casserole and brown the duck all over for 20 minutes. Sprinkle with the rest of the chopped tarragon and the flour, then add the water and wine. Season with salt and pepper. Cover the casserole and cook over a low heat for 1½ hours.

Spoon the Potato purée onto a warmed serving dish. Place the duck on top. Skim off the fat from the pan juices and pour the juices over the duck. Garnish with the whole tarragon leaves.

Duck with Brussels Sprouts

Serves 3 to 4

$3\frac{1}{2}$ lb Brussels sprouts
3 tablespoons peanut oil
$\frac{1}{2}$ lb bacon slices, rolled up
1 ($3\frac{1}{2}$-lb) duck
1 quart hot chicken broth
1 bouquet garni
salt and pepper
2 tablespoons white wine

Cook the sprouts in boiling salted water for 10 minutes. Drain and squeeze gently to get rid of excess water.

Heat the oil in a flameproof casserole and brown the bacon rolls and the duck, then add the broth, the bouquet garni and the sprouts. Season and cook for 1 hour over a low heat.

Place the duck on a warmed serving dish and surround with the sprouts and bacon rolls.

Discard the bouquet garni from the pan juices. Skim off excess fat. Pour in the wine. Reduce the juices over a high heat and pour over the duck.

Curried Chicken

Serves 4

¼ cup olive oil
5 shallots, thinly sliced
1 garlic clove, thinly sliced
1 (3½-lb) chicken, cut up
2 tablespoons curry powder
salt and pepper
2 tablespoons flour
1 cup red wine
1½ cups long-grain rice
1 cup Crème Fraîche (page 398)

Heat the oil in a flameproof casserole and brown the shallots and garlic. Add the pieces of chicken and fry them until golden brown.

Sprinkle in half the curry powder, and salt and pepper to taste. Add the flour and stir well, then stir in the red wine. Cover the casserole and cook over a medium heat for 1¼ hours.

Cook the rice in a pan of boiling salted water for about 15 minutes until just tender. Drain and transfer to a warmed serving dish. Arrange the chicken pieces on the rice.

Blend the rest of the curry powder with the Crème fraîche. Skim the excess fat from the casserole juices and pour in the cream mixture. Stir well until the sauce is smooth. Reduce the sauce by boiling for a minute or two. Pour a little sauce over the chicken, and serve the rest in a sauceboat.

Deviled Chicken

Serves 4

1 (3½-lb) chicken, cut into
    pieces
salt and pepper
½ cup butter
¼ cup strong mustard
3 tablespoons dried bread
    crumbs
1¼ cups white wine
2 shallots, finely chopped
1 cup chicken broth
⅛ teaspoon cayenne
1 cup Crème Fraîche (page 398)
lemon halves for garnish

Sprinkle the chicken with salt and pepper and put into an ovenproof dish. Melt half the butter and pour over the chicken. Bake in preheated 425° oven.

After 30 minutes, remove the dish from the oven, spread the chicken with the mustard, sprinkle with the bread crumbs and dot over the rest of the butter. Return to the oven to bake for a further 30 minutes.

Meanwhile, make the sauce: put the wine into a saucepan and boil to reduce by two-thirds. Add the shallots and the broth. Bring to a boil and boil for 3 to 4 minutes. Season with the cayenne. Keep warm.

When the chicken is cooked, remove from the oven and arrange the pieces on a warmed serving dish. Serve the sauce separately and accompany with the Crème fraîche and lemon halves.

Stuffed Chicken

Serves 4 to 6

6 tablespoons butter
$\frac{1}{4}$ cup ground bacon
3 oz lean boneless veal, cut into strips
3 oz chicken livers
1 ($4\frac{1}{2}$-lb) chicken, liver reserved
1 cup thinly sliced mushrooms
1 shallot, minced
salt and pepper
1 egg yolk
1 tablespoon chopped parsley
2 strips pork fat, for barding
$\frac{1}{4}$ cup brandy
5 tablespoons white wine
$\frac{1}{4}$ cup Crème Fraîche (page 398)

Melt $\frac{1}{4}$ cup butter in a large skillet with the bacon. Add the veal and brown it over a high heat. Add all the chicken livers, the mushrooms, and the shallot. Season with salt and pepper.

When everything is golden brown, grind all the ingredients finely and mix together thoroughly. Blend in the egg yolk and the chopped parsley.

Stuff the chicken with this mixture, then truss it. Wrap around the pork fat and tie with string. Place in a roasting pan, dot with the rest of the butter and roast for $1\frac{1}{2}$ hours in a preheated 425° oven. Baste with the juices once or twice during cooking.

Just before serving, remove the barding fat and the string and place on a warmed serving dish.

Skim the excess fat from the cooking juices. Add the brandy and white wine and reduce a little over a high heat, then add the Crème fraîche and boil for 1 minute. Whisk the sauce and pour half over the chicken. Serve the rest separately.

Casseroled Guinea Hen

Serves 2 to 4

1 (2½-lb) guinea hen, cleaned
1 strip pork fat, for barding
5 tablespoons peanut oil
1 bay leaf
¼ cup hot water
salt and pepper
2 cups whole kernel corn
2 tomatoes

Bard the guinea hen with the pork fat and truss the bird. Heat the oil in a flameproof casserole with the bay leaf, add the guinea hen and brown all over, for 10 minutes.

Pour over the hot water and season with salt and pepper. Cover and continue cooking over a moderate heat for 30 minutes, turning the bird twice during cooking. The second time, 10 minutes before the end of the cooking period, add the corn. Slash the skins of the tomatoes on top and add them also. Adjust the seasoning if necessary, and cover the casserole.

When the bird is cooked, remove the barding fat, and the trussing string. Spoon the corn onto a warmed serving dish, sit the guinea hen on top and garnish with the tomatoes.

Duck with Cherries

Serves 3 to 4

salt
1 (3½-lb) duck
½ cup butter
1 lb cherries, pitted
2 tablespoons sugar
pinch of ground cinnamon
⅔ cup port wine
grated rind and juice of 1
   orange
¼ cup red currant jelly
¼ cup cherry liqueur

Salt the inside of the duck and truss it. In a flameproof casserole, melt the butter and brown the duck all over, then lower the heat and leave to cook for about 1½ hours.

Meanwhile, put the cherries into a saucepan with the sugar and cinnamon, but no water. Cover and cook for 5 minutes over a low heat. Remove from the heat and leave to cool.

Remove the cooled cherries with a slotted spoon and set aside. Add the wine and the rind and juice of the orange to the cherry juices and reduce by half over a low heat.

Add the red currant jelly to the reduced juices and stir constantly until melted and the mixture is smooth. Return the cherries to the pan and keep warm.

When the duck is cooked, remove from the casserole and place on a warmed serving dish. Skim the excess fat from the juices and add the cherry liqueur. Pour over the duck and surround with the cherries. Pour over the cherry sauce.

Roast Chicken with Mushrooms

Serves 4 to 6

6 tablespoons butter
14 oz mushrooms, thinly sliced
1 slice stale bread
¼ cup milk
1 cup ground cooked ham
1 egg
3 tablespoons brandy
pinch of ground allspice
pinch of grated nutmeg
pinch of dried tarragon
salt and pepper
1 (3½-lb) chicken
2 lb potatoes
½ cup Crème Fraîche (page 398)
TO SERVE
a few leaves chicory
chopped parsley

Melt half the butter and gently fry the mushrooms. Soak the bread in the milk. In a large bowl, mix one-third of the mushrooms with the ground ham, egg, the soaked bread, 1 tablespoon of the brandy, the spices and the tarragon. Season and use to stuff the chicken. Sew up and place in a roasting pan. Sprinkle with salt and pepper and dot with the rest of the butter.

Roast in a preheated 450° oven for 15 minutes, then lower the oven temperature to 400° and continue roasting for 45 minutes. Meanwhile, cook the potatoes for 20 minutes in boiling salted water. Drain.

About 10 minutes before the end of the cooking time, add the potatoes and the rest of the mushrooms. Pour the Crème fraîche over. Return to the oven.

Warm the rest of the brandy in a small pan and light it. When the flames subside pour over the chicken. Transfer the chicken to a warmed serving dish, surround with the potatoes and mushrooms, and pour over the cooking liquid. Garnish and serve.

Fricasséed Chicken

Serves 4

1 (3½-lb) chicken, cut up
½ cup butter
⅔ cup white wine
20 pearl onions
1 quart water
1 bouquet garni
salt and pepper
2 tablespoons flour
1¼ cups thinly sliced button
 mushrooms
3 egg yolks
1 tablespoon chopped parsley

Put the chicken pieces, 3 tablespoons of the butter and the wine into a flameproof casserole. Cover and cook over a moderate heat to evaporate the wine.

Meanwhile, blanch the onions for a few minutes in boiling water.

When the wine has evaporated, add the water to the casserole with the onions and the bouquet garni. Season with salt and pepper and boil for 5 minutes. Blend the flour to a paste with a little cold water and stir into the casserole. Half-cover and cook over a moderate heat for 25 minutes.

Meanwhile, melt 3 tablespoons butter and gently fry the mushrooms. Add to the casserole 5 minutes before the end of the cooking time.

Just before serving, arrange the chicken pieces in a warmed serving dish. Remove the bouquet garni.

Beat the egg yolks, parsley and the rest of the butter into the cooking juices and pour over the chicken.

Guinea Hen with Apples

Serves 2 to 3

½ cup butter
1 (2½-lb) guinea hen, cleaned
¼ cup Calvados or applejack
1 lb onions, very thinly sliced
salt and pepper
1 cup Crème Fraîche (page 398)
2 lb apples

Melt half the butter in a flameproof casserole and brown the guinea hen.

Heat the Calvados in a small saucepan and pour over the guinea hen. Set the Calvados alight and continue cooking until the flames subside. Add the onions and season with salt and pepper. Pour in one-third of the Crème fraîche and stir gently. Cover and cook over a low heat until the Crème has turned a hazelnut color. Add the rest of the Crème and cook gently for 30 minutes.

About 15 minutes before the guinea hen is cooked, peel, core and slice the apples into rings. Melt the rest of the butter and fry them gently.

When the guinea hen is cooked, transfer the onions to a warmed serving dish. Place the guinea hen on top and surround with the golden apple slices.

Duck with Olives

Serves 4

1½ lb green olives (about 3
　cups), pitted
2 (3½-oz) tubes anchovy paste
1 (4-lb) duck
6 tablespoons butter
2 tablespoons olive oil
salt and pepper

Stuff the olives with anchovy paste. Fill the duck with stuffed olives and sew it up carefully. Reserve all the remaining olives.

Heat the butter and oil in a large flameproof casserole and brown the duck, making sure it is golden all over. Add the rest of the olives, season with just a little salt (since the olives are already salty) and pepper. Cover and simmer over a moderate heat for 2 hours. Serve the duck very hot surrounded by the olives.

Spit-Roasted Goose

Serves 10

1 (8-lb) goose, cleaned
salt and pepper
3 strips pork fat, for barding
1 lb tart apples
¼ cup sugar

Sprinkle the goose with salt and pepper and wrap in the pork fat. Tie with fine string to keep in place.

Put the goose on the spit and roast in the oven for 2 hours, basting occasionally with its juice.

Meanwhile, peel core and slice the apples, then put them in a saucepan with the sugar and heat gently until the juice runs. Continue to cook, stirring occasionally until the fruit is reduced to a pulp. Add a little water if necessary.

Before serving, remove the string and barding fat from the goose and transfer to a serving platter. Skim any excess fat from the pan juices and pour into a sauceboat. Serve with the apple purée.

Duck with Orange

Serves 3 to 4

½ cup butter
1 (3½-lb) duck
salt and pepper
2 tablespoons oil
5 oranges
4 brown sugar cubes
¼ cup Madeira
watercress for garnish

Put 2 tablespoons of the butter inside the duck and truss. Heat the oil and the rest of the butter in a flameproof casserole and brown the duck over a high heat – about 30 minutes.

Meanwhile, squeeze the juice of three of the oranges and reserve. Thinly peel the remaining oranges. Cut the peel into very thin strips and blanch for 2 minutes in boiling water. Segment the oranges and set aside.

Remove the duck from the casserole and skim off some of the fat from the juices. Pour the orange juice and strips of peel into the casserole and add the sugar. Return the casserole to a low heat and melt the sugar, stirring. Return the duck to the casserole and cook for another 40 minutes over a moderate heat.

Just before serving, remove the duck and place on a warmed serving dish. Skim the fat from the cooking juices. Add the Madeira to the cooking juices and stir in then pour over the duck. Surround with the reserved orange segments and garnish with watercress.

Royal Chicken

Serves 4

$\frac{1}{4}$ cup butter
1 (3$\frac{1}{2}$-lb) chicken, cut into large
    pieces
pinch of cayenne
1$\frac{1}{2}$ teaspoons dried chervil
pinch of grated nutmeg
salt and pepper
$\frac{2}{3}$ cup champagne
2 egg yolks
$\frac{2}{3}$ cup Crème Fraîche (page 398)
$\frac{3}{4}$ cup green olives
2 slices bacon, chopped

Melt the butter in a flameproof casserole and brown the chicken pieces. Add the cayenne, chervil and nutmeg and season with salt and pepper.

When the chicken is golden brown, pour over the champagne. Beat the egg yolks and the crème fraîche together and add to the casserole. Stir until thick.

Add the olives and the bacon. Cover and cook for 45 minutes over a moderate heat, stirring occasionally. Serve at once.

Chicken Galantine

Serves 6 to 8

1¼ lb ground bacon (about 2
  cups)
¼ cup ground cooked ham
1 cup ground lean veal
1 cup ground lean pork
3 eggs
1¼ cups Cognac
2 tablespoons pistachio nuts
salt and pepper
1 (4½-lb) chicken, boned (page
  83) but with drumsticks in
  place
2 carrots, sliced
1 onion, thinly sliced
1 bouquet garni
2 cups aspic, set in a shallow
  pan

Mix the bacon with the other meats thoroughly in a large
bowl. Add the eggs, one by one, then the cognac and
nuts. Adjust the seasoning, if necessary.

Spread the chicken out on a cloth and stuff with the
meat mixture. Gather together the edges of the skin and
sew it up, re-forming into a chicken shape. Wrap up
tightly in a scalded cloth and plunge the galantine into a
large pan of water. Add the sliced carrots, onion and
bouquet garni. Bring to a boil and cook for about 2
hours.

Drain the galantine, unwrap and place on an
ovenproof dish. Brown in a preheated 425° oven.
Garnish with diamonds of aspic.

Partridges on Canapés

Serves 6

6 partridges, cleaned
6 thin slices bacon
6 slices white bread
¼ cup butter
salt
cayenne
2 tablespoons peanut oil
¾ lb mushrooms, thinly sliced
watercress for garnish

Wrap each partridge in a slice of bacon and truss. Toast the bread on both sides and arrange in an Ovenproof dish. Place a partridge on each slice.

Melt the butter and pour over the partridges. Sprinkle with salt and add a pinch of cayenne to each bird. Roast in a preheated 325° oven for 30 minutes.

Meanwhile, heat the oil and fry the mushrooms. Serve the partridges on the slices of toast, surrounded with mushrooms. Garnish with watercress.

Turkey with Chestnuts

Serves 8 to 10

3 (1-lb) cans whole
   unsweetened chestnuts,
   drained
1½ lb bulk pork sausage meat
1 teaspoon dried thyme
1 bay leaf
1 tablespoon chopped parsley
salt and pepper
1 (6½-lb) turkey
¼ cup butter
6 slices bacon

Mix one-third of the chestnuts with the sausage meat and add the thyme, bay leaf and parsley. Season with salt and pepper. Use the mixture to stuff the turkey and then truss it. Place in a roasting pan and dot with the butter. Sprinkle with salt and pepper and roast in a preheated 425° oven for about 2½ hours. Baste occasionally with the pan juices.

Wrap six of the remaining chestnuts in the slices of bacon. About 15 minutes before the end of cooking time, arrange these and the rest of the chestnuts around the turkey. Return to the oven to complete the cooking time.

Transfer the turkey to a warmed serving platter and surround with the bacon rolls and chestnuts. Serve the pan juices separately.

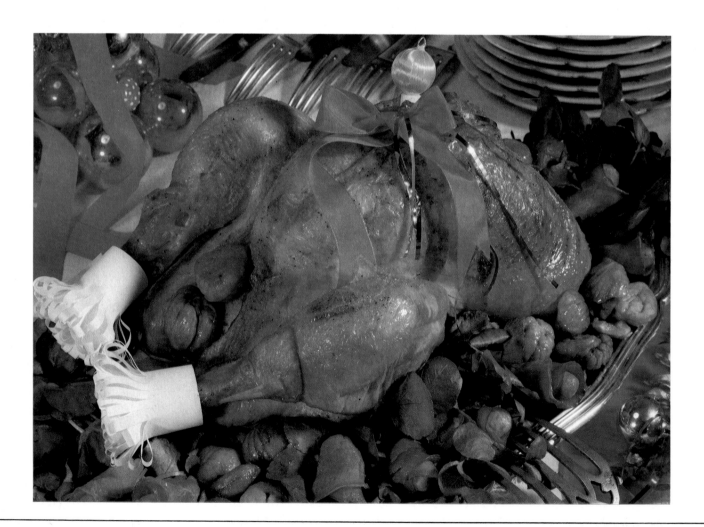

Rabbit with Mustard

Serves 4

1 (3½-lb) rabbit, cleaned
6 tablespoons strong mustard
3 tablespoons peanut oil
salt and pepper
1 tablespoon chopped tarragon
¼ cup water
2 lb small potatoes
3 tablespoons Crème Fraîche
   (page 398)

Brush the rabbit generously with the mustard. Heat the oil in a flameproof casserole and brown the rabbit all over. Sprinkle with salt and pepper, add the tarragon and pour over the water. Cook over a low heat for about 35 minutes, adding a little more water if necessary, and turning the rabbit occasionally so that it cooks evenly. Continue cooking for another 25 minutes.

Meanwhile, cook the potatoes in boiling salted water for 20 minutes.

Just before serving, remove the rabbit and place on a warmed serving dish. Skim any excess fat from the juices. Stir in the Crème fraîche and reduce over a high heat for 3 minutes. Pour over the rabbit. Drain the potatoes and serve with the rabbit.

Rabbit in a Pastry Case

Serves 4

1 (3½-lb) rabbit, skinned and
   cleaned
salt and pepper
double quantity Basic Pie
   Pastry (page 431)
¼ lb slab bacon, chopped
1 lb potatoes
¼ cup vegetable oil
TO SERVE
chicory

Sprinkle the rabbit with salt and pepper. On a lightly
floured board, roll out the pastry to ¼ inch thickness. Use
to wrap up the rabbit.

Put into a large roasting pan with the bacon and roast
for about 40 minutes in a preheated 450° oven, basting
occasionally with the pan juices.

Meanwhile, parboil the potatoes in salted water for 10
minutes. Heat the oil in a baking pan in the oven. Drain
the potatoes thoroughly and put into the baking pan.
Continue roasting with the rabbit for 30 minutes.

Serve the rabbit and roast potatoes garnished with
chicory.

Hare Pâté

Serves 6

1 (3½-lb) hare, skinned, cleaned
   and boned, with liver and
   heart reserved
½ lb fresh pork sides, chopped
¼ lb slab bacon, chopped
3 slices bread, crusts removed
5 tablespoons milk, warmed
2 eggs
1½ tablespoons chopped parsley
1 tablespoon salt
1 teaspoon pepper
2 tablespoons brandy
6 slices bacon

Ask your butcher to prepare the hare for you. Chop the hare roughly, together with the liver and heart. Put into a large bowl with the chopped pork sides and bacon. Soak the bread in the milk, then squeeze out and mix with the meat.

In another large bowl, beat the eggs and add the parsley, salt, pepper and brandy. Pour into the meat mixture and mix together thoroughly.

Butter an ovenproof (about 3-pounds in size) terrine and press the mixture down well in it. Spread the bacon slices over the top.

Cover with greased parchment paper and the lid and place the terrine in a roasting pan. Pour in water to come halfway up the dish. Bake in a preheated 425° oven until the water comes to a boil, then lower the oven temperature to 350° and cook for 2½ hours. Remove from the oven and cool completely.

Store for 24 hours before eating.

Chicken Liver Terrine

Serves 6

½ lb chicken livers, finely
   ground
¼ lb calf's liver, finely ground
½ cup finely ground bacon
2 egg yolks, beaten
1 shallot, minced
large pinch of grated nutmeg
salt and pepper
5 thin slices bacon, for barding
2 bay leaves

Mix together the ground livers and bacon. Add the egg yolks, shallot and nutmeg and season with salt and pepper.

Line the bottom and sides of a 1½-pound terrine or 9 × 5 × 3 inch loaf pan with the bacon slices. Spoon in the mixture and press down well. Arrange the bay leaves on top and cover with the lid. Place the terrine in a roasting pan. Pour in water to come halfway up the dish. Bake in a preheated 350° oven for 2 hours. Remove from the oven and cool completely.

Store for 24 hours before eating. Serve sliced on toast.

Duck Foie Gras

Serves 4

1 (1-lb) duck liver
salt and pepper
1 carrot, thinly sliced
1 onion, thinly sliced
1 bouquet garni
1½ quarts dry white wine

Separate the two lobes of the liver, sprinkle them with salt and pepper and lay "head to tail" in a terrine. Add the carrot, onion and bouquet garni. Cover with the wine and leave to marinate for 12 hours.

Remove the liver from the terrine and pour off the marinade, reserving it. Sprinkle the liver with salt and pepper and return to the terrine. Press it down, place a small wooden board on top and weight down. Leave for 1 hour.

After this time, pour over the white wine once more and place the terrine in a roasting pan. Pour in water to come halfway up the sides of the terrine. Bake in a preheated 375° oven for 20 to 30 minutes, making sure that the liver remains covered with the white wine.

When the liver is cooked, remove from the oven and cool. Place a small board on top and weight down for 1 hour. The pâté can be kept in a cool place for two weeks.

Flambéed Pheasant

Serves 4

1 (4-lb) pheasant, cleaned, with
  liver reserved
1 teaspoon sweet paprika
2 thin slices bacon, for barding
3 tablespoons peanut oil
salt and pepper
$\frac{2}{3}$ cup brandy
$\frac{2}{3}$ cup red wine
2 cups chicken broth
$\frac{1}{4}$ cup butter, softened
1 tablespoon flour
1 teaspoon Dijon-style mustard
TO GARNISH
2 oranges, segmented
green and black grapes
$\frac{1}{2}$ cup walnut halves

Sprinkle the inside of the pheasant with the paprika, wrap in the bacon slices and truss. Heat the oil in a flameproof casserole and brown the pheasant for about 10 minutes. Sprinkle with salt and pepper.

Warm the brandy in a small saucepan, pour into the casserole and set alight. When the flames subside, pour over the red wine with half the chicken broth. Cover and cook over a moderate heat for 40 minutes.

Meanwhile, grind the pheasant liver and mix together with the butter, flour and the mustard. When the pheasant is cooked, remove from the dish, discard the string and keep warm. Make the sauce by pouring the rest of the broth into the casserole. Boil gently and add the liver mixture, stirrring constantly until smooth.

Place the pheasant on a warmed serving platter and pour over the sauce. Garnish with the fruits and walnut halves.

Hunter's Rabbit

Serves 4

2 tablespoons peanut oil
3 slices bacon, chopped
3½ lb rabbit pieces, thawed if
    frozen
2 tablespoons olive oil
2 small onions, thinly sliced
2 shallots, thinly sliced
¼ cup flour
1¼ cups white wine
¼ cup brandy
1 bouquet garni
salt and pepper
1 (8-oz) can mushrooms,
    drained, with half the liquid
    reserved

Heat the peanut oil in a flameproof casserole and brown the bacon. Remove from the casserole and set aside. In the oil and bacon fat, brown the rabbit pieces.

Meanwhile, heat the olive oil in another pan and cook the onions and shallots until golden. Set aside.

When the rabbit pieces are well colored all over, pour off excess fat. Sprinkle with the flour and pour over the white wine and brandy. Mix well. Add the onions, shallots, bacon and bouquet garni, and season with salt and pepper. Cover and simmer over a low heat for 1 hour.

About 10 minutes before the end of the cooking time, add the mushrooms and their liquid to the casserole. Cook over a high heat to reduce the cooking liquid, stirring so that it does not stick. Serve very hot.

Rabbit with Prunes

Serves 4

2 cups prunes
$\frac{2}{3}$ cup rum
2 tablespoons peanut oil
$\frac{1}{4}$ lb slab bacon, chopped
3 onions, thinly sliced
$3\frac{1}{2}$ lb rabbit pieces, thawed if frozen
1 bouquet garni
salt and pepper
$1\frac{1}{2}$ lb potatoes
parsley sprigs for garnish

Put the prunes into a large bowl, pour over the rum, then add hot water to cover the prunes completely and soak for 2 hours.

Heat the oil in a flameproof casserole and brown the bacon and the onions. Add the rabbit pieces and cook until golden brown. Pour off excess fat.

Drain the prunes and set aside. Add their soaking liquid to the casserole with the bouquet garni. Season with salt and pepper. Cover and simmer over a moderate heat for 45 minutes.

Pit the prunes, add to the casserole and cook for another 15 minutes, then remove the bouquet garni.

Meanwhile, cook the potatoes in boiling salted water for 20 minutes. Serve the rabbit in a warmed deep dish. Surround with the bacon and prunes. Drain the potatoes and arrange around the dish. Garnish with parsley.

MEAT DISHES

There is a great temptation when it comes to meat cooking to adopt a repertoire of well-tried favorite recipes and never attempt anything else. It is usually the expense or the necessary planning and preparation involved in experimenting with new ideas which puts people off attempting to cook a different cut of meat or a different combination of hotpot ingredients.

Times and techniques for roasting meat are fairly personal; some people favor rare meat while others will eat only well-cooked roasts. The following times will offer a guide to achieving the result you prefer. Whether you opt for a quick roasting method or a slower method depends to an extent on individual preference but also on the quality of the meat. If you have a roast which is tender, then it will roast very successfully in a hot oven; if you think it may be tough, then put it in at a lower temperature. For beef on the bone, in a hot oven (425°), allow 15–20 minutes per pound plus 15 minutes extra. Off the bone allow 20–25 minutes per pound plus 5 minutes extra. In a moderate oven (350°), on the bone allow 20–25 minutes per pound plus an additional 25 minutes. Off the bone allow 30–35 minutes per pound plus an extra 35 minutes.

Pork must be well-cooked so it is best to calculate the time in a moderate oven (350°) at 25 minutes per pound plus an extra 25 minutes. To seal the roast and keep it juicy, the roast can be cooked in a hot oven (425°) for about 10 to 15 minutes first. Alternatively, the roast can be browned in a hot, dry heavy-based skillet for a few minutes before roasting.

Lamb is a tender, fatty meat which benefits from roasting in a hot oven (425°) for 15 to 20 minutes per pound on the bone plus an extra 20 minutes. Off the bone allow 20 to 25 minutes per pound plus an extra 25 minutes. If you think the lamb may be slightly tough, start it off in a hot oven and reduce the temperature to moderate (350°) after the first 20 or 25 minutes, then extend the cooking time slightly.

Calculating the cooking time by weight is a good starting point when you are roasting meat, but your own taste is the best guide. Check the roast as it cooks, using a meat skewer to pierce it or a meat thermometer. If you are roasting meat in a hot oven, have a piece of cooking foil at hand to cover the roast should it become too brown.

In addition to roasts, this chapter offers ideas for casseroles and hotpots, steaks and croquettes. Many of the recipes also include some interesting and full-flavored ingredients in sauces, stuffings or accompaniments.

Steak with Green Peppercorns

Serves 4

3 tablespoons butter
1 tablespoon peanut oil
4 filet mignons or boneless
   sirloin steaks (about 5 oz
   each)
2 tablespoons brandy
$\frac{2}{3}$ cup beef or chicken broth
$\frac{1}{2}$ cup Créme Fraîche (page 398)
$\frac{1}{4}$ cup green peppercorns
salt

Heat the butter and oil together in a skillet and seal the steaks over a high heat for 3 minutes. Turn them over and continue cooking for a further 3 minutes over moderate heat. Flame the steaks with the brandy, then arrange them on a serving dish, and keep hot.

Pour the broth into the skillet and leave to simmer for a few minutes. Scrape the bottom of the pan gently with a spatula to dissolve the glazed juices. Add the cream, the green peppercorns and salt to taste. Simmer gently until the sauce has reduced a little in quantity.

Pour the sauce over the steaks and serve them very hot, with fried tomatoes and watercress or French fried potatoes.

Steak Burgers

Serves 2 to 3

3 onions, finely chopped
3 tablespoons butter
1 lb ground sirloin
salt and pepper
$\frac{1}{4}$ cup flour
2 tablespoons peanut oil

For this recipe, choose meat with just a little fat; it will yield a softer burger.

Fry the onions gently in half the butter until golden. Season the steak, mix with the onion, then shape into 2 to 3 large balls with your hands. Flatten these balls and dust them lightly with flour. Heat the rest of the butter and the oil together in a skillet and fry the steak burgers over a high heat for 5 minutes each side.

The steaks can be served garnished with a poached egg, a pat of maître d'hôtel butter, half a fried tomato or a slice of bacon.

Steak Tartare

Serves 1

salt and pepper
6 oz very lean steak, ground
1 raw egg yolk
GARNISH
1 teaspoon capers
2 gherkins, finely chopped
1 shallot *or* 1 small onion, finely
   chopped
1 tablespoon finely chopped
   parsley plus a few extra
   sprigs
lemon slices

Season the meat, and shape it into a ball with a slight hollow in the middle. Place in the center of a serving plate and pour the egg yolk into the hollow very gently, so that it does not break.

Arrange the garnish ingredients around the steak on the serving plate. Each guest selects his ingredients and mixes them with the meat according to taste.

Grilled Rib of Beef

Serves 2

1 lb beef rib roast
1 tablespoon peanut oil
salt and pepper
1 tablespoon finely chopped
   parsley
watercress for garnish

Preheat the broiler to its hottest setting. Lightly trim and flatten the rib, so that it will cook more evenly. Brush with oil on both sides.

Place the meat under the broiler, close to the heat, and cook for a few minutes on both sides to seal in the juices. Move a bit further away from the source of heat and cook for a total of 7 minutes on each side for medium-done meat. (The cooking times given here are average ones. Allow less time if you like your steak rare, more if you like it well done. Cooking times will also vary slightly according to the thickness of the steak.)

When the steak is cooked to your liking season well on both sides with salt and pepper and sprinkle over the parsley. Place on a warmed serving plate and serve at once garnished with watercress.

Navarin of Lamb

2h 30m

Serves 6

2½ lb lamb for stew
¼ cup butter
4 onions, chopped
¼ cup flour
3 cups chicken broth
2 tablespoons tomato paste
2 carrots, sliced
1 bouquet garni
salt and pepper
2 cups dried navy beans, soaked
   overnight
1½ lb potatoes

Cut the meat into large pieces and trim off excess fat. Melt the butter in a large heavy kettle or flameproof casserole and fry the onions until soft. Remove the onions and fry the meat until golden brown on all sides. Remove from the pan.

Sprinkle in the flour and stir over a low heat until golden brown. Add the broth and tomato paste. Bring just to a boil and put back the meat and onions, together with the carrots and the bouquet garni. Season to taste, cover, and simmer gently for 1 hour.

In the meantime, drain and rinse the navy beans and cook in boiling, unsalted water for about 45 minutes. Peel the potatoes and cut into chunks.

When the meat has simmered for 1 hour, skim any fat from the top, then add the drained beans and the potatoes to the pan. Add a little boiling water if necessary. Cook for a further hour. Serve very hot.

Brain Fritters

Serves 4

1 carrot, roughly chopped
1 onion, roughly chopped
a few sprigs of parsley
salt and pepper
juice of $\frac{1}{2}$ lemon
2 cups cold water
$1\frac{1}{4}$ cups flour
2 tablespoons oil plus oil for
  deep frying
$1\frac{1}{2}$ cups lukewarm water
4 lambs' brains, soaked
  overnight
2 egg whites

Make a stock by placing the carrot, onion, one sprig of parsley, salt, pepper and the lemon juice in a saucepan with the cold water. Bring to a boil and simmer for 30 minutes. Strain and cool.

Prepare the batter by putting the flour into a bowl and making a well in the center. Add the 2 tablespoons oil, a pinch of salt and the lukewarm water. Mix thoroughly and leave to rest for 30 minutes.

Drain the brains. Carefully clean them, removing the membrane and the blood vessels. Place in the stock. Bring to a boil over a high heat, then reduce the heat and simmer for 7 minutes. Leave to cool in the stock.

Heat the oil for deep frying to 350°. Beat the egg whites until stiff and fold into the batter.

Season the brains, dip them into the batter one by one, then put them into the hot oil. Cook until golden brown, then drain on paper towels. Garnish and serve hot.

Sirloin Steak with Shallots

Serves 2

2 tablespoons butter
1 boneless sirloin steak (about
   1 lb)
salt and pepper
1 small onion, chopped
3 shallots, chopped
1 cup red wine
1 tablespoon finely chopped
   parsley

Heat the butter in a heavy skillet and fry the steak over a high heat for 3 minutes on each side. Season to taste with salt and pepper. Remove from the skillet, and keep hot. Put the chopped onion and shallots in the skillet and fry until golden brown, stirring. Reduce the cooking liquid almost completely, then add the wine. Bring to a boil and boil to reduce for 3 minutes.

Place the steak on a warmed serving dish and cover with the shallot sauce. Sprinkle with chopped parsley. This goes well with potatoes au gratin and a green salad.

Broiled Kidneys

Serves 6

12 lamb kidneys *or* 3 veal
   kidneys
3 tablespoons olive oil
salt and pepper

Preheat the broiler to high. Carefully clean the kidneys: cut them in half (not all the way through) and remove the fat, the core and all the excess tubes. Rinse in cold water and pat dry on paper towels. Skewer the kidneys right through so that they will stay as flat as possible during cooking. The veal kidneys, being larger, should be skewered on two crossed skewers. Brush the kidneys with oil, and broil for about 6 minutes on each side. Season the kidneys to taste and serve at once.

Variety meats

Variety meats (liver, heart, kidneys, heads, tongue, brain, sweetbreads, etc) are pieces of meat often considered to be gourmet fare. Some of them can only be obtained from a good old-fashioned butcher. You should demand faultless quality and freshness, which is essential not only for the flavor of these meats, but also for their nutritional value. Variety meat is very rich in vitamins, mineral salts and phosphates.

Beef and Red Wine Stew

Serves 6

3 lb beef chuck steak
$\frac{1}{4}$ cup lard
$\frac{1}{2}$ lb slab bacon, diced
$\frac{1}{4}$ lb pearl onions
2 tablespoons flour
$\frac{2}{3}$ cup beef broth
$1\frac{1}{4}$ cups red wine
1 (8-oz) can tomatoes
1 bouquet garni
a few sage leaves
salt and pepper
$\frac{1}{2}$ lb button mushrooms
chopped parsley for garnish

Cut the beef into large pieces. Melt the lard in a large kettle or flameproof casserole and brown the pieces of meat over a moderate heat. Remove from the pan. Add the bacon and onions and fry until golden brown, then remove them from the pan.

Pour off all but $\frac{1}{4}$ cup fat from the pan. Sprinkle with the flour and cook, stirring, until golden brown, then stir in the broth. When the sauce is smooth, put the pieces of beef, the bacon and onions back in the pan and add the wine (this should just cover the meat). Add the tomatoes, the bouquet garni and the sage. Season to taste and simmer very gently for about $2\frac{1}{2}$ hours. Alternatively cook in a preheated 325° oven.

Remove any fat from the top of the casserole and add the mushrooms. Cook for another 20 minutes. Serve the stew sprinkled with chopped parsley.

Oxtail Hotpot

Serves 6 to 8

$\frac{1}{4}$ cup butter
$4\frac{1}{2}$ lb oxtails, cut up
1 pig's foot, blanched (optional)
$1\frac{1}{4}$ cups white wine
2 quarts water
salt and pepper
1 medium-sized head cabbage
1 lb carrots, sliced
$\frac{1}{2}$ lb turnips, roughly chopped
3 onions, halved
1 bouquet garni

Melt the butter in a large kettle or flameproof casserole. Brown the oxtail on all sides with the pig's foot, if using. When brown, add the white wine and water, season and bring to a boil. Cover and leave to simmer for about 1 hour.

In the meantime, cut the cabbage into quarters and blanch it briefly in boiling water. Skim off any fat from the casserole. Add all the vegetables, together with the bouquet garni. Leave to simmer for a further $1\frac{1}{2}$ hours.

When serving, cut the pig's foot into pieces. Serve the meat and vegetables on a large dish. This goes well with plain boiled potatoes and tomato or horseradish sauce.

Pot-au-feu

Serves 6

1 (2½-lb) beef pot-roast
3 leeks
2 onions
2 cloves
½ lb carrots
1 celery stalk
½ lb turnips
salt
a few black peppercorns
1 marrow bone (optional)
1 lb potatoes

Plunge the meat into a large kettle of boiling water. Allow the water to come back to a boil and lower the heat to a gentle simmer.

Tie the leeks together. Stud one onion with the cloves. Cut up the carrots if large. Skim the fat from the liquid in the kettle, then add the celery, leeks, onions, carrots, turnips, salt to taste and the peppercorns. Cover and leave to simmer for 2½ hours.

About 30 minutes before the end of the cooking time, wrap the marrow bone (if using) in a cloth. Knot the corners diagonally, and add the bone to the kettle.

Cook the potatoes separately in boiling salted water for 20 minutes until they are tender. Drain.

Serve the meat and vegetables together. The marrow from the bone may be scooped out and spread on toast. You may also serve each guest with a bowl of the very hot stock.

Beef Tenderloin in Broth

Serves 6

3 quarts beef broth
1 onion
1 sprig thyme
1 bay leaf
salt
1 tablespoon black peppercorns
1 carrot
the white part of 1 leek
1 large turnip
1 (3-lb) piece beef tenderloin
12 medium-size potatoes

Bring the broth slowly to a boil in a kettle with the onion, thyme, bay leaf, a little salt and the peppercorns. Add the carrot, leek and turnip. Leave to simmer for 30 minutes.

Tie up the meat, leaving a loose piece of string which you can use to tie the meat to the handle of the kettle (enabling you to remove the meat without burning yourself). Place the meat in the broth and simmer for 45 minutes. Meanwhile boil or steam the potatoes.

Drain the steak, untie the string and serve the meat surrounded with the potatoes and the vegetables from the pot. Serve with condiments of your choice, for example mustard, pickled onions, gherkins as well as various sauces (béarnaise, bourguignonne, etc.).

Pork Shoulder with Cherries

Serves 6

2 tablespoons butter
1 boneless pork shoulder roast,
   weighing about 2½ lb
1 tablespoon each chopped
   fresh thyme and rosemary *or*
   1½ teaspoons each dried
   thyme and rosemary
salt and pepper
2 lb cherries
1 tablespoon sugar

This recipe, which is a subtle blend of sweet and salt flavors, will be enjoyed by those who are fond of more original cooking.

Grease an ovenproof dish with the butter and put the pork in it. Sprinkle with the thyme, rosemary and pepper. Roast in a preheated 450° oven for 20 minutes. Add 1¼ cups hot water to the pork and lower the oven temperature to 400°. Leave to cook for 1 hour longer, basting with the juices from time to time.

In the meantime, stalk and pit the cherries. Dissolve the sugar in ⅔ cup of water in a saucepan, and poach the cherries gently in this syrup for 10 minutes.

When the pork is cooked, remove from the oven, and surround with cherries and cherry juice from the pan. Adjust the seasoning, if necessary, and serve very hot.

French Country Hotpot

Serves 6

¾ lb slab bacon
6 Toulouse sausages or other
   garlic sausage
2 blood sausages
4 quarts cold water
1 head green cabbage, quartered
6 carrots
4 small turnips
3 onions
1 teaspoon cloves
1 bay leaf
1 teaspoon black peppercorns
salt
8 potatoes

Each region of France has its own version of this hotpot or "potée," but pork and cabbage are essential ingredients. You may wish to devise your own variations.

Put the bacon and sausages into a kettle with the cold water. Bring to a boil and skim, then add the cabbage, carrots, turnips, onions (studded with the cloves), bay leaf, peppercorns, and salt to taste. Cover the kettle tightly and simmer for 1¾ hours. Add the potatoes 10 minutes before the end of the cooking time.

You may use a pressure cooker if you have one large enough. Reduce the cooking time to 45 minutes. Remember to reduce the pressure before opening.

Serve the meat on the vegetables, together with some of the stock in a soup bowl and condiments such as gherkins and mustard which go well with this dish.

Leg of Lamb with Three Beans

Serves 6

2 cups dried red kidney beans,
  soaked overnight
$\frac{1}{4}$ lb slab bacon, chopped
2 onions
$1\frac{1}{4}$ cups red wine
2 cups dried navy beans, soaked overnight
2 cups dried green flageolet
  beans, soaked overnight
4 cloves garlic
2 carrots
2 bouquet garnis
1 leg of lamb, weighing about
  $3\frac{1}{2}$ lb
$\frac{1}{4}$ cup butter
salt and pepper
GARNISH
tomato roses
watercress

Place the kidney beans in a pan of cold water, bring to a boil and boil rapidly for 10 minutes. Reduce the heat and add the bacon, one onion and the wine. Simmer for 1 hour.

Meanwhile, put the navy and flageolet beans in boiling water to cook (separately) for 30 minutes with a clove of garlic, a sliced carrot and a bouquet garni.

While the beans are cooking, stud the leg of lamb with the remaining two cloves of garlic, sliced. Brush with butter and season with salt and pepper. Put the lamb in a roasting pan with the remaining onion, sliced and a little water. Roast in a preheated 425° oven for about 1 hour (the meat should be golden brown).

Drain the three types of beans when cooked and keep hot, without mixing them. Place the leg of lamb on a serving platter, garnish with the tomatoes and watercress, and surround it with the beans.

Ragoût of Lamb with White Beans

Serves 4 to 5

2 cups dried navy beans
2 lb lamb neck slices
2 tablepoons butter
2 tablespoons peanut oil
2 carrots, sliced
2 onions, chopped
½ lb Canadian bacon, diced
3 tablespoons flour
3 cups chicken broth
1 bouquet garni
salt and pepper

Soak the beans for 1 hour before cooking the ragoût. Drain and cook the beans in fresh water for 30 minutes.

Meanwhile trim the pieces of lamb, removing the fat. Melt the butter and oil together in a flameproof casserole and brown the pieces. When brown, remove and put to one side. Fry the carrots, onions and bacon in the same casserole until golden brown. Drain off excess fat. Put the meat back in the casserole. Sprinkle flour over the pieces of meat, then pour over the broth. Stir and add the bouquet garni. Season to taste, bring to a boil and simmer until the beans are ready.

Drain the beans and add them to the ragoût. Simmer gently for a further 1¼ hours. Serve the ragoût straight from the casserole. The casserole may also be cooked in a preheated 325° oven.

Casseroled Shoulder of Lamb

Serves 6

1 lamb shoulder roast, weighing
   about 3 lb
2 cloves garlic, sliced
3 tablespoons butter
salt and pepper
2 onions, sliced
3 bay leaves
2 sprigs of thyme
$\frac{2}{3}$ cup dry white wine
2 lb potatoes

Stud the lamb with slivers of garlic and spread the butter over it. Season with salt and pepper. Place the shoulder of lamb in a large flameproof casserole, and add the onions, the bay leaves and the sprigs of thyme. Cook the lamb over a high heat for 10 minutes, turning the meat over from time to time so that it browns on all sides.

When the meat has browned, pour the white wine into the casserole and add the potatoes. Bring to a boil, cover and leave to braise gently for $1\frac{1}{2}$ hours over a medium heat. Adjust the seasoning and serve the lamb straight from the casserole, after adjusting the seasoning if necessary.

Rack of Lamb Boulangère

Serves 4

1 rack of lamb consisting of 8
  chops
salt and pepper
6 tablespoons butter
1½ lb potatoes
⅔ cup water
a few sprigs watercress for
  garnish

Trim the lamb. Place it in an ovenproof dish. Season with salt and pepper and brush with the butter. Roast in a preheated 400° oven for 20 minutes.

Meanwhile, cook the potatoes in boiling salted water for 15 minutes. Drain. Take the meat out of the oven. Lower the oven temperature to 350°. Cut the potatoes into thick slices, and arrange them around the meat. Pour over the water. Put the dish back in the oven and roast for 15 minutes. The potatoes will finish cooking.

Garnish with the watercress before serving. Rack of Lamb Boulangère is traditionally served in the cooking dish.

Sauerkraut with Sausages

Serves 6 to 8

½ cup lard
1 2-lb smoked pork shoulder
  roll or half loin
½ lb slab bacon
5 lb sauerkraut, rinsed and
  drained
1 uncooked Toulouse sausage
  or other garlic sausage
8 large frankfurters
2 lb potatoes
salt

Melt the lard in a heavy kettle and add the pork and bacon. Cover with the sauerkraut. Cook over a medium heat for 30 minutes. Add the garlic sausage, and continue cooking for a further 30 minutes.

Meanwhile, poach the frankfurters for 10 minutes in boiling water, off the heat. Peel the potatoes and cook them in lightly salted boiling water for 20 minutes.

Drain the frankfurters and add them to the kettle. Cook for a further 15 minutes over a low heat. Before serving, test all the different meats with the point of a knife to ensure that they are cooked. Arrange the sauerkraut and meats on a serving dish with the boiled potatoes.

Pork with Mustard

Serves 6

salt and pepper
1 center loin of pork, weighing
   about 3 lb
3 tablespoons oil
2 onions, chopped
1¼ cups white wine
a few fresh tarragon leaves *or* ½
   teaspoon dried tarragon
¼ cup strong mustard

Season the pork, brush it lightly with the oil and place it in a roasting pan. Surround with the onions. Roast in a preheated 450° oven for 25 minutes or until golden brown.

Add the white wine and tarragon to the roasting pan. Spread the mustard over the meat. Put it back into the oven and reduce the temperature to 375°. Roast for a further 25 minutes.

Remove the pork from the oven, place on a warmed serving platter and keep hot. Skim any fat from the cooking juices, then deglaze them with a little warm water and strain.

Serve the pork with fried potatoes and a salad. Hand the sauce separately in a sauceboat.

Beef Fondue

Serves 4 to 5

2 lb boneless sirloin steak
1½ quarts good quality oil
TO SERVE
3 or 4 sauces of your choice (see pages 379–414)

Although the only Burgundy in this fondue is the name, your guests will still be delighted with it because it is fun. It is extremely simple to prepare, and very versatile because of all the permutations of sauces and accompaniments.

Prepare the various sauces in advance, using the recipes in the Sauces chapter. Try Green Sauce, Béarnaise Sauce and Tomato Sauce for example.

Cut the meat into bite-sized pieces (about 1-inch cubes). Put the fondue burner and the stand on the table.

The oil should be heated in the kitchen in the fondue pan and set over the fondue burner when very hot, but not smoking.

Each guest should skewer a piece of meat on a fondue fork, and cook it in the oil to taste. The meat is then dipped into one of the sauces and seasoned to taste. This goes well with fresh crusty bread and a crisp green salad.

Lamb Chops with Herbs

Serves 4

½ cup butter
2 tablespoons chopped fresh
   tarragon *or* 1 tablespoon
   dried tarragon
8 lamb rib chops
2 tablespoons chopped chervil
   or parsley
1 tablespoon chopped chives
salt and pepper
1¼ cups white wine

About 1 hour before the meal, make some tarragon butter by mashing 6 tablespoons of the butter with about two-thirds of the tarragon. Roll this butter into a cylinder, wrap in aluminum foil and chill in the refrigerator.

Sprinkle the chops with half the chopped chervil and chives and cook under a preheated hot broiler for 8 minutes. Turn them over halfway through the cooking time. Transfer the chops to a warmed serving plate.

Heat the remaining butter in a skillet. Add the white wine and sprinkle in the rest of the tarragon, chervil or parsley and chives. Leave to simmer for 5 minutes over a low heat.

Pour this herb sauce over the chops and garnish each with a slice of tarragon butter.

Calves' Liver with Oranges

Serves 4 to 5

6 tablespoons butter
5 slices of calves' liver weighing
 about 5 oz each
salt and pepper
4 oranges
few sprigs watercress for
 garnish

Heat $\frac{1}{4}$ cup of the butter in a skillet. Fry the slices of liver over a high heat for about 4 minutes on each side until browned. Season with salt and pepper when cooked.

In the meantime, squeeze two of the oranges to extract the juice. Peel the other oranges (removing all the pith) and cut into slices. Using the rest of the butter, fry the orange slices until golden brown in a separate skillet.

When the slices of liver are cooked, arrange them on a hot serving dish. Add the orange juice to the skillet and heat gently to dissolve the meat juices. Pour this sauce over the liver. Garnish the dish with the fried orange slices and sprigs of watercress.

Pork and Lamb Ragoût

Serves 6

$\frac{1}{2}$ lb onions
$\frac{1}{2}$ cup butter
3 lb mixed boneless pork and
 lamb
1 tablespoon flour
salt and pepper
1 cup dry hard cider
2 quarts chicken broth
1 bouquet garni
2 carrots, cut i.to sticks
2 cloves
1$\frac{1}{2}$ cups prunes, soaked
 overnight if necessary
2 lb apples, peeled, cored and
 quartered

Slice the onions, reserving one, which should be left whole. Brown the sliced onions in half the butter. Cut the lamb and pork into largish pieces and trim off any fat. Brown the meat in a heavy casserole in the rest of the butter. Sprinkle with the flour and stir thoroughly. Season with salt and pepper and add the cider. Mix well together and bring to a boil. Lower the heat and cover the casserole. After 5 minutes add the sliced onions and cover with the broth. Add the bouquet garni, the carrots and the whole onion (studded with the cloves). Adjust the seasoning and bring back to a boil. Add the prunes and apples and simmer gently for 5 minutes. Cover and cook for about 1$\frac{1}{2}$ hours over a low heat.

Serve with the pieces of meat arranged on top of the fruit and vegetables.

Breaded Pork Chops

Serves 4

2 eggs
salt and pepper
4 pork chops
$\frac{1}{4}$ cup flour
$\frac{2}{3}$ cup dried white bread crumbs
6 tablespoons butter
10 gherkins
1 (8-oz) can tomatoes

Break the eggs into a bowl and season, then beat to mix with a fork. Trim the pork chops. Dredge the chops with flour, then dip into the beaten egg and finally into bread crumbs. Press the bread crumbs onto the chops to help them adhere firmly. Heat the butter in a skillet and fry the chops over a medium heat for about 10 minutes each side or until browned and cooked through.

Reserve 6 whole gherkins for the garnish and thinly slice the remainder. Pour the tomatoes into a small saucepan and chop roughly. Add the sliced gherkins and seasoning and heat through gently.

Serve the pork chops with the tomato sauce and garnished with the reserved gherkins, sliced lengthwise into fan shapes.

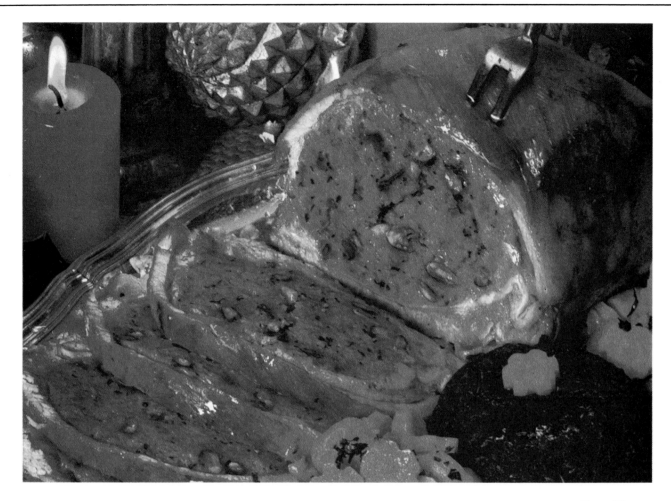

Stuffed Breast of Veal

Serves 4 to 6

2½ cups soft bread crumbs
4–6 tablespoons milk
2 onions, chopped
1 tablespoon chopped parsley
1¼ cups grated Gruyère cheese
⅔ cup ground smoked ham
1 cup chopped pistachio nuts
salt and pepper
1 egg, beaten
1 (2-lb) boned breast of veal
¼ cup butter
1¼ cups white wine
⅔ cup chicken broth
1 tablespoon tomato paste

First prepare the stuffing. Soak the bread crumbs in the milk. Add half the onion, the parsley, cheese, ham and pistachios. Season to taste and add the beaten egg to bind.

Lay the meat flat on the work top and spread the stuffing over it. Roll up tightly and tie with string.

Cook the remaining onion in the butter in a heavy casserole until beginning to brown. Add the veal and brown on all sides. Add the white wine, the broth and the tomato paste. Season with salt and pepper and put the lid on the casserole. Simmer over a low heat for about 1½ hours. Remove the string, place the meat on a warmed serving dish and cut it into slices. Serve with spinach or sorrel purée and a plain vegetable such as carrots.

Veal in Cream Sauce

Serves 4

2 lb boneless shoulder or breast
   of veal
⅔ cup white wine
1 onion
2 cloves
2 carrots, quartered
1 bouquet garni
2 cloves garlic, crushed
salt and pepper
2 tablespoons butter
¼ cup flour
2 egg yolks
½ cup Crème Fraîche (page 398)
juice of 1 lemon

Cut the meat into 2-inch strips. Place the meat in a heavy casserole and cover with water and the white wine. Bring to a boil and skim. Add the onion (studded with the cloves), the carrots, the bouquet garni and the garlic. Season to taste, then cover and simmer for 1 hour. Drain the pieces of meat and place in another heavy casserole with the butter. Strain the stock left from cooking the veal and skim off any fat. When the butter has melted, sprinkle with flour and mix well to obtain a pale roux then add the veal stock. Leave to cook over a low heat for 50 minutes.

About 10 minutes before the end of the cooking time, mix the egg yolks with the cream and add to the sauce to thicken it. Lastly, add the lemon juice and season to taste. Leave to cook very gently over a low heat for 10 minutes. It is important not to boil the sauce after adding the egg yolks or it will curdle. Serve with boiled rice.

Veal in Pastry

Serves 6

1 (3-lb) boned veal sirloin roast
2 tablespoons butter, melted
1 (1-lb) package frozen puff
   pastry, thawed
salt and pepper
3 tablespoons strong mustard
2 teaspoons chopped fresh
   tarragon or 1 teaspoon dried
   tarragon
1 egg yolk

Brush the meat with melted butter and brown in a preheated 450° oven for 10 minutes. While the meat is browning roll out the pastry to an oblong large enough to wrap around the veal. Take the meat out of the oven and season it. Brush with mustard, and sprinkle with tarragon. Wrap the veal in the pastry, sealing the seams carefully. Place seam-side down on a dampened baking sheet. Brush the pastry with beaten egg yolk and mark a lattice pattern with a knife.

Place in the oven and reduce the temperature to 400°. Cook for 25 minutes or until the pastry is golden brown. Serve with tartare sauce (see page 394) and mixed vegetables.

Croquettes with Herbs

Serves 4 to 5

1 large onion, finely chopped
1 lb raw or cooked ground beef,
   lamb or chicken (about 2
   cups)
2 eggs, beaten
½ cup grated Gruyère cheese
pinch of grated nutmeg
1 tablespoon chopped fresh sage
   and thyme *or* 2 teaspoons
   dried mixed herbs
salt and pepper
3–4 tablespoons flour
2 tablespoons oil
2 tablespoons butter
GARNISH
1 lemon, sliced
10 anchovy fillets
5 olives

Croquettes come in various shapes and can be made from many different ingredients. The basic ingredient is meat but you may add mushrooms, vegetables, spices etc. as you wish.

Mix the onion with the meat and add the egg, Gruyère cheese and nutmeg. Add the herbs and season to taste with salt and pepper. Mix thoroughly and shape into 4 to 5 balls. These should be flattened slightly, especially if they contain raw meat as this will help them to cook thoroughly.

Dredge lightly with flour, then fry in a mixture of oil and butter for at least 8 minutes, turning once. If the croquettes contain raw meat check to see that they are cooked thoroughly. Serve garnished with slices of lemon, anchovy fillets and olives as shown in the photograph, with spinach or another green vegetable.

Meatballs with Tomato Sauce

Serves 3

¾ lb bulk pork sausage meat, *or*
  6 oz lean boneless pork and
  6 oz slab bacon
salt
2 tablespoons chopped parsley
2 tablespoons flour
1 egg
3 tablespoons soft bread crumbs
2 tablespoons peanut oil
2 tablespoons butter
1¼ cups Tomato Sauce (page
  383)
parsley leaves for garnish

If you are not using the sausage meat, start by grinding the pork and bacon, using first a medium blade, then a fine one. Add a little salt, the chopped parsley, flour, egg and bread crumbs to this meat. If you are using ready-made sausage meat, leave out the salt. Mix thoroughly, then shape the meat into six balls and flatten them slightly. Dust each meatball lightly with flour.

Heat the oil and butter in a skillet then add the meatballs and cook over a medium heat. Allow about 10 to 15 minutes cooking time for each side and turn the meatballs once during cooking.

Pour the tomato sauce over the meatballs, and leave to heat up for a few minutes, stirring with a wooden spoon to deglaze the pan. Serve the meatballs garnished with parsley.

Veal Cutlet Parcels

Serves 4

4 thick veal cutlets
8 shallots, chopped
2 tablespoons butter
salt and pepper
$\frac{1}{4}$ cup oil
4 thin slices cooked ham
$\frac{1}{4}$ lb Gruyère cheese, thinly
   sliced
3 tablespoons bread crumbs

Ask your butcher to cut a pocket in the cutlets, without cutting all the way through. You can do this yourself with a thin, very sharp knife.

Fry the shallots in the butter until golden brown. Season to taste. Fill the pocket in the cutlets with the shallots and carefully close them with toothpicks or skewers. Heat the oil and fry the cutlets over medium heat. When the first side is brown, turn them over and fry for about 8 minutes or until cooked through. Arrange the cutlets in a gratin dish. Place a slice of ham and a thin slice of Gruyère on top of each cutlet, then sprinkle with bread crumbs. Cook under a preheated hot broiler until golden and bubbling.

Roast Pork with Prunes

Serves 4 to 6

1 (2½-lb) pork tenderloin roast
1½ cups prunes, soaked and
    drained
salt and pepper
2 tablespoons butter
1¼ cups hot water
3 oranges

Make an incision along one side of the pork, without cutting it completely in half, and stuff half the prunes into the pocket. Carefully tie up the roast with string to prevent the stuffing from coming out while it is cooking.

Season the pork and place in a roasting pan, greased with the butter. Roast in a preheated 425° oven for 20 minutes. Take the pan out of the oven and remove the excess fat. Pour in the hot water and put the roast back in the oven. Reduce the heat to 400° and roast for 40 minutes longer. Baste the meat several times.

About 10 minutes before the end of the cooking time, add the rest of the prunes to the dish, plus 2 of the oranges cut into thin slices. Finish cooking. Remove the roast from the oven, check that it is cooked through and remove the string. Place it on a serving dish surrounded by the prunes and orange slices. Cut the rind off the remaining orange in a thin strip to garnish the roast.

Beef in Aspic

Serves 6

1 onion, sliced
1 clove
3 carrots, sliced
1 bouquet garni
1½ quarts water
salt and pepper
1 (2½-lb) beef pot-roast
2 cups frozen or fresh shelled
    peas
2 envelopes unflavored gelatin
shredded lettuce for garnish

Place the onion, the clove, 1 carrot and the bouquet garni in a saucepan with the water. Bring to a boil, season and boil gently for 20 minutes. Place the beef pot-roast in the stock. Cover and simmer for 50–60 minutes.

In the meantime cook the remaining slices of carrot and peas separately in boiling salted water until just tender. The carrots may be cut into decorative shapes, if desired. Drain and set aside.

When the meat is cooked, remove it from the stock and allow to cool. When cool, cut into slices. Strain the stock. Dissolve the gelatin in a little of the stock, then add to the remaining stock. Stir to mix. Pour a little of this mixture into a dish or mold and tilt to coat the sides and bottom of the dish with a ½-inch layer. Leave to cool and set. Line the dish with slices of carrot and peas in a decorative design and place the slices of meat on top. Pour in the rest of the stock mixture and chill in the refrigerator for 2 or 3 hours. To serve place a serving plate over the top of the dish or mold and invert sharply. The aspic should fall onto the plate. It may be necessary to loosen the sides of the aspic carefully with a knife.

Surround with the shredded lettuce and serve with crusty French bread and salads of your choice.

Braised Beef with Turnips

Serves 4

1½–2 lb beef chuck or flank
    steak, cut into bite-sized
    pieces
6 tablespoons butter
¼ lb bacon slices
2 onions, chopped
1 carrot, sliced
2 cups beef broth
1 bouquet garni
1 lb small turnips
salt and pepper
1 tablespoon confectioners'
    sugar

Brown the pieces of beef all over in half the butter in a skillet. Line a heavy saucepan with the bacon and arrange the meat on it, surrounding it with the onions and carrot. Add the broth and the bouquet garni and leave to simmer very gently for at least 2½ hours. Alternatively cook in a preheated 325° oven.

In the meantime, put the turnips in a saucepan, cover with water and add salt and the sugar. Simmer over a low heat for about 30 minutes or until most of the cooking liquid has evaporated. Add the remaining butter and carefully turn the turnips over the heat to glaze them.

Arrange the beef and turnips on a warmed serving dish and keep hot. Strain the cooking juices from the beef. Boil to reduce the quantity and adjust the seasoning to taste. Skim off any fat and serve the gravy separately in a sauce boat.

French Shepherd's Pie

Serves 4

1½ lb potatoes
1 lb cooked beef *or* raw ground
   round
3 tablespoons butter
1 large onion, finely chopped
2 eggs plus 1 egg yolk
½ cup grated Gruyère cheese
3 tablespoons soft bread crumbs
salt and pepper
1 tablespoons chopped fresh
   mixed herbs *or* 2 teaspoons
   dried mixed herbs

Cook the potatoes in boiling salted water for 20 minutes. Drain and mash well.

Grind the cooked beef. If you are using raw ground round, fry it in half the butter for 5 minutes, then grind again when it has cooled. It will be softer. Mix together the onion, 2 whole eggs, half the grated Gruyère and the bread crumbs. Add the meat to this mixture. Season the mixture to taste and add the mixed herbs. Spread the mixture evenly over the bottom of a greased ovenproof dish.

Spread the potato over the meat. Sprinkle with the rest of the cheese, dot with the remaining butter, and brush with beaten egg yolk. Bake in a preheated 350° oven for 20–30 minutes until the top is brown.

BARBECUES

One of the great pleasures of summer is being able to cook and eat outside in the fresh air. It is not only the heightened appetites which make the food seem so full of flavor and goodness, but the way in which it is cooked.

Planning a barbecue is not difficult but the coals must be lit about 30–40 minutes in advance so that they will be hot enough to cook the food. It is a good idea to have a spray gun of water on hand to douse flames while the food is cooking.

Fish, meat and poultry can all be cooked over the barbecue; kabobs can be prepared from a variety of ingredients; potatoes can be foil-wrapped and baked in the coals or new potatoes can be skewered for baking on the grill. Pitta bread can be heated quickly over the coals, so too can garlic bread.

The barbecue can be simple – just some grilled fish, chicken or meat – with a crisp fresh salad and some hot crusty bread. Alternatively, a whole selection of kabobs, meat, fish or poultry and vegetables can be prepared and cooked over a period of several hours. Before cooking, the foods can be marinated with oil, vinegar, wine, herbs, seasoning and spices. More fresh herbs can be thrown on to the hot coals to flavor the food as it cooks.

This chapter also includes a selection of sauces, savory butters and accompaniments which can be served with the barbecued food. These are the important extras which will ensure that the meal is a success.

Pork Kabobs with Barbecue Sauce

Serves 4

2 zucchini
4 tomatoes
1 lb pork tenderloin
2 tablespoons olive oil
1 teaspoon chopped fresh basil
   or ½ teaspoon dried basil
1 teaspoon chopped fennel
   leaves or parsley
3 bay leaves (optional)
1 sprig fresh basil (optional)
salt and pepper
SAUCE
2 tablespoons olive oil
2 onions, chopped
1 lb tomatoes
2 cloves garlic, crushed
1 tablespoon vinegar
½ teaspoon celery salt
salt and pepper

Wipe and thickly slice the zucchini. Wash and halve the tomatoes. Cut the pork into large cubes. Onto skewers thread a slice of zucchini, a cube of pork, a tomato half, a cube of pork, a tomato half and finally a slice of zucchini. These can be held in place more firmly if you use two skewers for each kabob. Brush one side of each kabob with oil and sprinkle with half the chopped basil and fennel or parsley.

You will need to light the charcoal well in advance if it is to be red hot by the time you are ready to cook. It is ready when a fine layer of ash covers the glowing embers. When the charcoal is ready lay the kabobs across the grill. Don't have the grill too low over the charcoal as the pork needs to cook fairly slowly over a moderate heat. Toss the few bay and basil leaves, if using, into the charcoal for extra flavor.

Grill for 5 to 7 minutes, then remove the kabobs from the grill and brush the other side with oil. Return the kabobs to the grill and cook the second side for a further 5 to 7 minutes. Season to taste and sprinkle with the remaining chopped basil and fennel just before serving.

Barbecue sauce
Heat the oil in a saucepan and brown the sliced onions over a low heat. Plunge the tomatoes into boiling water for 10 seconds, then peel and quarter them. Add the tomatoes to the pan with the garlic, the vinegar and celery salt. Season to taste. Stir thoroughly and cover the pan. Simmer for 20 minutes over a low heat. If preferred this sauce can be puréed in a food processor or blender before serving and served either hot or cold.

Pilaff with Currants

Serves 4

⅔ cup currants
1 cup rice
3 tablespoons oil
2 cups boiling water
salt
sprig of thyme

Soak the currants in warm water. Sprinkle the rice into 3 tablespoons heated oil. Stir until the rice begins to become transparent. Add the boiling water. Stir and season to taste. Add the sprig of thyme. Cover the pan and cook over a low heat for 16 to 18 minutes without removing the lid. Drain the currants and stir into the rice just before serving. The rice should absorb all the liquid in the pan as it cooks.

Barbecued Sardines

Serves 6

24 fresh sardines or other small
   oily fish
3 tablespoons sea salt
6 sprigs rosemary
2 lemons
salt and pepper

To make this dish it is only necessary to wash the sardines and pat dry on a dish towel; there is no need to clean or scale them or remove the heads. About 1 hour before cooking, sprinkle the sardines with sea salt. When the charcoal is hot shake the sardines by the tail to remove excess salt. Place on the grill and cook for 2 to 3 minutes. Turn gently and cook for a further 2–3 minutes. Cooked in this way the skin comes away easily to reveal the delicate flesh. Just before you remove the sardines from the barbecue toss the rosemary onto the charcoal to give extra flavor. Sprinkle with lemon juice and season to taste. These are also delicious served with garlic butter or mustard sauce and pilaff with currants.

Garlic Butter

4 cloves garlic
½ cup butter
salt and pepper

Peel the garlic and crush in a pestle and mortar or garlic press to make a thick paste. Work into the butter until smooth. Season to taste. Shape the garlic butter into a roll and wrap in aluminum foil. Chill in the refrigerator for several hours. It will keep for several days in the refrigerator. To serve cut into slices and place on the cooked sardines.

Mustard Sauce

¼ cup butter
3 tablespoons Crème Fraîche
   (page 398) or sour cream
2 tablespoons Dijon-style
   mustard

Melt the butter in a small pan. When it has melted stir in the crème fraîche or sour cream and add the mustard. Heat gently without allowing the sauce to boil. Serve in a sauce boat with the barbecued sardines.

Barbecued Shrimp with Pineapple

Serves 4

1 fresh pineapple
4 thin slices cooked ham or lean
   bacon
16 raw shrimp in the shell
1 tablespoon oil
1 teaspoon sugar
pepper
$\frac{1}{4}$ cup butter

Peel the pineapple, remove the hard core, and cut into 8 slices. Leave 4 slices whole and cut the rest into cubes. Cut each slice of ham or bacon lengthwise into wide strips. Wrap each shrimp in a strip of ham or bacon. Make up one kabob per person by threading 4 shrimp and 4 cubes of pineapple alternately onto each skewer. Brush with the oil and sprinkle with sugar and pepper.

Place the kabobs on the barbecue grill. They take about 4 to 5 minutes to cook and should be golden brown but not black. If you allow the shells of the shrimp to burn the shrimp will taste bitter.

As soon as they are cooked serve the kabobs garnished with the slices of fresh pineapple and the remaining ham with a little melted butter. When buying shrimp for barbecueing make sure they are fresh, firm and shiny.

Scallops with Fennel

Serves 3

1¼ cups dry white wine
1 small bunch parsley
1 sprig thyme
½ teaspoon coarsely crushed
   black peppercorns
salt
¼ cup butter
6 scallops
2 shallots, chopped
6 small sprigs fresh fennel
   leaves

Place the white wine, 2 small sprigs parsley, thyme sprig and the crushed peppercorns in a small pan. Season lightly with salt. Bring to a boil and simmer for 15 minutes. Strain this stock. Add the butter and reduce by one-third over a high heat.

Finely chop the remaining parsley. Place the scallops in 6 scallop shells and sprinkle each with 2 to 3 tablespoons reduced stock. Sprinkle with the chopped shallots and parsley. Top with a small sprig of fennel. Cook over hot charcoal for about 10 minutes and serve immediately.

Herby Lamb Chops with Roquefort Sauce

Serves 2

2 double lamb chops
1 tablespoon oil
2 tomatoes
2 sprigs tarragon, chopped *or* $\frac{1}{2}$
   teaspoon dried tarragon
1 bay leaf, crushed
2 sprigs thyme, chopped *or* $\frac{1}{2}$
   teaspoon dried thyme
1 clove garlic, crushed
salt and pepper
GARNISH
1 lemon
small bunch watercress
ROQUEFORT SAUCE
1 oz Roquefort cheese
3 tablespoons cream cheese
cayenne
3 tablespoons mayonnaise

Lightly brush the chops with oil. Cut the top off the tomatoes. When the charcoal is very hot place the chops on the grill with the tomatoes. Sprinkle the tarragon, bay leaf and thyme over the meat and tomatoes and sprinkle with garlic. Cook the chops for 6 to 7 minutes each side. When cooked, season with salt and pepper.

Serve the chops and tomatoes with the Roquefort sauce and garnish with lemon slices and sprigs of cress.

Roquefort sauce
Mash the Roquefort in a bowl. Beat in the cream cheese with cayenne to taste, then fold in the mayonnaise. Serve in a sauceboat.

Filet Mignons with Red Wine Sauce

Serves 4

4 filet mignons
1 tablepoon oil
salt and pepper
4 slices beef marrow, each
   1-inch thick (optional)
2 tablespoons finely chopped
   parsley
SAUCE
3 slices bacon, chopped
2 cups red wine
3 shallots, chopped
1 bouquet garni
2 tablespoons flour
$\frac{1}{4}$ cup butter

Brush the steaks on both sides with oil and sprinkle generously with pepper. Leave to stand for 30 minutes.

Brown the bacon in a saucepan. Pour off the excess fat. Add the wine, shallots and bouquet garni. Season to taste. Reduce by half over a low heat and remove the bouquet garni. In a small bowl work the flour into half the butter. Whisk this into the sauce a little at a time and simmer for 3 to 4 minutes. Whisk in the remaining butter. Poach the beef marrow, if using, in 1 cup seasoned water for 3 to 4 minutes.

Cook the steak under a preheated hot broiler. Allow 3 minutes per side if you like your steak very rare, 4 minutes per side for medium rare and 6 minutes per side for well done. Transfer the steaks to a skillet. Top each with a slice of beef marrow, if using, and pour over a little sauce. Heat through briefly. Sprinkle with chopped parsley. Serve with the remaining sauce.

Pork Chops with Sage

Serves 5

5 pork chops
few stems fresh sage
¼ cup oil
1 tablespoon strong mustard
salt and pepper

Rub the pork chops each side with a few bruised fresh sage leaves. Then brush with a mixture of the oil and mustard. Season to taste with salt and pepper. White meat cooked on a barbecue needs to be more highly seasoned than when it is cooked by traditional methods, otherwise it seems flavorless.

Place the chops over the charcoal which should not be too hot. Cook for 5 to 7 minutes each side depending on thickness. Turn the chops from time to time as they cook. Serve on a hot plate sprinkled with sage leaves.

Note: It is not always possible to get hold of fresh sage and dried sage has little flavor, so you may prefer to serve these barbecued chops with a choice of either rémoulade or charcutière sauce.

Rémoulade Sauce

1 egg yolk
1 teaspoon vinegar
1 tablespoon strong mustard
salt and pepper
1 cup oil
1 tablespoon capers, chopped
3 gherkins, chopped
1 tablespoon chopped parsley

Make up a bowl of mayonnaise by whisking together the egg yolk, ½ teaspoon of the vinegar and the mustard. Season to taste. Then whisk in the oil one drop at a time. When the sauce begins to thicken you can add the oil more quickly but keep whisking continuously. Finally add the remaining vinegar with the capers, gherkins and chopped parsley. Adjust the seasoning. Serve immediately or keep in the refrigerator until ready to serve.

Charcutière Sauce

1 onion, chopped
3 tablespoons butter
2 tablespoons flour
⅔ cup white wine
1¼ cups water
salt and pepper
1 teaspoon prepared mustard
2 gherkins, chopped
1 tablespoon chopped parsley
1 tablespoon capers, chopped

Fry the chopped onion in the butter. Sprinkle over the flour and stir well. Cook gently for a few minutes. Stir in the wine and water. Season to taste and cook for 10 minutes. Then add the mustard, gherkins, chopped parsley and capers. Serve separately in a sauceboat or pour over the barbecued chops.

Ham and Fruit Kabobs

Serves 6

6 thick slices cooked ham *or* 6
   ham steaks
1 (16-oz) can mangoes in syrup
24 bay leaves
1 tablespoon runny honey
1 teaspoon vinegar
1 clove, crushed
salt and pepper

Cut the ham into squares or quarter the ham steaks.
Drain and quarter the mangoes. Reserve a little of the
syrup. Using two skewers for each kabob, thread with a
bay leaf, a square of ham and a mango quarter. Repeat,
using 4 pieces of ham for each kabob, finishing with a
piece of ham.

In a bowl mix together the honey, 2 tablespoons of the
reserved mango syrup, the vinegar, the crushed clove
and seasoning to taste. Cook the kabobs under a
preheated broiler for about 10 minutes, brushing from
time to time with the honey mixture. Cover the kabobs
liberally with the mixture and allow to caramelize
slightly. Don't forget to turn the kabobs occasionally
during the cooking time.

The mangoes can be replaced with canned peach
halves, apricots or cubes of fresh pineapple. Serve these
delicious kabobs with a dish of rice.

Gipsy-Style Beef Kabobs

Serves 4

1 lemon
½ cup oil
salt and pepper
1 teaspoon paprika
1½ lb flank steak
2 green peppers
¼ lb slab bacon, chopped
2 onions, chopped
16 bay leaves

Thinly pare the rind from the lemon. In a bowl, make a marinade with the juice of the lemon, ¼ cup oil, salt, pepper and paprika. Cut the meat into large cubes (to make about 32). Place in the marinade. Stir well and leave to stand for 3 hours in a cool place, but not in the refrigerator. Cut the green peppers in half, remove the seeds and cut into strips. Brown the bacon in a skillet, then add the onions and peppers and season to taste. Cook for about 10 minutes over a low heat.

Drain the beef thoroughly. On each skewer thread 1 bay leaf, 1 piece lemon rind and 1 cube meat. Repeat until there are four pieces of meat on each skewer. Finish with a bay leaf. Brush each kabob with oil and cook close to the charcoal or under a preheated broiler for about 10 minutes, turning two or three times as they cook. When cooked season to taste.

Serve the kabobs very hot with the drained pepper and bacon mixture and boiled rice.

Monkfish and Prune Kabobs

Serves 4

15 prunes
2 lemons
1 lb monkfish fillet
12 stuffed olives
3 tablespoons olive oil
salt and pepper
¼ cup butter, melted
1 teaspoon dried oregano

Soak the prunes in warm water for 2 hours, if necessary. Drain and remove the pits. Squeeze the juice of the lemons into a shallow dish. Skin the fish. Wash and pat dry. Cut into largish cubes (about 20 in all) and marinate in the lemon juice for 1 hour. Thread the prunes, olives and fish onto the skewers as shown in the photograph. Brush with olive oil and place on a grill over very hot charcoal. Cook for 15 minutes, turning several times. Season to taste and sprinkle with melted butter and oregano. Serve with wedges of lemon.

You can replace the olives with mussels, opened by heating in a large pan for 5 minutes. Shake the pan as they heat. When open remove the mussels and thread onto the skewers in place of the olives. (Discard any mussels which do not open.)

Flambéed Barbecued Lobster

Serves 6

3 medium-size live lobsters
¼ cup unsalted butter, melted
3 tablespoons dried white bread
  crumbs
⅛ teaspoon cayenne
½ cup cognac
SAFFRON SAUCE:
½ cup Crème Fraîche (page 398)
⅛ teaspoon powdered saffron

Plunge the lobsters into boiling water and boil for 1 minute. Drain and cool. Cut in half lengthwise using a very sharp knife. Remove the inedible parts.

Brush the meat of the lobsters with the melted butter, keeping a little to one side to use during cooking. Place, cut side down, on a grill over hot charcoal. Cook for 10 minutes, then turn over. Pour 1 tablespoon melted butter over each lobster half and sprinkle with bread crumbs. Season with cayenne and cook for a further 12 minutes. Sprinkle repeatedly with butter during this time. Place on a warmed plate.

Make the saffron sauce. Season the crème fraîche with the saffron and warm over a low heat. When the cream begins to boil pour it into a hot sauceboat. Warm the cognac in a small pan. Remove from the heat and light the cognac with a match. Pour over the lobster immediately. Serve with the saffron sauce and a salad.

Sole Kabobs

Serves 4

12 sole fillets
12 slices bacon
4 tomatoes
2 lemons
8 bay leaves
pepper
3 tablespoons oil

Roll up each fillet in a bacon slice. Wash and quarter the tomatoes. Wash, scrub and slice 1 lemon.

Using two skewers for each kabob thread with the soles wrapped in bacon, tomatoes, lemon slices and bay leaves as shown in the photograph. Season with pepper. There is no need to season with salt as the bacon is salty enough.

Brush the kabobs with oil and cook over a moderately hot barbecue for 15 minutes, brushing repeatedly with the oil and turning the kabobs from time to time. Serve with the remaining lemon cut into wedges and potatoes baked in foil with green or curry sauce.

Green Sauce

6 stems watercress
1 bunch chervil
1 bunch chives
1 cup Crème Fraîche (page 398)
salt and pepper

Wash the watercress and herbs and purée in a blender or food processor to give a green paste. Add the crème fraîche and season to taste. Blend for a few seconds more. Serve immediately or keep in the refrigerator until ready to use.

Curry Sauce

2 tablespoons butter
2 tablepoons flour
1 teaspoon curry powder
1 cup chicken broth
salt and pepper
3 tablespoons Crème Fraîche
  (page 398)

Over a low heat melt the butter and stir in the flour and curry powder. Heat gently for 1–2 minutes, stirring with a wooden spoon. Add the cold broth. Season to taste. Stir until the sauce boils. Simmer for 10 minutes. Add the crème fraîche. Reheat for 2 minutes and when the sauce begins to boil pour into a warmed sauceboat and serve.

Barbecued Chicken

Serves 4

1 chicken
¼ cup oil
salt and pepper
5 bay leaves
1 lb tomatoes
1 clove garlic, crushed

Remove the breastbone from the chicken by cutting along both sides with a sharp knife and easing it out. Beat the chicken to flatten it. Rub both sides with oil and season to taste with salt and pepper. Place 4 of the bay leaves over the top. Cook for 15 minutes each side on the barbecue grill, brushing it with oil from time to time as it cooks. Check that the chicken is cooked through.

While the chicken is cooking make a tomato sauce. Peel the tomatoes and cut into large pieces. Peel the garlic. Pour a little oil into a saucepan and when it is hot add the tomato, garlic and 1 bay leaf. Season to taste. Simmer for about 30 minutes. Sieve the purée to remove seeds, skin and herbs.

When the chicken is cooked serve it with the tomato sauce handed separately.

Orange Barbecued Chicken

Serves 6

3 oranges
1 chicken, cut into 6 pieces
2 tablespoons oil
6 thin slices bacon
salt and pepper
1¾ cups rice
sprigs of parsley for garnish
ORANGE SAUCE
2 oranges
1 cup chicken broth

Peel 2 oranges to remove both peel and pith and remove the segments. Wash and finely slice the remaining orange. Brush each chicken portion with oil, place a slice of orange on each portion and wrap in a slice of bacon secured with a wooden toothpick. Brush with oil and season. Cook over red hot charcoal then over cooler embers for about 30 minutes in all. Turn the chicken once and brush with oil occasionally.

While the chicken is cooking cook the rice. Tip the cooked rice into a shallow serving dish and top with the chicken portions and wedges of orange. A simple orange sauce will go well with this dish. Scrub 1 orange, remove the rind and bring to a boil in a pan of cold water. Thickly peel both oranges and cut into wedges. Add the orange wedges with the chicken broth. Simmer over a low heat for 10 minutes and serve separately in a sauceboat. Garnish with sprigs of parsley.

Barbecued Shrimp Corsaire

Serves 3

15 raw shrimp in the shell
2 cloves garlic
1 small sweet or hot pepper
2 tablespoons oil
cayenne
LEMON BUTTER
1 lemon
½ cup softened butter
salt and pepper
SPICY SAUCE
¼ cup oil
2 onions, finely chopped
2 cloves garlic, crushed
1 (1-inch) piece cinnamon stick
⅛ teaspoon ground allspice
½ teaspoon sugar
½ cup ground peanuts
½ cup coconut milk
1 lime

First make the spicy sauce. Heat 2 tablespoons oil in a heavy-bottomed pan. Fry the onions and garlic without allowing them to brown. Add the cinnamon, allspice, sugar and peanuts. Stir over the heat for 1 minute using a wooden spoon. Then add the coconut milk with remaining oil and the juice of the lime. Simmer, uncovered, over a very low heat for 15 minutes. Keep hot.

Now make the lemon butter. Scrub the lemon and finely grate the rind taking care not to grate any of the bitter white pith. Mix into the butter. Season to taste and pack into a small pot.

Wash, drain and dry the shrimp. Place a metal sheet on the barbecue grill over very hot coals. Peel and very finely chop the garlic. Cut the sweet or hot pepper (whichever you prefer) into small rings. Brush the shrimp with oil and place on the hot metal sheet. Sprinkle with the garlic and pepper rings. Cook for 5 to 6 minutes, taking care not to let the shells burn as this makes the shrimp bitter. Turn each shrimp using tongs. Season with cayenne.

Serve the shrimp very hot with the spicy sauce and lemon butter.

Cook's tip
Barbecuing shrimp on a metal sheet or large slate tile is the way they are cooked in the Vendée region of France. You should clean the plate or tile by holding it in a flame before use. Never wash them with detergents. Simply rub clean with paper towels. The metal sheet is hot enough when a slice of bread toasts in 30 seconds. A metal plate is also used to cook crayfish and other types of shellfish and can also be used for opening shellfish such as cockles or mussels and grilling sausages and slices of vegetables.

Lamb Chop Kabobs

Serves 3

3 lemons
1 green pepper
6 lamb chops
2 tomatoes, halved
3 bay leaves
2 onions, halved
3 tablespoons olive or herb-
   flavored oil
salt and pepper

Halve the lemons by cutting a zig-zag around the center. To do this first trim the two ends. With one hand hold the lemon vertically on a chopping board and using a small pointed knife cut into the center of the lemon about halfway up. Turn the knife and repeat until you have cut a zig-zag all the way around the lemon. Lift off the top. Halve the pepper, remove seeds and pith and cut into strips.

Use two skewers for each kabob to make them more secure. Thread with a lemon half, a chop (with the narrow end tucked around and secured on the skewers), a piece of pepper, a tomato half, a bay leaf, an onion half, a second chop and finally a second lemon half. Brush with oil and place the kabobs on a fairly hot barbecue. Brush with oil from time to time as they cook for 4 to 5 minutes each side. Season and serve very hot.

Pork Chops with Orange

Serves 4

4 pork loin chops
2 tablespoons oil
salt and pepper
2 oranges
1½ lb sweet potatoes
¼ cup butter
1 avocado
1 tablespoon chopped parsley

Brush the chops with oil, season to taste and cook under a preheated broiler for 5 to 6 minutes each side depending on thickness. Turn and brush with oil again, then broil for a further 5 minutes each side. Wash and thickly slice the oranges to broil with the chops.

Meanwhile peel the sweet potatoes and cut into slices. Heat the butter in a skillet and fry the sweet potatoes until golden brown, about 20 minutes, turning carefully from time to time.

Spoon the flesh from the avocado and mash with the chopped parsley. Season to taste and add a few small pieces of orange. Mix thoroughly.

Serve the chops on a hot plate garnished with the orange slices and a little of the avocado mixture. Serve the fried sweet potatoes and the rest of the avocado mixture separately.

Chicken Liver Kabobs

Serves 5

20 chicken livers
3 tablespoons butter
1 sprig thyme *or* $\frac{1}{2}$ teaspoon
   dried thyme
salt and pepper
20 thin slices bacon
1$\frac{1}{3}$ cups rice

Trim the chicken livers. Melt 2 tablespoons of the butter in a skillet and add the thyme leaves and then the livers. Stir until completely sealed. Season to taste. Remove the livers from the heat and leave to cool. Thread the livers onto skewers, alternating with rolls of bacon.

Cook the rice for 15 to 20 minutes in an large pan of boiling Salted water. Drain, season and stir in the remaining butter. Fluff up with a fork. Tip into a serving dish and keep hot.

Broil the kabobs for about 10 minutes, turning repeatedly. Arrange over the rice and serve immediately. This simple recipe makes a delicious meal and is very good accompanied by a crisp green salad.

Spit-Roasted Duck

Serves 6

1 (3½- to 4-lb) duck
3 tablespoons oil
juice of 1 lemon
salt
cayenne
1 lb apples
1⅓ cups green olives

Rub the duck with oil, lemon juice, salt and cayenne. Leave to soak in well and repeat the seasoning twice more. Peel and core the apples and cut into thick rings. Pit the olives. Thread the duck onto the rotisserie spit and secure the wings to the body with string. Cook for about 1¼ hours or until the juices from the thickest part of the thigh are clear, brushing from time to time with oil and lemon juice. About 25 minutes before the end of the cooking time place the apple rings and olives in the dripping tray where they will cook gently in the juices from the duck. To carve the duck, first remove the legs and cut in two. Cut along the breastbone, remove the breasts and carve into slices. Remove the wings, leaving only the carcass. Serve the duck meat with the olives and apple rings. You can also cook one or two whole apples in the dripping tray but these will take 10 minutes longer to cook than the rings.

Barbecued Steak with Two Butters

Serves 4

1 large slice boneless sirloin
    steak (about 1 to 1½-inches
    thick)
⅓ cup oil
salt and pepper
10 bay leaves

Choose a steak "marbled" or flecked with fat as this will be both tasty and tender.

Place the steak in a shallow dish and pour over the oil. Work the oil gently into both sides of the meat. Give four twists of a pepper mill over each side of the steak and allow the pepper to be absorbed. Place the bay leaves both under and on the steak to flavor it. Oil the grill rack and prepare a very hot barbecue.

Drain the steak. Keep the bay leaves to one side. Place the steak on the grill and seal the first side for 3 minutes. Then toss the bay leaves one at a time into the embers. Make sure that the charcoal does not flame from the dripping cooking juices as this gives the meat a burnt taste. Turn the steak and cook the second side for 3 to 4 minutes. Do not prick the meat with a fork but use a spatula or tongs to turn it. If you like steak very rare, a 1½-inch sirloin will cook in 5 minutes; for a rare steak allow 6 to 7 minutes, for medium steak allow 10 minutes. When the meat is cooked season to taste and leave to stand for 1 to 2 minutes before serving with a choice of anchovy or garlic butter.

Anchovy Butter

5 anchovy fillets
1 clove garlic
½ cup butter, softened
pepper

In a mortar, thoroughly pound the anchovies, then pound in the chopped garlic to make a paste. Work this mixture into the butter. Season with pepper, but not salt as the anchovies are salty enough.

Garlic Butter

½ cup butter
2 cloves garlic, crushed
2 shallots, finely chopped
1 tablespoon chopped parsley
salt and pepper

Place the butter in a bowl at room temperature to soften. Add the crushed garlic, shallots and parsley and season to taste. Work in thoroughly with a fork. Transfer the butter to a small pot and leave in the refrigerator to harden.

Lamb and Sausage Kabobs

Serves 4

1 lb boneless shoulder of lamb
2 tablespoons olive oil
salt and pepper
1 green pepper
8 pearl onions
2 large onions, quartered
8 small pork link sausages
1 tomato, quartered

Cut the lamb into 1-inch cubes. Place the meat in a shallow dish and sprinkle with the olive oil. Season to taste. Wash and halve the pepper, remove the seeds and pith and cut into strips.

Make up the kabobs by threading each skewer with 1 pearl onion, 1 strip pepper, 1 cube meat, 1 onion quarter, 1 sausage, 1 tomato quarter, 1 cube meat, 1 strip pepper and 1 pearl onion as shown in the photograph. Cook over hot charcoal for about 10 minutes, turning frequently and brushing with the oil from the marinade. Serve on a bed of boiled rice. This colorful dish can be served with a fresh tomato sauce and a green pepper sauce.

Chicken-Filled Lamb Parcels

Serves 6

6 thin slices of leg of lamb
6 slices bacon
3 tablespoons white wine
2 tablespoons Crème Fraîche (page 398)
MARINADE
2 tablespoons oil
juice of 1 lemon
1 tablespoon chopped parsley
1 tablespoon chopped chives
1 clove garlic, crushed
salt and pepper
STUFFING
½ lb boneless chicken meat
2 tablespoons butter
salt and pepper
pinch freshly grated nutmeg
1 tablespoon chopped parsley
2 cups soft bread crumbs
⅔ cup chicken broth

Mix the marinade ingredients in a shallow dish and marinate the lamb for 2 hours, turning the slices from time to time.

Finely dice the chicken and fry gently in the butter until cooked through. Season with salt, pepper and nutmeg. Add the chopped parsley and bread crumbs together with the broth. Simmer for 15 minutes. Drain the stuffing and mash with a fork. Drain the lamb and keep the marinade to one side. Divide the stuffing between the slices of lamb. Roll up and wrap the bacon around the lamb to seal the two ends and prevent the stuffing escaping. Tie the parcels with fine string and thread on to a kebab skewer.

Cook the lamb rolls over very hot charcoal for 15 minutes, turning them repeatedly and brushing with the marinade diluted with the white wine. Catch the cooking juices, stir with the crème fraîche and serve the rolls very hot with the sauce handed separately in a sauceboat.

Chicken Kabobs with Olives

Serves 4

4 chicken pieces (thigh or breast
  and wing)
2 small zucchini
2 tomatoes
salt and pepper
1 head lettuce, shredded
$\frac{2}{3}$ cup ripe olives
MARINADE
3 tablespoons oil
1 lemon
salt and pepper

In a bowl mix the oil and the juice of the lemon with the salt and pepper to make the marinade. Marinate the chicken pieces for 1 hour, turning every 15 minutes.

Peel the zucchini, leaving thin strips of peel. Cut into thick slices. Blanch the zucchini in boiling salted water for 3 minutes. Drain and wipe dry. Wash and halve the tomatoes. Drain the chicken and keep the marinade to one side.

Using two skewers for each kabob, thread with a slice of zucchini, a chicken piece, a tomato half and a second slice of zucchini. Cook over hot charcoal for 12 to 15 minutes until the chicken is cooked through, turning and brushing with the marinade from time to time. Season to taste. Serve on a bed of shredded lettuce with the ripe olives.

Cook's tip
For a special meal serve the kabobs with a tapenade sauce and provençal zucchini.

Tapenade Sauce
Tapenade is a sauce made with ripe olives in the south of France. Pit $1\frac{1}{3}$ cups ripe olives and purée in a blender with 4 oz canned anchovy fillets and $\frac{1}{3}$ cup capers. Add enough olive oil to give a smooth consistency and mix thoroughly. Work in the juice of 1 lemon. Season with pepper and beat well. Serve with hot toast.

Provençal Zucchini
Allow 2 small zucchini per person and cut into thick slices. In a pan heat 2 tablespoons olive oil. When the oil is hot seal the zucchini and season to taste. When the zucchini are golden brown drain in a sieve for 15 minutes. Pour the oil that drips from the zucchini into a pan over a low heat. Add 5 chopped tomatoes, 1 pinch sugar, the leaves from 1 sprig thyme, 1 bay leaf and 1 tablespoon chopped parsley. Cook for 5 minutes. Add the zucchini and stir gently. Cover the pan and cook for a further 25 minutes.

Stuffed Veal Chops

Serves 4

4 veal chops
6 shallots, chopped
2 tablespoons butter
salt and pepper
4 slices cooked ham
$\frac{1}{4}$ lb Gruyère cheese in 4 thin
   slices
$\frac{1}{4}$ cup oil

Make sure you buy thick veal chops and ask your butcher to cut through the lean end to the bone to make a pocket. You can do this yourself using a thin pointed knife.

Brown the shallots in half the butter. Season to taste. Fry the ham slices in the remaining butter for 1 minute each side. Stuff the veal chops with a slice of ham, some fried shallots and a thin slice of Gruyère. Seal using two wooden toothpicks.

Brush the stuffed chops all over with oil and cook over hot charcoal for 8 to 10 minutes each side, brushing with oil from time to time. Serve hot with potatoes baked in foil with melted butter.

Paris-Style Steak Kabobs

Serves 4

¾ lb boneless sirloin or
  tenderloin steak
4 button mushrooms, trimmed
2 tomatoes, quartered
4 thin slices bacon
1 onion, quartered
2 tablespoons oil
sprigs of watercress for garnish
MARINADE
1 lemon
salt and pepper
¼ cup oil

In a bowl mix a marinade with the juice of the lemon, salt, pepper and oil. Cut the meat into large cubes and stir into the marinade. Leave to marinate for 3 hours.

Wipe the mushrooms and sprinkle with lemon juice to keep them white. Drain the steak. Thread each skewer with a tomato quarter, a bacon roll, a cube of steak, an onion quarter, a cube of steak and finally a mushroom (threaded from bottom to top). Brush the kabobs with oil and cook close to the embers for 8 to 12 minutes depending on how well you like your steak cooked. Turn from time to time as they cook, then season to taste. Serve on a bed of boiled rice and garnish with a few sprigs of watercress.

Liver Kabobs with Herb Crêpes

Serves 6

KEBABS
10 slices bacon
6 pearl onions
2 green peppers
10 chicken livers
1 thick slice calves' or lamb's
    liver (about ¾ lb)
2 tablespoons oil
CRÊPES
¼ cup flour
salt and pepper
1 egg
⅔ cup milk
¼ cup butter
1 tablespoon chopped fresh
    mixed herbs (for example
    parsley, chives, thyme)

Make the crêpe batter by beating the flour, salt and egg with a wooden spoon until you have a smooth paste. Gradually beat in the milk and a pat of the butter (about half), just melted. Beat in the herbs. Set aside.

Blanch the bacon in boiling water for 2 minutes. Drain. Blanch the onions in boiling water for 3 minutes. Drain on paper towels. Wash and halve the peppers, remove seeds and pith and cut into strips. Trim and halve the chicken livers. Cube the other liver.

Make up the kabobs with the chicken livers and pearl onions, calves' liver with pepper or with bacon.

Cook the crêpes in a very hot skillet or crêpe pan over a high heat, adding a little butter to the pan before frying each one. Keep hot. Brush the kabobs with oil and cook over very hot charcoal for 10 minutes, turning occasionally. Season and serve with the crêpes.

LUNCH AND SUPPER DISHES

Planning one main meal a day is usually enough for anyone to cope with. So having to think up some ideas for lunch or supper, particularly over a busy weekend when all the family are at home or guests are staying, is often just too much.

For times when you want to make a quick and tasty dish or if you would prefer a light supper instead of a hearty dinner, then you will find a wide range of tempting ideas in this chapter. Vegetables and eggs are both economical and easy to prepare so these ingredients often form the backbone of many light meals. Too often the answer to lunch or supper is a simple cheese omelette, poached eggs or a quick dish of scrambled eggs with toast. Many of these traditional favorites have been transformed by the addition of some interesting ingredients, seasonings and accompaniments to offer a selection of ideas which offer familiar appeal but with a new slant on flavor.

For example, why not try a Zucchini Omelette, Scrambled Eggs with Mussels or Soft-cooked Eggs with Herb Mayonnaise? Remember to try and keep the diet balance in your lunches and suppers as well as in the main meal, so make a simple green salad if you have time. Alternatively, prepare a few sticks of scrubbed celery, sticks of carrot and an apple to add a little freshness to the snack. Have some crusty whole wheat bread, crisp savory bran crackers or a slice of whole wheat toast as an accompaniment. Fresh fruit juice or sparkling spring water will quench the thirst without increasing the calorie content.

Even though the dishes in this chapter are intended to be served for lunch or supper you will find that many of them are equally well suited to opening the meal – try offering small portions of Scrambled Eggs with Ratatouille or Apple-stuffed Eggs as the first course, for example. You may even find that some of the ideas are good candidates for breakfast dishes or for a relaxed weekend brunch party.

The less important meals of the day are often the ones in which one hopes to make use of leftovers, frozen foods or pantry items. So don't be afraid of using the odd convenience food now and then – canned cooked rice, canned tomatoes or mushrooms, tuna fish or prepared bottled or frozen mussels for example. A jar of mayonnaise is another good standby; frozen chopped or leaf spinach and some rolls, brioches or croissants are all useful ingredients to keep in the freezer. It is easy to strike a happy balance between fresh foods and convenience foods and you will find that several of these recipes can be used to transform a few handy cans or freezer packages.

Baked Eggs with Mushrooms

Serves 4

2 shallots
$\frac{1}{2}$ lb mushrooms
$\frac{1}{4}$ cup butter
salt and pepper
$\frac{1}{4}$ cup Crème Fraîche (page 398)
4 eggs

Peel and thinly slice the shallots. Wipe the mushrooms, trim the stalks, then rinse quickly and dry. Thinly slice the mushrooms.

Heat 2 tablespoons of the butter in a skillet and fry the mushrooms without allowing them to brown. Fry until all the moisture has evaporated. Season to taste. Grease 4 ramekins with the remaining butter. Place the mushrooms at the bottom of the ramekins and then pour over the cream. Break the eggs into the ramekins, taking care that the yolks do not break. Place the ramekins in a bain maire (water bath) or roasting pan containing 1-inch hot water and cook for 10 minutes in a preheated 350° oven. Serve hot with toast and parsley butter.

Variations

You can also make Baked eggs with spinach or sorrel. Remove the stalks from the leaves, then wash and wipe dry. Fry gently in a skillet with a little butter. Season. Butter the ramekins, and place the spinach or sorrel in them. Add a little cream, then gently break the eggs into the ramekins, taking care not to break the yolks. Cook in a water bath for 10 minutes.

Instead of the mushrooms, you could also use ratatouille, fried artichoke bottoms, or sliced zucchini fried gently in a little butter. As soon as all the moisture has evaporated, arrange the zucchini in the bottom of the ramekins, add the eggs, and cook as above. You can also use asparagus tip purée. Cook the asparagus in boiling salted water until tender, then drain and purée in a blender or food processor. Strain the purée. Add 2 tablespoons crème fraîche and mix together. Season. Add the eggs, and cook in a water bath.

Simpler still, just cook the Baked eggs with cream. Heat 1 tablespoon of crème fraîche per egg in a small saucepan, then divide the cream between the ramekins, which should have been warmed in hot water. Sprinkle with chopped chives. Break an egg into each ramekin, season with salt and pepper and place a pat of butter on each one. Cook in a water bath for 10 minutes.

Princess Scrambled Eggs

Serves 4

¾ lb cooked ham
8 slices of bread
½ cup butter
8 eggs
2 pinches freshly grated nutmeg
salt and pepper
a few sprigs chervil or parsley

Cut the ham into pieces, reserving some for the garnish. Fry the bread in half the butter and keep hot. Prepare a water bath by pouring about 1-inch of boiling water into a roasting pan. Break the eggs into a bowl. Add 1 tablespoon water. Whisk the eggs briefly, then add 2 tablespoons butter cut up into pieces and the nutmeg. Season. Pour the mixture into a saucepan in the water bath over a low heat. Using a wooden spoon, stir constantly and gently, scraping the sides, until the eggs thicken. The water in the water bath must never boil, only simmer very gently.

When the eggs have thickened, remove the pan from the heat and add the remaining butter in small pieces and the ham. Stir for another 1 to 2 minutes. Pour the eggs into a hot serving dish and garnish with the fried bread and reserved pieces of ham (cut into fancy shapes, if desired) and a few sprigs of chervil or parsley.

Darioles on Toast

Serves 5

1 sweet red or green pepper
1 tablespoon olive oil
1 onion, chopped
2 cloves garlic, crushed
1 lb tomatoes, quartered
2 tablespoons chopped parsley
salt and pepper
1 tablespoon flour
2 pinches freshly grated nutmeg
5 eggs, separated
3 tablespoons Crème Fraîche
   (page 398)
3 tablespoons butter
5 round slices of bread
5 sprigs parsley for garnish

Halve the pepper, remove the seeds and cut into pieces. Place the oil, onion, garlic, tomatoes, pepper and parsley in a saucepan, stir, season and cook gently for 30 minutes. Purée the mixture, add the flour and leave to thicken over a low heat for a few minutes, stirring to prevent lumps forming. Keep hot.

Add the nutmeg, salt and pepper to the egg yolks, then the crème fraîche. Beat the whites until stiff but not dry and fold them gently into the yolks. Pour the mixture into 5 greased dariole molds, leaving $\frac{1}{2}$ inch space at the top. Cook in a water bath in a preheated $325°$ oven for 15 minutes. Fry the bread in the butter.

Turn the molds out on the slices of bread. Top with a little sauce and a sprig of parsley. Serve the remaining sauce separately.

Multicolored Eggs

Serves 4

8 eggs
$\frac{1}{4}$ cup tomato paste
$\frac{1}{2}$ sweet red or green pepper
3 tablespoons Crème Fraîche
  (page 398)
salt and pepper
$\frac{1}{2}$ cup Mayonnaise (page 409)
1 slice (about 1 oz) of salmon
1 bunch of chives
2 tablespoons puréed spinach
2 canned anchovy fillets
a few capers
2 teaspoons anchovy paste
2 lemons, sliced
sprigs parsley for garnish

Hard-cook the eggs then remove the shells. Carefully cut them in half. Cover four of the egg halves with tomato paste, and garnish with a triangle of pepper. Carefully remove the yolks from another two egg halves, then mash the yolks and add the crème fraîche and seasoning. Pile this mixture into the egg whites.

Cover another four egg halves with mayonnaise then cut up the salmon and place on the mayonnaise. Cover two more egg halves with mayonnaise. Cut the chives into $1\frac{1}{2}$-inch lengths and make them into bundles. Place the bundles on the mayonnaise then place two strips of pepper on the chives. Place a dollop of spinach on two egg halves then roll up an anchovy with a caper and place on the egg.

Cover two egg halves with anchovy paste then place a caper and a triangle of lemon on top. Arrange on a serving platter garnished with slices of lemon and sprigs of parsley. Serve cold with aperitifs, crusty French bread and ripe olives.

Zucchini Omelette

Serves 4

4 small zucchini
2 tablespoons oil
2 cloves garlic, crushed
1 tablespoon chopped parsley
salt and pepper
1 small dried hot red pepper
  (optional)
6 eggs
3 tablespoons milk
$\frac{1}{2}$ cup grated Parmesan cheese
2 tablespoons butter

Trim the ends off the zucchini, then wash, dry and slice them. Heat the oil in a skillet and fry the garlic and parsley over a medium heat for 2 minutes. Add the zucchini. Season with salt and crumble in the dried hot pepper if used (previously rinsed and wiped dry). Cook without a lid over a medium heat for 15 minutes, stirring frequently.

Beat the eggs in a bowl with the milk and 3 tablespoons of the Parmesan cheese. Season with salt and pepper. Melt the butter in a skillet. When it begins to brown, pour in the eggs and leave the omelette to set over a medium heat. After 1 minute add the zucchini and leave to cook for another 1 to 2 minutes. Sprinkle with the remaining Parmesan cheese and allow to melt. Serve immediately.

Scrambled Eggs with Kidneys

Serves 4

4 lambs' kidneys
6 tablespoons butter
2 cloves garlic, crushed
salt and pepper
8 eggs, beaten
2 tablespoons Crème Fraîche
  (page 398)
2 pinches freshly grated nutmeg
4 sprigs parsley for garnish

Cut the kidneys in half and remove the white parts from the center. Melt 2 tablespoons of the butter in a skillet. Brown the kidneys in it for 2 minutes on each side over a low heat, then add the garlic. Season with salt and pepper and put the lid on the pan. Cook for a further 4–5 minutes over a very low heat, then remove from the heat and keep hot.

Scramble the eggs as for Princess Scrambled Eggs (page 218) and add the cream and nutmeg when they have thickened. Continue stirring for another 1 to 2 minutes.

Pour the scrambled eggs onto warmed serving plates and place the kidney halves on each dish. Garnish with the sprigs of parsley and serve immediately with a green salad and small garlic-flavored croûtons.

Blue Cheese Soufflés

Serves 8

½ cup butter
6 tablespoons flour
2 cups milk
¼ lb blue cheese (Roquefort
   type)
salt and pepper
⅛ teaspoon freshly grated
   nutmeg
6 eggs, separated

Melt 6 tablespoons of the butter in a saucepan over a low heat. Add the flour and then the milk (a little at a time). Leave to cook, stirring constantly, for 10 minutes.

Take the pan off the heat and crumble in the cheese. Stir carefully. Season with pepper and adjust the seasoning if necessary. Add the nutmeg and the egg yolks, beating each one in lightly. Beat the egg whites until they form stiff peaks. Fold them gently into the mixture.

Generously grease 8 ramekins with the remaining butter. Pour the mixture into the ramekins up to ½ inch from the top. Pass the blade of a knife around the edge of each ramekin. Bake in a preheated 325° oven for 15 to 20 minutes.

The soufflés are cooked when they have risen and turned golden brown. Serve immediately with a well-seasoned chicory salad.

Scrambled Eggs with Ratatouille

Serves 4

3 tomatoes
2 zucchini
1 sweet red pepper
1 green pepper
2 tablespoons oil
1 onion, chopped
2 cloves garlic, crushed
1 small bunch of chervil or
　chives, chopped
1 small bunch of parsley,
　chopped
salt and pepper
8 eggs
6 tablespoons butter
2 pinches freshly grated nutmeg
sprigs parsley for garnish

Peel, seed and chop the tomatoes. Wash and wipe the zucchini and cut into thin slices. Halve, seed and slice the peppers.

Heat the oil in a skillet and add the tomatoes, zucchini, peppers, onion, garlic and herbs. Season and leave to cook over a medium heat for 35 minutes. If the mixture is very liquid, turn up the heat and allow to boil in order to evaporate the moisture in the vegetables. Stir the mixture as you do this to prevent burning.

Prepare a water bath (see page 218). Break the eggs into a bowl. Add a tablespoon of water and whisk briefly. Add $\frac{1}{4}$ cup of the butter cut up into pieces and the nutmeg. Season. Pour the mixture into the pan in the water bath and, using a wooden spoon, stir constantly, scraping the sides, until the eggs thicken. The water in the water bath must never boil, only simmer gently.

Once the eggs have thickened, take the pan off the heat. Add the remaining butter in small pieces. Finally add the ratatouille. Mix well and continue to stir for 1 to 2 minutes. Pour the eggs into a warmed serving dish and garnish with parsley. Serve immediately.

Cook's tip
It is better to cook scrambled eggs in a high vessel rather than a wide one. When the egg is in a thicker layer, it will stay (when gently stirred) at the same distance from the heat source. It will cook more slowly, not stick together and will be softer.

The water bath is the best way to cook scrambled eggs, but you can also use a thick-bottomed saucepan or a flameproof porcelain vessel over a heat-diffuser.

Scrambled Eggs with Mussels

Serves 4

1 quart mussels, scrubbed
$\frac{1}{2}$ cup butter
1 onion, chopped
2 cloves garlic, crushed
$\frac{2}{3}$ cup dry white wine
1 small bunch of parsley,
   chopped
salt and pepper
8 eggs
2 pinches grated nutmeg

Tap each mussel sharply and discard any which do not close. Melt $\frac{1}{4}$ cup butter in a saucepan and add the onion and garlic. Brown for 1 minute then add the white wine, mussels and parsley. Season with pepper, cover, and cook until the mussels open. Discard shells and closed mussels.

Prepare a water bath (see page 218). Break the eggs into a bowl. Add a spoonful of water and stir briefly. Add 2 tablespoons butter cut into pieces and the nutmeg. Season, pour into the water bath and gently stir, scraping the sides, until the eggs thicken.

Once the eggs are smooth, take the pan off the heat and add the remaining butter cut into pieces and then the mussels, reserving a few for garnish. Stir for 1 to 2 minutes and serve garnished with the reserved mussels.

Eggs in Paprika Sauce

Serves 4

1½ lb fresh spinach
½ cup butter
3 tablespoons flour
⅔ cup white wine
2½ cups beef broth
½ teaspoon paprika
½ lb button mushrooms
salt and pepper
6 eggs

Stalk and wash the spinach and blanch it for 5 minutes in boiling salted water. Drain and stew in a saucepan with 3 tablespoons butter. Season and keep hot.

Melt 3 tablespoons butter in a heavy saucepan and add the flour, then the white wine and broth. Cook for 10 minutes, stirring continuously, then add the paprika and put to one side. Fry the mushrooms gently in the remaining butter. Season. Soft-cook the eggs and peel them.

Arrange the spinach on a warmed serving dish and place the eggs on top. Arrange the mushrooms in the center. Coat the eggs with the paprika sauce, and serve immediately. Instead of paprika, you could use another spice such as curry powder which goes well with eggs.

Spanish-Style Omelette

Serves 4

2 tomatoes
1 sweet red pepper
1 green pepper
3 tablespoons olive oil
2 onions, chopped
2 cups frozen or fresh, shelled
    peas
2 slices cooked ham, diced
salt and pepper
6 eggs
sprig fresh basil, chopped *or* $\frac{1}{2}$
    teaspoon dried basil
1 tablespoon chopped chives
1 tablespoon chopped parsley
$\frac{1}{4}$ cup butter
sprig of basil or parsley

Peel, seed and chop the tomatoes. Halve, seed and dice the peppers. Heat the oil in a skillet and gently fry the onions without allowing them to brown. Add the peas, tomatoes, peppers and ham. Season, stir well and leave to cook over a low heat for 35 minutes. If necessary, add a little water.

Beat the eggs with a fork, getting as much air into them as possible. Season. Add the herbs and vegetables and stir well. Heat the butter in a skillet. When it is nut brown in color, pour in the egg mixture and leave to cook over a medium heat, distributing the eggs and vegetables evenly over the pan.

When the omelette is cooked, slide it onto a serving dish. Garnish with a sprig of basil or parsley and serve immediately.

Cook's tips

Cook omelettes in a good-quality enamel or cast iron skillet, with a thick, very flat bottom. Ideally, you should keep a pan like this especially for omelettes. If so, never wash it, merely wipe with a wad of paper towels while still hot.

To peel tomatoes, put them in a pan of very hot water for 10 seconds. You can then peel off the skin easily with a small knife.

This omelette can also be made with various meats: finely ground pork, ground beef, and chicken breast cut up into small pieces and mixed with chopped chives. The meats should be browned for 10 minutes in a skillet and then mixed with the beaten egg.

Another alternative is to make a green herb omelette. Beat the omelette as described above, then add a tablespoon of chopped parsley, a tablespoon of chopped chervil, and a tablespoon of chopped chives. Do not add tarragon to these herbs as the strong taste will dominate the other herbs.

Eggs Poached in Spinach

Serves 6

$\frac{1}{2}$ lb fresh bulk spinach and $\frac{1}{2}$ lb
   sorrel *or* 1 lb spinach
1 head lettuce
1 tablespoon chopped fresh
   chervil
1 tablespoon chopped fresh
   parsley
$\frac{1}{4}$ cup butter
salt and pepper
6 eggs
3 tablespoons Crème Fraîche
   (page 398)

Select green, fresh spinach. If the spinach is young and new (at the beginning of the season) merely cut off the stalk flush with the leaf; otherwise, cut out the stalk all the way along the leaf. Cut the stalks off the sorrel, if using. Wash in several changes of water and shake dry. Wash the lettuce and cut out the core.

Chop the spinach, sorrel, lettuce and herbs. Heat 3 tablespoons of the butter in a skillet and stew the spinach, sorrel, lettuce and herbs in it. Season.

Grease a gratin dish with the remaining butter. Put the greens in the dish, make 6 hollows and drop in the eggs, taking care not to break the yolks. Pour over the cream. Season. Bake in a preheated 350° oven for 8 minutes and serve hot.

Eggs in Brioches

Serves 4

4 brioches
¼ cup Crème Fraîche (page 398)
1 tablespoon chopped fresh
  chives
salt and pepper
4 eggs

Cut the round tops off the brioches, then hollow out the buns without damaging the sides. Mix the crumbled brioche centers and the cream in a bowl, then add the chopped chives and seasoning. Mix thoroughly.

Stuff the brioches with the mixture, leaving space for the eggs. Break the eggs into the buns, taking care not to break the yolks. Season. Place the buns on a baking sheet and put into a preheated 350° oven. Increase the oven temperature to 375° and bake for 7–8 minutes.

Take the buns out of the oven and serve hot with spinach or sorrel. You can also serve this dish with tomato and chive sauce or you could add one tablespoon of mushroom ketchup per bun to the crumb-cream mixture or some finely chopped ham.

Party Eggs

Serves 4–5

2 envelopes unflavored gelatin
1 quart chicken broth
$\frac{1}{2}$ lb frozen mixed vegetables,
   cooked, drained and cooled
$\frac{1}{2}$ cup mayonnaise
1 canned truffle (optional)
$\frac{1}{2}$ lb green beans, cooked,
   drained and cooled
1 sweet red pepper
6 eggs

Dissolve the gelatin in the broth and leave this aspic to cool. Mix the vegetables and mayonnaise together in a bowl. Add $\frac{2}{3}$ cup aspic and turn into a small round mold. Chill until set. Pour the rest of the aspic into a shallow container and set in the refrigerator.

Cut the truffle into thin slices, then cut out 10 crescent moon and flower shapes with a cookie-cutter. Trim the green beans, and cut in half. Cut the sweet pepper in half and remove the stalk, seeds and pith. Then poach it in boiling water for 15 minutes; drain. Soft-cook 5 of the eggs and hard-cook the sixth egg. Leave to cool.

Take the set aspic out of the refrigerator, and, using a dampened knife, cut it into small pieces. Use this aspic to decorate the rim of the serving dish. Dip the mold holding the vegetable and mayonnaise mixture in hot water for 30 seconds, then turn the mold out in the center of the serving dish. Place the prepared pieces of truffle (previously cut out) on the mold.

Carefully shell the soft-cooked eggs and lay them gently in position. Arrange the beans between them, in bunches, each wrapped with a strip of sweet pepper. Remove the yolk from the hard-cooked egg, and press it through a sieve. Decorate the tops of the eggs with a little of this yolk. Serve chilled.

Note: this recipe is a little complex, but success is ensured if you chill and set everything thoroughly. The chilling time is not counted in the time it takes to prepare the recipe. You can make this dish in the morning to eat in the evening, or make it the day before you eat it. The sieved egg yolk decoration should be added at the last moment.

Green Eggs in Lettuce Leaves

Serves 4

8 tomatoes
3 tablespoons olive oil
salt and pepper
1 tablespoon chopped fresh dill
   or fennel plus a few sprigs
1 head lettuce
4 slices cooked ham
1½ cups cooked rice
4 eggs

First make a tomato sauce. Peel, seed and chop the tomatoes and fry them in olive oil. Season them. Add the chopped dill or fennel and leave to simmer for 30 minutes. Clean the lettuce and remove the largest leaves, reserving the heart for a salad. Blanch in boiling salted water for 1 minute, then drain. Spread out the leaves in four piles of two or three leaves, depending on size. Lay a slice of ham on top and then a heap of rice. Make hollows in the rice and drop in the eggs. Season. Carefully close up the eggs in the rice and leaves, place in the basket of a steamer with the sprigs of dill or fennel and steam for 8 minutes. Serve hot with the tomato sauce.

Apple-Stuffed Eggs

Serves 3

6 eggs
2 small apples
½ cup butter
2 lemons
salt and pepper
2 pinches freshly grated nutmeg

Hard-cook 3 eggs, then peel them and keep them in hot water.

Peel the apples and cut them into quarters. Cook the apple quarters in a heavy skillet with half the butter and the juice of half a lemon. Season and keep hot.

Scramble the remaining eggs in a water bath (see page 218) with the remaining butter. Season with salt, pepper and nutmeg. Take half the apple quarters and chop them roughly. Add the scrambled eggs and keep hot.

Cut the remaining lemons into thin slices and cut the hard-cooked eggs in half. Top them with scrambled egg and apple and a small piece of lemon. Decorate the dish with the remaining slices of apple and lemon. Serve immediately.

Eggs in a Nest

Serves 4

4 large tomatoes
salt and pepper
1 clove garlic, crushed
$\frac{1}{3}$ cup grated Gruyère cheese
4 eggs
$\frac{1}{2}$ teaspoon dried thyme
2 tablespoons olive oil

Open and seed the tomatoes, then carefully remove and reserve the flesh. Season the inside of the tomatoes with salt and put them upside down on paper towels. Mix the garlic with the tomato pulp and season.

Turn the tomatoes the right way up and bake in a preheated 350° oven for 10 minutes. Take the tomatoes out of the oven and put a little of the grated Gruyère cheese inside. Break the eggs one by one gently into the tomatoes, taking care not to break the yolks. Season.

Place the whole tomatoes in a gratin dish and surround with the tomato pulp. Sprinkle with thyme and olive oil. Bake for 8 to 10 minutes and serve immediately.

Variation
You can make this dish with other vegetables, for example potatoes. Use two small or 1 large potato per person. Bake them in a preheated 400° oven for $1-1\frac{1}{4}$ hours. Check to see if they are cooked using a needle (they should not be squashed). Cut a small lid out of the potatoes, and hollow them out with a small spoon. Reserve the insides and mix together with a large pat of butter and some chopped parsley. Sprinkle a little grated Gruyère cheese into the hollowed-out potatoes then drop in the egg. Bake for 6 to 8 minutes. The eggs will cook more quickly in the still hot potatoes than they will in the tomatoes. Serve with the potato and parsley mixture.

Tuna-Stuffed Eggs

Serves 4

4 eggs
$\frac{1}{4}$ cup butter
3 tablespoons flour
2 cups milk
salt and pepper
$\frac{1}{2}$ (7-oz) can tuna fish
1 tablespoon chopped parsley
1 tablespoon dry white bread
  crumbs

Hard-cook the eggs, cool under running cold water and peel them.

Make the béchamel sauce. Melt 3 tablespoons butter in a saucepan and add the flour. Stir well, then pour in the cold milk, stirring all the time. Season, bring slowly to a boil and simmer for 2–3 minutes.

Cut the eggs in half. Carefully remove the yolks and mash them with a little béchamel sauce. Drain and flake the tuna, then blend it to a smooth paste in a blender or food processor. Mix the fish into the sauce with the chopped parsley. Stuff the egg whites with this mixture, piling it up high. Pour the rest of the sauce into a gratin dish. Lay the stuffed eggs on top, sprinkle with bread crumbs and bake in a preheated 350° oven for 10–15 minutes or until the bread crumbs are brown. Serve hot.

Soft-Cooked Eggs with Herb Mayonnaise

Serves 5

8 eggs and 1 yolk
salt and pepper
1 teaspoon Dijon-style mustard
1 cup oil
1 tablespoon vinegar
1 tablespoon chopped parsley
1 tablespoon chopped chervil
1 tablespoon chopped chives
1 few tarragon leaves, chopped
sprigs of fresh herbs for garnish

First make the mayonnaise. Whisk up one egg yolk, the salt, pepper and mustard in a bowl until the mixture is perfectly smooth and uniform, then add the oil, drop by drop. When the mixture begins to thicken a little, you can add the oil more quickly, but do not stop whisking. Pour in the vinegar and whisk well. Taste, and adjust the seasoning if necessary. Fold in the chopped herbs.

Soft-cook the eggs, put them under running cold water and gently peel them. Arrange 5 whole eggs on the serving dish. Cut the remaining eggs in half and place in the middle of the dish. Coat with the herb mayonnaise and garnish with the sprigs of herbs. Chill well before serving.

Poached Eggs with Grapes

Serves 4

4 shallots
1 lb large green grapes
$\frac{1}{2}$ cup butter
1$\frac{1}{4}$ cups dry white wine
salt and pepper
4 round slices of bread
4 eggs

Peel and slice the shallots. Wash, peel and seed the grapes (if necessary).

Heat 2 tablespoons of the butter in a small saucepan and gently fry the shallots without allowing them to brown. Put to one side. Heat half the remaining butter in a deep skillet and fry the grapes, then add the shallots and white wine. Season and leave to simmer over a low heat for 15 to 20 minutes.

Fry the slices of bread in the remaining butter and keep hot. Poach the eggs. Pour the sauce and grapes onto a hot serving dish, then arrange the slices of bread on top and gently lay the poached eggs on the bread. Garnish with a grape. Serve immediately.

Variations
You can use plums, apricots or other fruit (depending on the season) in this recipe instead of grapes. Proceed in the same way.

Poached eggs with red wine
Make these poached eggs with red wine and onions instead of grapes. To do this, peel 1 lb onions and thinly slice them. Cook the onions gently in a heavy skillet in 2 tablespoons butter, but do not allow the onions to brown. Season and add a clove. Sprinkle with a teaspoon of flour, mix well, then gradually add 1 cup red wine. Simmer for 7 to 8 minutes then pour the mixture onto a hot serving dish. Arrange the poached eggs on top and serve immediately with toast.

Provençale-Style Eggs

Serves 3 or 4

5 tomatoes
¾ lb mushrooms
¼ cup olive oil
2 onions, chopped
2 cloves garlic, crushed
a few fresh basil leaves,
   chopped *or* a pinch of dried
   basil
1 teaspoon chopped fresh thyme
   or ½ teaspoon dried thyme
salt and pepper
7 eggs

Peel the tomatoes after blanching them in boiling water for 1 minute, then seed and chop them. Trim the mushrooms, wash them quickly and slice them.

Heat 1 tablespoon of the olive oil in a small saucepan and gently fry the mushrooms without allowing them to brown. Heat the rest of the oil in a deep skillet and add the onions and garlic, then the tomatoes, mushrooms, basil, thyme, salt and pepper. Cook over a low heat for 30 minutes.

Pour the mixture into a gratin dish. Make 7 hollows, and break in the eggs, taking care not to break the yolks. Bake in a preheated 350° oven for 8 to 10 minutes or until the egg whites are just set. Serve immediately with toast which has been rubbed with garlic.

French-Style Eggs and Bacon

Serves 3

¾ lb bacon
3 tablespoons butter
pepper
3 eggs

Cut the bacon into strips, then blanch the strips for 2 minutes in boiling water, to extract the excess salt. Drain, and pat with paper towels. Heat the butter in a skillet and fry the bacon until brown. Drain to remove excess fat.

Place the bacon strips in a flameproof dish and season with pepper, then break the eggs onto the bacon and cook over a low heat until the whites are opaque. Alternatively bake them in a preheated 350° oven for 4 to 5 minutes or until the whites are just set. Serve hot.

Variations
If you wish, you can add some chicken livers and chopped parsley to this dish, or you can use a mixture of bacon and ham, fried in butter with a chopped shallot. Pour over ½ cup white wine and stir to dissolve the bacon juices just before adding the eggs.

Omelette Cake

Serves 6

4 tomatoes
3 canned artichoke bottoms
2 chicken breasts, cooked
$\frac{1}{2}$ lb (2 sticks) butter
3 cloves garlic, crushed
1 large bunch of parsley,
 chopped
salt and pepper
10 eggs

Peel, seed and chop the tomatoes. Slice the artichokes and chicken meat.

Heat 2 tablespoons of the butter in a skillet and fry the tomatoes until brown. Add a little garlic and parsley, season and leave to cook for about 20 minutes over a low heat. Mix the remaining parsley and garlic in a bowl and set to one side. Heat 2 tablespoons of the butter in a skillet and brown the artichoke slices. Season and reserve. Brown the chicken in 2 tablespoons of the butter and season.

Make 5 small 2-egg omelettes, cooking them one by one in the remaining butter and keep them hot. Place one omelette on an ovenproof dish and cover it with chicken. Place the second omelette on top and cover it with fried artichoke. Place the third omelette on top and cover it with garlic and parsley. Place the fourth omelette on top and cover it with tomato, then finally place the last omelette on top of this. Bake the omelette cake in a preheated 325° oven for 4 minutes and serve hot with a chicory salad.

Variations
You can fill this omelette cake with other ingredients, depending on the contents of your refrigerator and pantry.

A seafood omelette cake can be made with four omelettes: the first one with $\frac{1}{2}$ lb peeled, cooked shrimp, the second one with mussels (1 pint of mussels opened over a high heat), the third one with two handfuls of clams, prepared in the same way as the mussels, and also shelled, and the fourth one with a small can of crabmeat. Save a few crumbs of crabmeat to sprinkle over the top of the cake.

A few of the many other fillings for this omelette cake are as follows: ratatouille, ham, fried potatoes, spinach, asparagus tips, small croûtons, chicken livers, etc. We leave it to your imagination!

Baked Ham and Egg Omelette

Serves 4

$\frac{1}{3}$ cup flour
$\frac{1}{2}$ cup milk
8 eggs
salt and pepper
1 onion, chopped
4 slices of cooked ham, diced
$\frac{1}{4}$ cup grated Gruyère cheese
2 tablespoons butter

Place the flour in a bowl and add the cold milk, a little at a time and then the eggs, one by one, beating steadily all the time. Season with salt and pepper. Add the onion, ham and Gruyère cheese.

Generously grease a shallow ovenproof dish with the butter and pour in the mixture. Bake in a preheated 325° oven for 20 minutes. Serve hot with a green salad.

Variations

Leftover beef or breast of chicken cut into small pieces make tasty alternatives to ham. This dish can also be made with smoked salmon cut into thin strips, or any other smoked fish. In this case, leave out the onion and Gruyère cheese.

Toulouse-Style Eggs

Serves 8

2 Toulouse sausages or other
  garlic sausages
1 bouquet garni
3 tablespoons butter
8 eggs
pepper

Poach the sausages for 20 minutes in simmering water with the bouquet garni. Drain and slice. Place the sausage slices in a gratin dish which has been greased with the butter, then carefully break the eggs into the dish. Season with pepper, and bake in a preheated 350° oven for 6 to 7 minutes. Serve hot with potato salad.

Eggs Florentine

Serves 3

2 lb fresh bulk spinach
$\frac{1}{4}$ cup butter
salt and pepper
6 eggs
$\frac{1}{4}$ cup Crème Fraîche (page 398)

Stalk and wash the spinach. Heat 2 tablespoons of the butter in a saucepan and cook the spinach gently in it until limp. Add a little water, season and leave to simmer for 15 minutes. Generously grease a gratin dish with the remaining butter and fill with the spinach. Make 6 hollows in the spinach and break in the eggs. Season, then pour over the crème fraîche. Bake in a preheated 350° oven for 8 to 10 minutes or until the eggs are just set. Remove from the oven and serve hot.

You can also make this dish using frozen spinach, and also with salad greens instead of the fresh spinach. This dish goes well with cold roast pork or veal, as well as with ham.

VEGETABLE DISHES

The role of vegetables is not merely that of adding color, texture and a filling ingredient to the main dish and this chapter certainly goes a long way to proving the versatility of this often neglected group of ingredients.

The fact that freezers are now commonplace appliances means that a wide range of vegetables are available all the year round – cauliflowers, zucchini, green and lima beans, carrots, peas and corn are just a few types of vegetables for which we no longer rely on seasonal availability. However, it is good to make the most of fresh items in the market. Look out for seasonal produce – baby carrots, young leeks, new beans and fresh peas – buy those which are unblemished, bright and fresh but avoid any limp, faded vegetables which are bruised or damaged. Often it is not necessary to peel good quality new vegetables, so just scrub or scrape early carrots, potatoes and zucchini and they will retain their goodness and flavor to the full.

As well as a variety of familiar recipes like ratatouille, stuffed tomatoes, Potatoes Lyonnaise and Cauliflower Mornay, this chapter offers lots of interesting new ways in which to prepare and cook a good selection of easily available vegetables. Many will lend themselves to becoming a supper dish, vegetarian main dish or tasty appetizer in addition to going well with a roast, broiled steaks, chops or burgers. With fish, poultry, pies and quiches you may like to serve some Mushrooms Provençal, Zucchini with Bacon, Cauliflower Antibois or Spinach with Croûtons.

So next time you are stuck for ideas, bored with making a fuss of the main dish and fed up with offering up some plain boiled potatoes to compensate for the vegetable dishes, then have a look through the pages which follow and you will find some inspired creations which will do justice to any occasion.

Stuffed Onions

Serves 5

5 large onions
¼ cup butter
2 tablespoons soft bread crumbs
5 oz bulk pork sausage meat
salt and pepper
1 egg, beaten
2 (10-oz) packages frozen
   spinach, thawed
20 bay leaves
5 tablespoons broth
1 cup Tomato Sauce (page 383)

Cook the onions in a pan of boiling salted water for 10 minutes. Drain and leave to cool for 5 minutes. Slice off the top from each onion. Carefully scoop out the inside of the onions with a small spoon and reserve.

Melt the butter in a skillet and fry the bread crumbs for 2 minutes until golden brown. Add the sausage meat and the reserved onion flesh. Season and cook over a low heat for 5 minutes.

Remove from the heat, add the egg and mix thoroughly. Fill each onion with the stuffing, then add 2 tablespoons of spinach. Surround each with 4 bay leaves, and tie with fine string to keep the stuffing and bay leaves in place.

Place the onions in an ovenproof dish. Pour the broth over them, and bake in a preheated 375° oven for 45 minutes. Garnish each onion with 1 teaspoon Tomato sauce. Hand the rest of the sauce separately.

Mushrooms Provençale

Serves 6

$4\frac{1}{2}$ lb mushrooms, caps and
   stems separated
juice of $1\frac{1}{2}$ lemons
6 tablespoons oil
salt and pepper
3 garlic cloves, chopped
2 tablespoons chopped parsley

Wash the mushroom stems and caps in water with two-thirds of the lemon juice added. Drain on paper towels, and cut into large pieces.

Heat half the oil in a skillet over a high heat, then add the mushrooms. Stir frequently and cook until they release their moisture. Drain and dry again, on paper towels.

Heat the rest of the oil in the rinsed out skillet and add the mushrooms. Season, then brown for 15 minutes, stirring. Just before serving, stir in the garlic and parsley and the remaining lemon juice.

Spinach with Croûtons

Serves 4

4½ lb spinach, central rib
   removed
6 tablespoons Crème Fraîche
   (page 398)
salt and pepper
2 tablespoons butter
4 slices bread, halved diagonally
2 lemons, cut into wedges, for
   serving

Bring a large pan of salted water to a boil and cook the spinach for 10 minutes. Drain, cool under running water to stop the cooking process and drain again, then squeeze in your hands without crushing the spinach too much.

Put the spinach into a pan over a low heat, mixing in half the cream. Stir gently and adjust the seasoning. Cook for 20 to 30 minutes. If too much juice is released, increase the heat to evaporate it, stirring constantly with a wooden spoon to prevent the spinach from sticking.

Melt the butter and fry the bread until golden brown. Arrange the spinach on a hot dish, garnish with the hot croûtons, and top with the rest of the cream. Serve with lemon wedges.

Spinach prepared in this way can be served as an accompaniment to sweetbreads, liver, fried veal cutlets, or roast veal. Or it can be served in a gratin dish, with 4 slices of rolled-up ham, and topped with ½ cup grated Gruyère cheese. It should be browned under the broiler for 8 minutes.

This dish goes well with fried or baked eggs. It can also be served with soft-cooked eggs laid on pieces of bread fried in butter and served without the lemon.

Spinach Gratin
To make a delicious spinach gratin, put the cooked spinach in an ovenproof dish. Make 1 quantity Bechamel Sauce (see page 384) and stir 1 cup grated cheese into it. When the cheese has completely melted pour the sauce over the spinach. Top with 2 tablespoons fresh bread crumbs mixed with 2 tablespoons grated Parmesan cheese and 2 tablespoons chopped chives. Sprinkle this mixture over the sauce, then place the dish under a hot broiler and cook until golden and bubbling. This gratin can be served with cooked whole wheat pasta, brown rice or lentils to make a tasty vegetarian supper dish. Alternatively, the gratin will taste good with broiled meats or fish.

Green Beans with Onions and Tomatoes

Serves 6

¼ cup butter
2 tablespoons olive oil
1 lb tomatoes, peeled, halved and seeded
3 onions, coarsely chopped
2 garlic cloves, coarsely chopped
salt and pepper
3½ lb tender green beans
1 teaspoon chopped parsley

Heat the butter and oil in a saucepan and gently fry the tomatoes, onions and garlic. Season with salt and pepper.

Bring a large pan of salted water to a boil and cook the beans for 8–10 minutes. They should still be slightly crunchy. Drain.

Remove the tomato and onion mixture from the saucepan, and reserve. Add the beans to the pan and brown for 5 minutes. Season.

Arrange the beans on a dish. Spoon the onion and garlic mixture into the center and top with the tomatoes. Sprinkle with chopped parsley.

Braised Brussels Sprouts

Serves 4

2 lb Brussels sprouts
1 tablespoon vinegar
5 oz bacon, cut into small strips
$\frac{1}{4}$ cup butter
salt and pepper

Rinse the sprouts in water with the vinegar added then put into a pan of boiling salted water and cook for 6 to 8 minutes. Drain and rinse.

Blanch the bacon in a pan of boiling water for 2 minutes. Drain and put into a saucepan with the butter. When golden brown, add the sprouts and season with pepper and a little salt. Cover and leave to simmer for 30 minutes.

Serve on a warmed serving dish as an accompaniment for a roast, pork chops, or roast duck.

Braised Fennel

Serves 5

2 lemons
10 fennel bulbs
$\frac{1}{4}$ cup butter
2 cups chicken broth
salt and pepper
$\frac{1}{4}$ cup chopped parsley

Squeeze the juice of 1 lemon and cut the other into fluted slices.

Put the fennel into a pan of boiling salted water with the lemon juice. Cook for 10 minutes and drain.

Melt the butter in a saucepan and add the fennel, arranging it in one layer. Add the broth and season lightly, then cover and simmer for about 45 minutes. The fennel is cooked when the broth is absorbed.

Serve the fennel in a hot serving dish, sprinkled with the parsley, and surrounded with fluted slices of lemon.

Peas Bonne Femme

Serves 4

$\frac{1}{4}$ cup butter
1 lettuce heart
10 pearl onions
3 tomatoes, peeled and
   quartered
$4\frac{1}{2}$ lb peas, shelled
1 bouquet garni
salt and pepper
5 tablespoons water
1 sugar cube (optional)

Melt two-thirds of the butter in a heavy-based saucepan and add the lettuce heart, onions, tomatoes, peas and bouquet garni. Season and add the water. Cover, and leave to cook over a low heat for 40 minutes, checking from time to time that the peas are not sticking to the pan; if they do, add a little extra water.

About 5 minutes before the end of cooking time, stir in the sugar, if using. Remove the bouquet garni and lettuce heart. Add the rest of the butter in small pieces to the peas and serve immediately.

Corn on the Cob with Maître d'Hôtel Butter and Crème Fraîche

Serves 4

4 ears of corn
2 sugar cubes
$\frac{1}{2}$ cup butter
juice of 1 lemon
2 tablespoons chopped parsley
salt and pepper
$\frac{2}{3}$ cup Crème Fraîche (page 398)

Remove the husks and silk from the corn. Bring a large pan of water to a boil and add the corn – they should be completely covered. Add the sugar cubes and cook for 4–10 minutes after the water comes back to a boil. Remove the corn and drain it.

Prepare the maître d'hôtel butter: melt the butter in a heavy saucepan over a low heat. Add half the lemon juice, sprinkle with the parsley, and season. Serve in a warmed sauceboat.

Gently beat the Crème together with the remaining lemon juice. Season, and serve in a warmed bowl. Arrange the corn on a serving dish covered with a folded napkin and serve with the two sauces.

Serve as a vegetable with broiled pork chops or as an appetizer with Tomato sauce (see page 383).

Flavored Cream Cheese
Any of the following savory cream cheese mixtures will complement plain cooked corn on the cob. With these accompaniments, the corn can be served for the first course of a meal or as a light lunch with warm crusty bread.
Stilton Cream: Crumble, then mash $\frac{1}{2}$ cup blue cheese and beat in $\frac{1}{2}$ cup cream cheese. Add 1 tablespoon chopped chives and black pepper to taste.
Cream Cheese with Bacon: Finely chop and fry $\frac{1}{2}$ lb lean smoked bacon. When crisp, drain on kitchen paper towels and leave to cool. Stir the bacon into 1 cup cream cheese and add 2 tablespoons chopped parsley.
Cream Cheese with Smoked Oysters: Drain and chop 1 (4-oz) can smoked oysters then stir in 1 cup cream cheese with the grated rind of $\frac{1}{2}$ lemon.

Stuffed Tomatoes

Serves 10

10 large tomatoes
2 onions, chopped
2 garlic cloves, chopped
½ lb (1 cup) ground beef or
  leftover cooked chicken or
  ham
½ lb bulk pork sausage meat
2 eggs, beaten
3 tablespoons chopped parsley
salt and pepper
¼ lb bacon, finely chopped
2 bay leaves
⅔ cup dried white bread crumbs
3 tablespoons butter

Cut off the tops of the tomatoes and reserve. Scoop out the flesh with a teaspoon, without damaging the skins. Reserve a little juice and pulp. Sprinkle the insides with salt and leave the tomatoes upside down on a rack to drain for 15 minutes.

Put the onions and garlic into a bowl with the beef, sausage meat, eggs, 5 tablespoons tomato juice and pulp, and the parsley. Season with salt and pepper and mix thoroughly.

Fill the tomatoes with the mixture, then put into a buttered baking dish with the rest of the stuffing, surrounded with the bacon pieces and bay leaves. Sprinkle with the bread crumbs and pats of butter.

Bake in a preheated 400° oven for 30 minutes, then put the tops back on the tomatoes and bake for 10 minutes longer. Discard the bay leaves and serve hot.

Potatoes Niçoise

Serves 6

2 lb potatoes, cut into $\frac{1}{4}$ inch
  slices
4 large tomatoes, cut into $\frac{1}{4}$ inch
  slices
2 cups beef broth
salt and pepper
1 cup grated Gruyère cheese
2 tablespoons butter, diced
2 tablespoons chopped parsley
  (optional)

Butter an ovenproof dish, and arrange a layer of potatoes on the bottom, followed by two layers of tomatoes and another layer of potatoes. Next, reverse the sequence, putting the tomatoes on the potatoes, and the potatoes on the tomatoes. Continue layering until all the ingredients are used, finishing with a layer of potatoes and tomatoes. Add the broth and season with pepper and a little salt. Sprinkle with Gruyère cheese and dot with the butter.

Bake in a preheated 400° oven for about 40 minutes until the top is golden brown. Serve sprinkled with the parsley if wished. Serve with all broiled meats: lamb chops, steaks.

French-Fried Onion Rings

Serves 5

1 cup flour
2 eggs, separated
2 tablespoons oil plus oil for
    deep frying
1 cup beer
salt and pepper
5 large onions, sliced into quite
    thick rings and separated

Make the batter: mix the flour in a bowl with the egg yolks and the 2 tablespoons oil. Gradually add the beer, then season with salt, and leave to stand for 1 hour.

Heat the oil for deep frying to 375° or until a bread cube browns in 50 seconds. Beat the egg whites into stiff peaks, and fold into the batter just before you use it.

Season the onion rings and coat in the batter. Put them into the hot oil. When the rings return to the surface and turn golden brown, lift them out with a slotted spoon, and drain on paper towels.

Serve with roast meats and broiled fish such as cod or tuna.

Vegetable Charlotte with White Sauce

Serves 8

1 lb carrots
½ lb turnips
5 oz mushrooms
juice of 1 lemon
¼ cup oil
2 lb peas, shelled
salt and pepper
3 eggs
⅔ cup Crème Fraîche (page 398)
2 tablespoons butter
2 tablespoons flour
2 cups milk
2 tablespoons chopped parsley

Cut 2 carrots and 1 turnip into short lengths and slice the remainder. Rinse the mushrooms in water with the lemon juice added, then slice.

Heat the oil in a saucepan, and add the sliced carrots and turnips, the mushrooms and peas. Season, cover and cook over a low heat for 15 minutes.

Meanwhile, beat the eggs with the Crème fraîche in a bowl, and season. Drain the vegetables, and mix gently with the eggs and cream.

Butter a charlotte mold, then pour in the prepared mixture. Put the mold into a water bath in a preheated 375° oven and cook for 45 minutes.

Melt the butter over a low heat. Add the flour and stir for 1 to 2 minutes. Remove from the heat and add the milk gradually. Season and return to the heat. Stir for 5 minutes until thickened. Add the parsley.

Remove the cooked mold from the oven and leave to cool for a few minutes. Turn out onto a dish; garnish with the lengths of vegetables and top with the sauce.

Cauliflower with Mornay Sauce

Serves 4

1 cauliflower
$\frac{1}{4}$ cup butter
1 tablespoon flour
2 cups milk
salt and pepper
$\frac{1}{2}$ cup grated Gruyère cheese
1 egg yolk

Cook the cauliflower in a large pan of boiling salted water for 30 minutes.

Meanwhile, prepare the Mornay sauce: melt 3 tablespoons butter over a low heat. Add the flour and stir for 1 to 2 minutes. Remove from the heat and gradually add the milk. Season and return to the heat. Stir for about 5 minutes until the sauce thickens.

Remove the sauce from the heat and mix in the grated cheese and egg yolk. Blend thoroughly. Taste, and adjust the seasoning if necessary.

Carefully drain the cauliflower so that it does not break and place in a flameproof dish. Pour over the Mornay sauce, dot with the remaining butter, and place under a preheated broiler for a few minutes to brown. Serve in the same dish so that the cauliflower stays hot. Serve with all white meats – pork and veal as well as ham.

Variations
Cauliflower Mornay with Mushrooms
Sauté $\frac{1}{2}$ lb small button mushrooms in 1 tablespoon butter. Add 2 tablespoons chopped parsley and transfer to the dish. Add the cauliflower and pour in the sauce, then finish as above.
Savory Cauliflower Mornay
Sprinkle $\frac{1}{4}$ lb chopped garlic sausage over the cauliflower before pouring in the sauce. Continue as above.
Seafood Cauliflower Mornay
Mix $\frac{1}{2}$ lb peeled, cooked shrimp and $\frac{1}{4}$ lb shelled mussels or clams into the sauce. Add 2 tablespoons chopped parsley and continue as above.

Leek Gratin

Serves 6

$3\frac{1}{2}$ lb leeks
$\frac{1}{2}$ cup butter
$\frac{1}{4}$ cup flour
2 cups milk
salt and pepper
$1\frac{1}{4}$ cups grated Comté or
  Gruyère cheese
pinch of grated nutmeg

Cut off the top parts of the leeks leaving only the white and tender green. Halve the leeks lengthwise, wash and put into boiling salted water. Simmer gently for 20 minutes. Drain on a dish towel.

Prepare a white sauce: melt $\frac{1}{4}$ cup butter over a low heat. Add the flour, and stir for 1 to 2 minutes. Remove from the heat and gradually add the milk. Season and return to the heat. Stir for about 5 minutes, until the sauce thickens. Stir in 1 cup grated cheese and the nutmeg.

Put the leeks into a buttered gratin dish and cover with the white sauce. Sprinkle with the rest of the cheese and dot with the remaining butter. Bake in a preheated 325° oven for 8 to 10 minutes, then put under the broiler and brown for 5 minutes.

Soufflèd Zucchini

Serves 4

4 large zucchini, halved
   lengthwise
$\frac{1}{4}$ cup butter
1 tablespoon flour
1 cup milk
salt and pepper
$\frac{3}{4}$ cup grated Gruyère cheese
2 eggs, separated

Hollow out the zucchini halves with a teaspoon and purée the flesh in a blender or food processor. Set aside. Blanch the zucchini shells in boiling salted water for 3 minutes. Drain and place in a buttered gratin dish.

Make a thick white sauce: melt half the butter over a low heat. Add the flour and stir for 1 to 2 minutes. Remove from the heat and gradually add the milk, stirring. Season and return to the heat. Stir for about 5 minutes until the sauce thickens.

Remove the sauce from the heat, and add the Gruyère, egg yolks and zucchini purée. Beat the egg whites until standing in stiff peaks. Carefully fold into the zucchini mixture. Spoon the mixture into the zucchini shells and bake in a preheated 400°–425° oven for 25 minutes.

Serve as a main dish with a salad or as an accompaniment to broiled steak or roast beef.

Mushrooms with Green Peppercorns

Serves 4

1½ lemons
1¾ lb mushrooms
¼ cup butter
3 tomatoes, peeled and chopped
15 green peppercorns
5 tablespoons white wine
1 bouquet garni
salt
1 tablespoon chopped parsley

Squeeze the juice from 1 lemon. Wash the mushrooms in water with the lemon juice added, then slice thickly.

Melt the butter in a pan, and fry the mushrooms for a few minutes over a high heat until golden. Slice the half lemon and add to the pan with the tomatoes, green peppercorns, wine and bouquet garni. Season with salt, cover and cook over a medium heat for 15 minutes.

Remove the bouquet garni and serve the mushrooms sprinkled with parsley.

Mushrooms prepared in this way can be eaten hot or cold. When hot, serve with chicken, or rabbit, or with roast meats. When cold, serve with a hot omelette. They can also be added to a stewed meat dish.

Ratatouille

Serves 5

2 eggplants, peeled and sliced
2 green peppers
1 quart olive oil
4 zucchini, sliced
4 onions, sliced
5 tomatoes, peeled, quartered
   and seeded
2 garlic cloves, sliced
1 bouquet garni
salt and pepper

Sprinkle the eggplants with salt to draw out the bitter juices. Leave for 20 minutes.

Skin the peppers: put on a baking sheet in a preheated 375° oven and bake for 5 to 7 minutes. Turn the peppers fRom time to time so they roast evenly. When the skin has blistered, remove the peppers from the oven and leave to cool. When cool, halve the peppers, seed and peel them. Cut them into strips.

Heat the oil in a deep fryer to 375° or until a bread cube browns in 50 seconds. Rinse and dry the eggplants, deep fry for 2 minutes, then drain and put into a saucepan. Deep fry the zucchini for 2 minutes and then the onions. Add to the pan with the eggplants. Add the tomatoes, peppers, garlic and bouquet garni. Season, cover and simmer for $1\frac{1}{2}$ hours. If the ratatouille releases too much juice, boil fast, uncovered, for 3 to 4 minutes at the end of the cooking time. Remove the bouquet garni before serving.

Zucchini with Bacon

Serves 8

½ lb bacon, chopped
1 tablespoon oil
8 small zucchini, sliced
1 lb tomatoes, peeled, quartered
  and seeded
2 garlic cloves, sliced
salt and pepper
2 tablespoons chopped parsley

Blanch the bacon pieces in boiling water for 2 minutes to extract the excess salt. Drain.

Heat the oil in a pan, and fry the bacon, then add the zucchini, tomatoes, garlic and a little salt and pepper. Simmer over a very low heat for 1 hour, stirring occasionally to ensure that the zucchini do not stick.

Serve hot, sprinkled with chopped parsley. This dish goes well with roasts or fried pork chops, and also chicken, turkey, or a white rice dish.

Red Cabbage Fondue with Apples

Serves 4

¼ cup butter
1 head red cabbage, weighing
  2 lb, shredded
3 tablespoons wine vinegar
salt and pepper
4 apples
½ (1-lb) can whole chestnuts,
  drained and rinsed
2 teaspoons confectioners' sugar

Use a little of the butter to grease a heavy saucepan. Add the cabbage and vinegar. Season, cover and simmer over a very low heat for 1 hour.

Peel, quarter and core the apples and add to the saucepan 30 minutes before the end of cooking time, together with the chestnuts and confectioners' sugar.

Serve hot, adding the remaining butter at the last minute.

Serve with roast pork, pork chops or fried sausages. This dish also goes well with all game dishes.

Potatoes Lyonnaise

Serves 4

2 lb potatoes, unpeeled
$\frac{1}{2}$ cup butter
1 tablespoon oil
$\frac{3}{4}$ lb onions, thinly sliced into
    rings
salt and pepper
1 tablespoon chopped flat-
    leaved parsley

Cook the potatoes in boiling salted water for about 20 minutes until tender. Drain and leave to cool, then peel. Cut into slices $\frac{1}{4}$ inch thick.

Heat half the butter and the oil in a large skillet and add the potatoes. Fry over a medium heat for 10 minutes.

Heat the rest of the butter in another skillet over a low heat, and gently fry the onions until golden – do not allow them to brown, or they will make the dish taste bitter. When the potatoes and onions are cooked, put them together in the same skillet, and season. Leave over the heat for 2 or 3 minutes, stirring thoroughly.

Arrange the potatoes on a serving dish in concentric circles, interspersed with the onion rings. Sprinkle with parsley and serve.

Note: This dish is a traditional recipe which tastes particularly good with roast veal or chicken. If you would like to vary the flavor of the dish, add crushed garlic cloves, caraway seeds or a mixture of chopped fresh herbs.

Cauliflower Antibois

Serves 5

1 cauliflower
1 tablespoon vinegar
½ lemon, sliced
3 tablespoons olive oil
5 tomatoes, peeled, seeded and
    chopped
2 garlic cloves, sliced
3 sprigs thyme or parsley
salt and pepper
½ lb mushrooms, sliced
20 ripe olives

Wash the cauliflower whole in water with the vinegar added. Fill a large pan with salted water, add the lemon slices and bring to a boil. Add the cauliflower and cook for 30 minutes.

Meanwhile, heat the olive oil in a pan, and add the tomatoes, garlic and thyme. Season, add the mushrooms and simmer over a low heat for 25 minutes.

Add the olives 5 minutes before the end of cooking time and discard the thyme.

Carefully drain the cauliflower and place on a dish. Cut off the top, and scoop out the cauliflower's center. Purée the top slice and the scooped-out cauliflower in a blender or food processor. Pile the cauliflower purée into the cauliflower and then pile half the tomato and mushroom mixture on top. Pour the rest of the mixture around the cauliflower.

Potatoes Auvergnates

Serves 6

6 large baking potatoes
2 tablespoons butter
salt
2 pinches cayenne
$\frac{1}{4}$ lb Monterey Jack cheese,
    diced
2 tablespoons Crème Fraîche
    (page 398)
2 tablespoons chopped parsley

Scrub the potatoes and prick all over. Bake in a preheated 350° oven for 2 hours until cooked.

Remove the potatoes from the oven, and cut the top off each. Scoop out the centers with a teaspoon and reserve.

Melt the butter in a skillet, and brown the reserved potato over a high heat for 6 to 7 minutes. Season with salt and cayenne and mix in the cheese and Crème fraîche.

Fill each potato shell with the cheese mixture, and sprinkle with parsley. Place in a baking dish and broil for 5 minutes.

Serve with a chicory salad mixed with chopped crisp bacon.

Picardy Endive

Serves 6

12 French or Belgian endives
2 tablespoons butter
2 tablespoons water
½ teaspoon confectioners' sugar
salt and pepper
2 egg yolks
3 tablespoons Crème Fraîche
   (page 398)
2 lemons, cut into wedges

Hollow out the inside of the endive stem which is often bitter. Melt the butter in a pan, and fry the endives on all sides until golden brown. Add the water and sugar. Season, cover and leave to cook over a very low heat for 30 minutes.

Put the endives into a warmed serving dish and keep hot. Make the sauce: if the endive releases too much water during cooking, reduce the liquid over a high heat before adding the egg and cream. Remove the pan from the heat, whisk in the egg yolks and cream and cook very gently until slightly thickened. *Do not boil.* Season and pour the sauce over the endives. Serve with lemon wedges to squeeze. This dish goes well with roast chicken.

Cauliflower Soufflé

Serves 4

1 cauliflower, broken into
  florets
$\frac{1}{4}$ cup butter
2 tablespoons flour
$2\frac{1}{2}$ cups milk
salt and pepper
$\frac{1}{8}$ teaspoon grated nutmeg
$\frac{1}{2}$ cup grated Gruyère cheese
3 eggs, separated

Cook the cauliflower florets in boiling salted water for about 20 minutes.

Meanwhile, melt the butter over a low heat. Add the flour and stir for 1 to 2 minutes. Remove from the heat and gradually add the milk. Season with salt, pepper and nutmeg. Return to the heat and stir for about 5 minutes until the sauce thickens.

Drain the cauliflower and purée in a blender or food processor. Mix the cauliflower purée with the sauce and add the grated Gruyère and the egg yolks. Add a pinch of salt to the egg whites and beat into stiff peaks. Fold into the purée with a metal spoon. Butter a soufflé dish and pour the mixture into it. Bake in a preheated 375° oven for 45 minutes. Serve immediately.

Springtime Beans

Serves 4

$5\frac{1}{2}$ lb fresh broad or lima beans,
  shelled
10 pearl onions
$\frac{1}{4}$ cup butter
5 tablespoons water
1 tablespoon chopped fresh
  thyme *or* $1\frac{1}{2}$ teaspoons dried
  thyme
salt and pepper
2 pinches grated nutmeg

Put the beans and onions into a large pan of boiling water and cook for 5 minutes. Drain, cool the beans with cold water, and squeeze each one to remove the thick skin.

Melt the butter in a pan over a low heat. Add the beans and onions, the water and the thyme. Season, and add the nutmeg. Cover and bring to a boil over a high heat. Lower the heat and continue to cook, covered, over a low heat for 30 minutes. Serve the beans in their juices.

These beans go very well with lamb. Combine them also with fresh peas and chopped fried bacon.

Carrot Soufflé

Serves 4

1 lb carrots
2 onions
2 tablespoons butter
2 tablespoons flour
1¼ cups milk
salt and pepper
a pinch of confectioners' sugar
2 eggs, separated
flat-leaved parsley for garnish
  (optional)

Cook the carrots and onions in boiling salted water for 30 minutes. Drain the vegetables. Slice 2 carrots and cut the rest into pieces. Reserve the carrot slices and purée the rest of the vegetables in a blender or food processor.

Prepare a white sauce: melt the butter over a low heat. Add the flour and stir for 1 to 2 minutes. Remove from the heat and gradually add the milk. Season and return to the heat. Stir for about 5 minutes until the sauce thickens.

Mix the sauce with the carrot purée. Add the sugar and the egg yolks, one at a time.

Beat the egg whites until standing in stiff peaks, and fold carefully into the carrot mixture. Pour into a buttered soufflé dish, and bake in a preheated 400–425° oven for about 35 minutes. Unmold and serve immediately, garnished with the reserved carrot slices and parsley.

Tomatoes Stuffed with Corn

Serves 6

12 small tomatoes
2 tablespoons oil
3 thin slices cooked ham, cut
    into strips
salt and pepper
1 (16-oz) can whole kernel corn,
    drained
5 tablespoons Crème Fraîche
    (page 398)
1¼ cups grated Gruyère cheese

Cut the tops off the tomatoes and scoop out the centers with a teaspoon. Salt the insides, and leave upside down on a rack to drain for 15 minutes.

Lightly oil a skillet, and gently fry the ham. Season with pepper and a little salt. Add the corn and mix in. On a very low heat pour in the Crème fraîche, stir and heat through for 3 to 4 minutes.

Fill the tomatoes with the mixture and arrange in a generously buttered ovenproof dish. Sprinkle with grated cheese and bake in a preheated 400° oven for 25 minutes. Serve hot.

Serve as an accompaniment for roast beef or shoulder of lamb, or with lamb's liver or kidneys. They can also be served as a main dish with a green salad.

Potato Pancake

Serves 4

2 lb potatoes, coarsely grated
5 tablespoons oil
1 large onion, chopped
salt and pepper

Rinse the potatoes in plenty of water to extract the starch and squeeze dry carefully.

Heat the oil in a skillet and fry the onion until golden. Add the potatoes. Season and stir gently, then shape into a thick pancake in the pan with a spatula.

Cook over a high heat for 6 to 7 minutes, shaking the pan so that the pancake does not stick. When the edge of the pancake is crisp, invert a plate over the pan and turn the pancake out. Lower the heat and slide the pancake back into the pan to cook the other side for 10 minutes.

This is an excellent accompaniment for all roast meats and poultry.

Carrots with Cream

Serves 4

2 lb carrots, sliced
¼ cup butter
1 teaspoon confectioners' sugar
5 tablespoons Crème Fraîche
  (page 398)
2 egg yolks
salt and pepper
1 tablespoon finely chopped
  parsley
1 lemon, quartered

Put the carrots into a saucepan and add salt and just enough water to cover. Cook over a high heat, uncovered, for 20 minutes. Drain.

Melt the butter in a pan and brown the carrots over a high heat. Stir in the sugar, and leave to simmer, covered, over a very low heat for about 15 minutes – the carrots should still be slightly firm.

Beat the cream with the egg yolks. Add to the carrots a few minutes before the end of cooking time. Season and leave to simmer for 3 to 4 minutes. Transfer to a hot serving dish, sprinkle with the parsley and serve with the lemon.

This dish goes very well with all braised, roasted or fried meats.

Creamed Brussels Sprouts

Serves 4

1 lb Brussels sprouts
salt and pepper
1 small onion
2 tablespoons butter
6 tablespoons Crème Fraîche
  (page 398)
2 tablespoons chopped parsley

Trim the sprouts, then cook them in boiling salted water for 5 to 7 minutes. Drain thoroughly and set aside.

Meanwhile, chop the onion finely and cook it in the butter until soft but not brown. Add the sprouts, crème fraîche and parsley and heat gently without boiling. Season to taste and serve at once.

Cauliflower Gratin

Serves 5

1 cauliflower, broken into
  florets
2 tablespoons vinegar
3 tablespoons butter
3 tablespoons flour
2 cups milk
salt and pepper
2 pinches grated nutmeg
1 cup grated Gruyère cheese
1 tablespoon Crème Fraîche
  (page 398)

Wash the cauliflower in water with the vinegar added. Put into boiling salted water and cook for 15 minutes.

Meanwhile prepare a white sauce: melt 2 tablespoons butter over a low heat. Add the flour and stir for 1 to 2 minutes. Remove from the heat and gradually add the milk. Season and add the nutmeg. Return to the heat and stir for about 5 minutes until the sauce thickens, then add two-thirds of the cheese and the crème fraîche.

Drain the cauliflower and pack the florets, heads up, in an ovenproof dish. Cover with the sauce, sprinkle with the rest of the cheese and dot with the rest of the butter.

Heat in a preheated 300° oven for 10 minutes, then put under the broiler for 5 minutes to brown the top.

SALADS

To some a salad is a collection of lettuce leaves and tomatoes, served during the summer months to save on the cooking; to others a salad is a special creation of complementary ingredients with a dressing which marries the whole dish in a refreshing flavorsome recipe which offers a pleasing texture.

There are one or two guidelines to follow when preparing a salad. Firstly, if there are lots of crisp vegetables included, then make sure that they are at their best – fresh, crisp lettuce, crisp green celery and bright scallions. Avoid any ingredients which are limp or damaged or this will result in a very tired, miserable salad. If the salad consists of cooked ingredients as well as fresh ones, then make sure that these too are in tip-top condition. Cooked meats should be perfectly cooked, not stale or dry and lightly seasoned before cooking to bring out their flavor to the full. Eggs and fish should be cooked until they are just ready, not overcooked or they will be dry and unappetizing.

Prepare the fresh ingredients as near to serving the salad as possible: tear lettuce leaves into pieces with your fingers, slice or chop other ingredients evenly and cut meats, fish or eggs into similar-sized pieces. If the salad includes rice, pasta or potatoes, then it may be advantageous to prepare them in advance and allow the mixed ingredients to stand for a while so that the flavors combine and mingle with the dressing.

Salad dressings can be good or bad – a good one will bring out the flavor of the main ingredients, at the same time moistening and enhancing them with seasonings or herbs. If the salad is meant to be a crisp green one, then prepare the dressing in advance but toss it with the ingredients at the very last second, otherwise the lettuce and other ingredients will become limp and lifeless. If, on the other hand, the salad includes rice, pasta or potatoes, then it may be best to pour the dressing over the hot, freshly cooked ingredients and leave them to marinate until cold, so that the flavors are thoroughly mingled, or enhanced by the dressing.

A note about dressings – whether made from a simple mixture of oil and vinegar, seasoned and flavored with just a little mustard, or concocted from cream, eggs and lemon juice, the dressing should always be tasted before it is poured over the salad. Bottled mayonnaise is a good standby, but other creamy dressings can be prepared from sour cream, heavy cream or plain yogurt. Mustard, garlic, herbs and spices can all be used to flavor salads. The key to a good salad is freshness – bear this in mind and success is ensured.

Salade Niçoise

Serves 4

1 sweet red pepper
1 green pepper
1 garlic clove
½ head lettuce
1 onion, finely sliced
4 tomatoes, peeled and
   quartered
½ cucumber, sliced
½ bunch radishes, sliced
4 hard-cooked eggs, quartered
⅔ cup ripe olives
1 celery stalk, finely chopped
12 anchovy fillets in oil, drained
1 teaspoon chopped parsley
⅔ cup Vinaigrette Dressing
   (page 410)

Cut off the stalk end of the peppers. Remove seeds and pith and thinly slice the peppers.

Rub the garlic around the inside of a salad bowl and line with the lettuce. Arrange the onion, peppers, tomatoes, cucumber and radishes on the lettuce and then add the egg quarters. Add the olives and celery and garnish with the anchovy fillets. Sprinkle with the chopped parsley and serve, without stirring in the ingredients. Hand the Vinaigrette dressing separately.

Salad Platter

Serves 4

½ bunch watercress
2 tablespoons vinegar
1 cooked beet, sliced
4 French or Belgian endives
celery leaves
8 slices Parma ham, rolled
4 large gherkins, sliced
1 celery stalk, diced
⅔ cup Vinaigrette Dressing
  (page 410)

Soak the watercress in water with the vinegar added for 15 minutes. Rinse and drain.

Arrange the watercress in the center of a plate and then arrange the beet on one side and the endive on the opposite side. Between them arrange the celery leaves and ham rolls with the gherkins. Sprinkle the celery leaves with the celery. Serve with the Vinaigrette dressing handed separately.

Royal Salad

Serves 4

2 avocados
juice of 2 lemons
¼ small cucumber, thinly sliced
1 (7-oz) can crab, drained
1 small sweet red or green
   pepper
salt and pepper
1 cup Mayonnaise (page 409)
pinch of cayenne
lettuce leaves, shredded

Halve and seed the avocados. Carefully spoon out the flesh and reserve the skins. Dice the avocado flesh, put into a large bowl and sprinkle with the lemon juice. Add the cucumber and the crab.

Cut off the stalk end of the sweet pepper, remove seeds and pith and thinly slice. Add to the salad. Season with salt and pepper.

Season the Mayonnaise with a pinch of cayenne. Pour three-quarters of the mayonnaise into the salad and stir in gently, taking care not to break up the crab and avocado.

Fill the avocado skins with the salad and arrange on a bed of lettuce on a serving plate. Dot with the reserved Mayonnaise. Chill before serving.

Angelès Salad

Serves 4

4 lettuce leaves
1 (16-oz) can artichoke hearts,
   drained and rinsed
juice of 2 lemons
1 lb tomatoes, cut into eighths
1 teaspoon Dijon-style mustard
3 tablespoons Crème Fraîche
   (page 398)
1 garlic clove, finely chopped
1 tablespoon chopped parsley
   and basil
salt and pepper
⅓ cup ripe olives, pitted

Line a salad bowl with the lettuce leaves. Sprinkle the artichokes with half the lemon juice. Leave to marinate for 5 minutes and then finely dice.

Place the tomatoes and artichokes on the lettuce in the salad bowl.

In a small bowl, stir the mustard into the Crème fraîche. Stir in the garlic, parsley and basil and season with salt and pepper to taste. Gently stir in the remaining lemon juice.

Pour the dressing over the salad and sprinkle with the olives. Stir in just before serving.

Fisherman's Salad

Serves 5

1 quart clams
1 quart mussels, scrubbed
1 onion, finely sliced
3 shallots, finely sliced
1 cup dry white wine
1 cup water
$1\frac{3}{4}$ lb potatoes, cut into large
   slices
juice of 1 lemon
2 tablespoons olive oil
salt and pepper
$1\frac{1}{2}$ teaspoons chopped chervil

If any of the clams or mussels are open, tap them and discard if they do not close. Put them into a large pan with the onion and shallots, the white wine and water. Bring to a boil. Simmer for 5 to 6 minutes until the shells open. Discard any that do not open. Drain, reserving 3 tablespoons liquid. Remove the fish from their shells and put into a bowl.

Cook the potatoes in boiling salted water for 20 minutes. Drain and transfer to a salad bowl. Top with the fish.

Gently beat together the lemon juice, olive oil and strained cooking liquid. Season with pepper and pour over the salad. Serve immediately sprinkled with chervil.

Mussel Salad Vinaigrette

Serves 4

2 quarts mussels, scrubbed
2 cups white wine
6 shallots, 2 chopped and 4 very
   finely sliced
1¾ lb potatoes, cut into large
   cubes
1 tablespoon vinegar
2 teaspoons sugar
3 tablespoons olive oil
1 teaspoon chopped chives
salt and pepper

If any of the mussels are open, tap them and discard them if they do not close. Put them into a large pan. Add the white wine and the chopped shallots. Bring to a boil. Simmer for 5 to 6 minutes until the shells open. Discard any that do not open. Drain reserving 3 tablespoons liquid, and remove the mussels from the shells.

Cook the potatoes in boiling salted water for 20 minutes. Drain. Put the sliced shallots into a skillet with the vinegar and sprinkle with the sugar. Cover and cook for 3 minutes. Reserve.

Make the dressing: pour the reserved cooking liquid into a bowl. Add the olive oil, chives and sliced shallots with their juice. Season with salt and pepper and mix well.

Arrange the potatoes in the center of a shallow dish and surround with the mussels. Pour over the dressing and serve warm.

Watercress Salad

Serves 6

1 bunch watercress
3 tablespoons vinegar
1¼ lb potatoes
4 hard-cooked eggs
1 tablespoon Dijon-style
    mustard
salt and pepper
2 tablespoons oil

Soak the watercress in water with 2 tablespoons vinegar added, for 15 minutes. Rinse and drain.

Cook the potatoes in boiling salted water for 20 minutes. Drain and leave to cool slightly before peeling and slicing. Arrange on the bottom and around the sides of a salad bowl. Add the watercress.

Slice three eggs. Halve the remaining egg and separate the yolk and white. Crush both with a fork.

In a bowl beat the mustard into the remaining vinegar. Season with salt and pepper and briskly whisk in the oil.

Pour the dressing over the salad, coating the potatoes well. Arrange the egg slices around the edge of the salad and spoon the crushed egg into the center on top of the watercress.

Tomato Salad with Anchovies

Serves 6

6 anchovy fillets
2 lb tomatoes, peeled and cut
    into thin wedges
2 hard-cooked eggs, halved
3 tablespoons olive oil
salt and pepper
juice of 1 lemon

Soak the anchovies in 2 tablespoons warm water for 15 minutes. Put the tomatoes into a salad bowl. Separate the egg yolks and whites. Crush the yolks in a bowl and slowly add the oil, stirring briskly to give a smooth dressing. Season the dressing with salt and pepper and beat in the lemon juice. Pour the dressing over the salad. Garnish with the finely diced egg white and the drained anchovy fillets and serve immediately.

Pepper Salad with Anchovies

Serves 6

6 sweet red peppers
2 tomatoes, sliced
juice of 1 lemon
salt and pepper
4 hard-cooked eggs, sliced
12 anchovies in oil, drained
12–15 ripe olives
1¼ teaspoons chopped chervil
⅔ cup Vinaigrette Dressing
   (page 410)

Skin the peppers: put on a baking sheet and bake in a preheated 375° oven for 5 to 7 minutes. Turn the peppers from time to time so they scorch evenly. When the skin has blistered, remove the peppers from the oven and leave to cool. When cool halve the peppers, remove the seeds and peel them.

Spread the peppers out to cover a serving plate and add the tomatoes. Sprinkle with the lemon juice and salt and pepper.

Garnish the peppers and tomato with egg slices and make a lattice with the anchovy fillets. Dot with the olives and sprinkle with chervil. Pour the Vinaigrette dressing over the salad.

White Beans with Basil

Serves 8

1 onion
1 clove
1 carrot
3 tablespoons olive oil
5 oz slab bacon, chopped
2 cups dried navy beans, soaked
   overnight
salt and pepper
1 tablespoon chopped basil *or* 1
   teaspoon dried basil
basil leaves for garnish
   (optional)

Stud the onion with the clove and put into a pan of cold water with the carrot. Bring to a boil and cook for 15 minutes. Strain the liquid, discarding the vegetables.

Pour 1 tablespoon oil into a pan, and gently fry the bacon until golden brown. Drain the beans and add to the oil with 2 cups of the reserved cooking liquid. Cover and simmer over a low heat for $1\frac{1}{4}$ hours, adding a little more cooking liquid occasionally as the beans swell. Season with salt and pepper halfway through the cooking time.

Mix the basil with the remaining oil in a large bowl.

When the beans are cooked, transfer them to the bowl of basil and oil, and garnish with a few basil leaves, if wished.

This dish goes very well with roast leg of lamb, bro led pork and sausages.

Dandelion Salad

Serves 4

1 garlic clove
$\frac{2}{3}$ cup Crème Fraîche (page 398)
salt and pepper
$\frac{1}{2}$ lb dandelion leaves
2 thick slices (about $\frac{1}{2}$ lb)
    cooked ham, cubed
1 tablespoon olive oil
juice of 1 lemon

Rub the garlic over the inside of a salad bowl. Season the Crème fraîche with salt and pepper and lightly whip.

Arrange the dandelion leaves around the edge of the salad bowl. Pour the Crème fraîche into the center and top with the ham cubes.

Make the dressing: using a fork, beat the olive oil with the lemon juice. Season and pour over the salad. Do not mix in. Leave to stand for 5 minutes before serving.

Chicory with Croûtons

Serves 4

1 head chicory
1 teaspoon Dijon-style mustard
juice of 1 lemon
salt and pepper
3 tablespoons peanut oil
$\frac{1}{4}$ lb bacon, chopped
4 slices bread
2 garlic cloves

Arrange the chicory in a salad bowl.

Make the dressing: mix the mustard with the lemon juice. Season and gradually beat in the oil until it is all incorporated.

Fry the bacon in a skillet. Drain and set aside. Fry the bread in the bacon fat. When golden brown on each side, remove from the pan and drain on paper towels. Rub the garlic on the bread and cut the bread into cubes (croûtons).

Pour the dresing onto the chicory and toss. Garnish with the bacon and croûtons and serve immediately.

Tuna Salad

Serves 4

1 (7-oz) can tuna in oil, drained
   and broken into pieces
1 head fennel, cut into fine
   strips
3 hard-cooked eggs, halved
$\frac{2}{3}$ cup ripe olives
1 teaspoon Dijon-style mustard
2 tablespoons vinegar
salt and pepper
3 tablespoons olive oil

Put the tuna into a shallow dish. Sprinkle with the fennel strips and garnish with the egg halves and ripe olives.

Make the dressing: mix the mustard with the vinegar. Season and gradually beat in the oil until it is all incorporated.

Pour the dressing over the salad but do not stir in.

Warm Herring Salad

Serves 4

3 onions, sliced
2 carrots, sliced
1 cup herb vinegar
2 lb potatoes, quartered
1 lb smoked herring fillets, half
   cut into chunks, half chopped
salt and pepper
$\frac{1}{4}$ cup olive oil
1 tablespoon chopped parsley

Put the onions and carrots into a salad bowl with 1 tablespoon vinegar. Mix well and leave to marinate for 30 minutes.

Cook the potatoes in boiling salted water for 20 minutes. Put the herring chunks into the salad bowl with the carrots and onions. Stir in.

Drain the potatoes and add to the salad. Sprinkle immediately with the rest of the vinegar, most of which will be absorbed. Season with salt and pepper.

Sprinkle the chopped herring over the salad and pour over the olive oil and parsley. Serve the salad steaming hot without stirring.

Mushroom Salad

Serves 4

$\frac{3}{4}$ lb small button mushrooms,
  sliced
1 cup dry white wine
juice of 2 lemons
salt and pepper
1 medium-size onion, finely
  chopped
2 garlic cloves, finely chopped
1 tablespoon chopped parsley

Blanch the mushrooms in the white wine and half the lemon juice for 2 minutes. Drain thoroughly and transfer to a shallow dish. Season and sprinkle with the onion and garlic. Sprinkle over the remaining lemon juice. Serve garnished with chopped parsley.

Ham and Cheese Salad

Serves 6

1 lb potatoes, cut into chunks
½ lb green beans
2 hard-cooked eggs, quartered
¼ lb Emmental cheese, cubed
¼ lb thickly sliced cooked ham, cubed
parsley sprigs
2 shallots, chopped
salt and pepper
1 tablespoon vinegar
1 cup Mayonnaise (page 409)

Cook the potatoes in boiling salted water for 20 minutes. Drain and put into a shallow dish. Cook the beans in the same way for 15 minutes. Drain and arrange decoratively in small bundles around the edge of the dish with the eggs, cheese and ham. Garnish with parsley.

Season the shallots with salt and pepper and sprinkle with the vinegar. Spoon over the potatoes and serve with a fairly thin mayonnaise handed separately.

Endive Salad with Nuts

Serves 4

2 apples
5 French or Belgian endives
¼ lb Roquefort cheese, crumbled
1 teaspoon Dijon-style mustard
juice of 1 lemon
salt and pepper
3 tablespoons peanut oil
½ cup walnut halves
1 teaspoon chopped chives

Peel, quarter, core and thinly slice the apples. Cut a wedge from the base of each endive head as the stalk is often bitter, then slice the endive. Put into a salad bowl with the apples and Roquefort.

Make the dressing: mix the mustard with the lemon juice. Season and whisk the oil in briskly.

Coat the endive in the dressing and garnish with the nuts. Mix in gently. Sprinkle with chives and serve chilled.

Apple Salad with Raisins

Serves 4

⅓ cup raisins
juice of 2 lemons
1 head green cabbage, shredded
5 apples
1 cup cubed Gruyère cheese
2 thin slices bacon, chopped
2 tablespoons olive oil
salt and pepper
¼ cup walnut halves for garnish

Macerate the raisins for 10 minutes in half the lemon juice.

Put the cabbage into a salad bowl. Peel, core and finely slice the apples. Sprinkle with the juice of the remaining lemon to prevent discoloring and add to the salad bowl with the cheese.

Fry the bacon in a skillet in its own fat. Drain on paper towels.

Sprinkle the raisins and the bacon over the salad. Pour over the oil, season with salt and pepper to taste, garnish with walnut halves and serve immediately.

Haddock Salad

Serves 6

1 cup long-grain rice
1 lb haddock
1 cup milk
1 apple
3 canned artichoke hearts,
   drained and halved
1 celery stalk, chopped
3 shallots, chopped
12 ripe olives
salt and pepper
$\frac{2}{3}$ cup Mayonnaise (page 409)

Cook the rice in a pan of boiling salted water for 15 minutes, until just tender. Drain and transfer to a salad bowl.

Put the haddock into a flameproof dish. Pour over the milk together with enough water to cover the fish completely. Poach for 20 minutes, making sure that the liquid does not boil.

When cooked, drain the haddock, leave to cool and cut into fairly large pieces. Arrange over the rice.

Peel, quarter, core and chop the apple and arrange with the artichoke hearts, celery and chopped shallots on the salad. Add the olives and season with salt and pepper.

Serve with the Mayonnaise handed separately.

Avocado with Mushrooms

Serves 8

$\frac{1}{2}$ lb mushrooms, chopped
3 shallots, finely sliced
1 garlic clove, crushed
2 tablespoons olive oil
1 tablespoon cider vinegar
salt and pepper
4 avocados
juice of 1 lemon

Put the mushrooms in a salad bowl. Add the shallots and garlic. Pour over the oil and vinegar and season with salt and pepper to taste. Leave for 2 hours to marinate.

Just before serving, halve the avocados lengthwise and remove the seeds. Arrange on a serving dish and sprinkle with the lemon juice.

Fill the hollow in each avocado with a generous tablespoon of marinated mushrooms.

Pea Salad

Serves 6

1 (8-oz) can whole kernel corn
½ (16-oz) can chick peas
1 (8-oz) can peas
⅔ cup Mayonnaise (page 409)
1 (7-oz) can shrimp, drained
1 celery stalk, diced
salt and pepper
1 head romaine lettuce
1 tomato, quartered
1 tablespoon chopped parsley
chopped chives

Tip the corn, chick peas and peas into a strainer. Rinse and drain, then transfer to a bowl. Add the Mayonnaise and toss to coat.

Add the shrimp to the vegetables with the celery. Season with salt and pepper and mix all the ingredients together well.

Line a serving dish with lettuce leaves and tip in the mayonnaise salad. Arrange the tomato in the center. Sprinkle with chopped parsley and chives. Serve chilled.

Radish Salad with Soft Cheese Dressing

Serves 5

5 large lettuce leaves
2 bunches radishes, sliced
1 large Japanese radish (*daikon*),
   peeled and grated
1½ cups cream cheese
⅓ cup milk
3 tablespoons chopped chives
   and parsley
salt and pepper

Line a salad bowl with the lettuce leaves and put the sliced radishes in the center. Garnish with the grated radish. Chill.

Make the dressing: put the cheese into a bowl with the milk and mix thoroughly. Sprinkle with the chopped parsley and chives. Season to taste with salt and pepper and stir thoroughly. Pour into a sauceboat and hand separately.

Tomatoes à la Rémoulade

Serves 4

1 head celeriac, thickly sliced
1 celery stalk, cut into julienne
1 tablespoon Dijon-style
  mustard
1 cup Mayonnaise (page 409)
8 large tomatoes
salt and pepper
2 hard-cooked eggs, sliced
8 stuffed green olives
celery leaves for garnish

Cook the celeriac in boiling salted water for 6 minutes. Drain, rinse and cut into julienne. Put into a bowl with the celery. Stir the mustard into the mayonnaise and stir into the vegetables.

Cut a lid from the tomatoes and remove a little of the flesh from the tomatoes using a teaspoon. Season with salt and pepper and fill with the celeriac mixture.

Arrange the tomatoes on a serving plate and top with a slice of egg and an olive. Garnish the plate with celery leaves.

Cauliflower Salad

Serves 4

1 (2-lb) cauliflower, broken into
  florets
1 tablespoon Dijon-style
  mustard
1 tablespoon vinegar
salt and pepper
3 tablespoons olive oil
1 tablespoon chopped tarragon
  leaves *or* 1½ teaspoons dried
  tarragon
4 tomatoes, quartered
4 hard-cooked eggs, halved

Drop the cauliflower florets into a pan of boiling salted water, bring back to a boil and cook for 10 to 15 minutes.

Meanwhile, make the dressing: mix the mustard with the vinegar. Season with salt and pepper and gradually beat in the oil until it is all incorporated. Stir in the tarragon.

Drain the cauliflower and rinse under cold water to cool it slightly. Drain thoroughly and put into a salad bowl.

Garnish with the tomatoes and eggs. Pour on the dressing and serve immediately while still warm.

Lentil Salad

Serves 4

2 cups brown lentils, soaked for
   2 hours
1 large onion, sliced
2 carrots, sliced
2 bay leaves
1 teaspoon Dijon-style mustard
2 tablespoons vinegar
salt and pepper
3 tablespoons olive oil
1 shallot, finely chopped
2 tablespoons chopped chives
4 slices bacon, finely chopped

Put the lentils into a pan with 1 quart of salted water and bring to a boil. Add the onion, carrot and the bay leaves. Simmer over a low heat in a covered pan for at least 1 hour.

Make the dressing: mix the mustard with the vinegar. Season and gradually beat in the oil until it is all incorporated. Fold the shallot into the dressing with half the chives.

Drain the lentils, transfer to a salad bowl and stir in the dressing. Top with a little extra mustard if you like. Fry the bacon in a skillet in its own fat. Add to the lentil salad while still hot and serve immediately garnished with the rest of the chives.

Fried Salad

Serves 4

4 sweet red or green peppers
$\frac{1}{4}$ cup butter
5 tomatoes, sliced
12 lettuce leaves
onion salt
garlic salt
pepper
juice of 1 lemon
3 tablespoons olive oil
1 teaspoon chopped parsley

Remove the stalk from the peppers, remove the seeds and pith then cut the peppers into fine strips.

Sauté the strips of pepper in the butter over a high heat for about 5 minutes, stirring from time to time. Remove from the pan and set aside.

In the same butter, cook the tomatoes over a moderate heat for 2 minutes.

Line a salad bowl with the lettuce leaves. Tip the pepper and tomato into the center. Season with onion salt, garlic salt and pepper. Pour over the lemon juice and olive oil. Sprinkle with chopped parsley and serve warm.

Cucumber Salad with Mint

Serves 4

1 cucumber, peeled and thinly
  sliced
salt and pepper
¼ cup plain yogurt
2 tablespoons Crème Fraîche
  (page 398)
⅔ cup crumbled Roquefort
  cheese
1 bunch mint leaves

Sprinkle the cucumber with salt to draw out some of the juice. Leave for 10 minutes.

Meanwhile, pour the yogurt and Crème fraîche into a shallow dish. Add the Roquefort, season with pepper and whisk for 2 minutes to give a smooth, creamy sauce.

Drain the cucumber and put three-quarters of the slices into the sauce. Chop and stir in three-quarters of the mint. Adjust the seasoning and garnish with the remaining cucumber and whole mint leaves. Serve well chilled.

Cabbage Salad

Serves 4

$\frac{1}{4}$ head red cabbage, finely
    shredded
juice of 2 lemons
$\frac{1}{2}$ head green cabbage, finely
    shredded
2 teaspoons Dijon-style mustard
2 tablespoons vinegar
salt and pepper
$\frac{1}{4}$ cup peanut oil

Tip the red cabbage into a small bowl and sprinkle with half the lemon juice. Stir in well and then arrange in the center of a shallow dish.

Repeat with the green cabbage, using the same bowl and the remaining lemon juice, but arranging the shredded green cabbage around the red cabbage.

Make the dressing: mix the mustard with the vinegar. Season and gradually beat in the oil until it is all incorporated. Pour over the cabbage.

Leave to marinate for 10 minutes before serving, but do not stir in. Serve at room temperature or well chilled.

Eggplant Salad

Serves 4

4 eggplants
2 garlic cloves, crushed
1 tablespoon chopped parsley
1 large onion, thinly sliced
2 hard-cooked eggs, quartered
1 teaspoon Dijon-style mustard
juice of 1 lemon
salt and pepper
3 tablespoons olive oil

Wrap each eggplant in foil and place on a baking sheet. Bake in a preheated 350° oven for 40 minutes. Turn the eggplants from time to time to ensure that they cook evenly.

Remove the foil and leave the eggplants to cool. Cut into fairly large cubes.

Put the eggplants into a salad bowl and sprinkle with the garlic and parsley. Garnish with onion rings and egg quarters.

Make the dressing: mix the mustard with the lemon juice. Season and gradually beat in the oil until it is all incorporated. Pour the dressing over the salad. Stir the salad and serve warm.

Zucchini Salad

Serves 4

2 lb small zucchini, half sliced
   lengthwise, half sliced into
   rounds
1 teaspoon Dijon-style mustard
2 tablespoons vinegar
salt and pepper
1 teaspoon chopped parsley or
   coriander
3 tablespoons olive oil

Put all the zucchini into a large pan of water, bring to a boil and cook for 2 minutes over a moderate heat.

Meanwhile, make the dressing: mix the mustard with the vinegar. Season, add the parsley and gradually beat in the oil until it is all incorporated.

Drain the zucchini and arrange in a serving dish. Cover with the dressing and serve warm.

Vegetable Salad

Serves 6

4 potatoes, cut into cubes
2 carrots, cut into cubes
$\frac{1}{4}$ lb green beans
$1\frac{1}{4}$ cups shelled peas
4 gherkins, sliced
salt and pepper
1 cup Mayonnaise (page 409)
2 hard-cooked eggs, quartered

Cook the potatoes and carrots together in boiling salted water for 20 minutes.

In a second pan, cook the beans and peas together in boiling salted water for 20 minutes.

Drain the vegetables and chop the beans. Put the gherkins into a salad bowl and add all the cooked vegetables. Season the Mayonnaise and gently stir most of it into the vegetables, taking care not to break them up.

Garnish with the egg quarters and reserved spoonful of Mayonnaise and chill for at least 30 minutes before serving.

Melon Salad

Serves 4

4 small melons
juice of 1 lemon
salt and pepper
4 thin slices Parma ham, cut
  into strips
4–5 tablespoons dry white wine

Cut off the top third of the melons or, if the melons are fairly large cut each in half (and allow half a melon per person).

Using a teaspoon remove the seeds. Cut the flesh into small balls and reserve the shells. Put the melon balls into a bowl and sprinkle with lemon juice. Season and mix gently.

Fill each melon shell with the melon balls. Roll up the ham strips and arrange between the melon balls. Sprinkle the salad with the dry white wine. Serve well chilled.

Green Salad with Oranges

Serves 4

1 head lettuce
1 head chicory
3 oranges
salt and pepper
1 tablespoon vinegar
3 tablespoons olive oil
sorrel leaves

Put the lettuce and chicory leaves into a salad bowl.

Make the dressing: squeeze the juice from 1 orange and season it with salt and pepper. Add the vinegar and gradually beat in the oil until it is all incorporated. Pour the dressing over the salad and toss gently.

Cut the remaining unpeeled oranges into slices. Arrange the slices around the sides of the salad and one in the center. Garnish with sorrel leaves.

Carrot Salad with Limes

Serves 4

1 lb carrots, grated
2 apples
3 limes, unpeeled and thinly
  sliced
1 tablespoon Dijon-style
  mustard
$\frac{2}{3}$ cup plain yogurt
1 tablespoon Crème Fraîche
  (page 398)
salt and pepper
juice of 1 lemon

Put the carrots into a salad bowl. Peel, halve, core and finely dice the apples and add, with most of the limes, to the carrots.

Make the dressing: mix the mustard with the yogurt. Add the Crème fraîche, season and gradually beat in the lemon juice. Taste and adjust the seasoning.

Pour the dressing over the salad and stir in very gently. Serve garnished with the reserved slices of lime.

Tongue Salad

Serves 6

¼ lb macaroni
1 lb cooked tongue, cut into
    strips
4 tomatoes, peeled and
    quartered
1 (16-oz) can artichoke hearts,
    drained, rinsed and quartered
salt and pepper
juice of 1 lemon
2 hard-cooked eggs, sliced
5 tablespoons Mayonnaise (page
    409)

Cook the macaroni in boiling salted water for about 12 minutes until just tender. Drain and leave until cold.

Put the tongue into a bowl and add the tomatoes and artichoke hearts. Add the macaroni. Season and sprinkle with the lemon juice and stir in gently.

Arrange the salad in a serving dish and garnish with the egg slices and mayonnaise. Serve chilled.

Beet Salad

Serves 4

1 onion, finely sliced
2 cooked beets, peeled and
   sliced
½ lb lamb's lettuce (corn salad)
1 teaspoon Dijon-style mustard
1 tablespoon vinegar
salt and pepper
3 tablespoons peanut oil

Put the onion in the bottom of a salad bowl. Pile the beets into the center of the bowl and arrange the lettuce around the sides.

Make the dressing: mix the mustard with the vinegar. Season and gradually beat in the oil until it is all incorporated.

Pour the dressing over the salad but do not toss. Leave to stand for 5 minutes in a cool place before serving.

Chick-Pea Salad

Serves 4

1 (16-oz) can chick-peas,
  drained
1 onion, chopped
1 garlic clove, chopped
juice of 1 lemon
1 green pepper
1 sweet red pepper
salt and pepper
2 tablespoons Dijon-style
  mustard
2 shallots, finely chopped
2 tablespoons vinegar
$\frac{1}{4}$ cup olive oil
1 (7-oz) can tuna in oil, drained
  and flaked

Put the chick-peas into a salad bowl with the onion and garlic. Sprinkle with the lemon juice and stir in.

Remove the stalks from the peppers, halve the peppers and remove the seeds and pith. Cut the peppers into short, fairly thin strips. Add to the chick-peas, arranging them around the edge of the dish.

Make the dressing: add 1 teaspoon salt, 3 pinches pepper and the mustard to the shallots. Add the vinegar and gradually beat in the oil until it is all incorporated.

Put the tuna into the center of the salad. Serve with the dressing handed separately.

Fennel Salad

1 lb fennel, sliced
3 oranges
1 apple
½ lb thinly sliced Parma ham,
  cut into triangles
1 teaspoon Dijon-style mustard
juice of 1 lemon
salt and pepper
3 tablespoons olive oil

Put the fennel into the center of a salad bowl.

Cut 2 oranges into thin slices. Peel the remaining orange and divide into segments. Peel, quarter, core and thinly slice the apple.

Arrange the whole slices of orange around the edge of the bowl and cover with the ham. Fill the center with apple and top with the orange segments.

Make the dressing: mix the mustard with the lemon juice. Season and gradually beat in the oil until it is all incorporated. Serve the dressing separately.

Lemon and Fennel Salad

Serves 4

1 garlic clove
½ (7-oz) can tuna in oil, drained
    and broken into chunks
2 heads fennel, sliced, leafy tops
    reserved
3 lemons
1 teaspoon Dijon-style mustard
salt and pepper
3 tablespoons peanut oil
1 sprig parsley or chervil for
    garnish

Rub a salad bowl with the garlic and tip the tuna into the bowl. Add the sliced fennel. Peel the skin and pith from 2 lemons and thinly slice, then add to the salad.

Make the dressing: mix the mustard with the juice of the remaining lemon. Season and gradually beat in the oil until it is all incorporated.

Pour the dressing over the salad and toss gently. Serve garnished with parsley or chervil and fennel leaves.

Lettuce with Onion

Serves 4

1 head lettuce
¾ lb very mild onions, thinly
    sliced
1½ cups crumbled Roquefort
    cheese
5 tablespoons cream or small-
    curd cottage cheese
⅔ cup plain yogurt
juice of 1 lemon
salt and pepper

Arrange the lettuce in a salad bowl. Add half the onions.

Put the Roquefort into a bowl and gradually work in the cream cheese. When smooth, whisk briskly.

Make the dressing: mix the yogurt with the lemon juice and season to taste. Pour over the salad and stir in. Add the cheese mixture and garnish with the reserved onion rings. Serve immediately.

Chicken Salad

Serves 4

1½ cups long-grain rice
½ green pepper, seeded and
   diced
½ sweet red pepper, seeded and
   diced
1 tomato, diced
1 tablespoon Dijon-style
   mustard
1 tablespoon vinegar
salt and pepper
3 tablespoons peanut oil
2 hard-cooked eggs, chopped
¾ lb skinless, boneless chicken
   breast, cooked and sliced
chopped chives for garnish

Cook the rice in boiling salted water for 15 minutes until just tender. Drain and transfer to a salad bowl. Add the peppers and tomato.

Make the dressing: mix the mustard with the vinegar. Season and gradually beat in the oil until it is all incorporated. Pour over the salad. Heap the chopped eggs in the center and arrange the chicken around the sides of the bowl. Garnish with chopped chives.

Argenteuil Asparagus Salad

Serves 4

2 lb asparagus
2 tablespoons sea salt
2 hard-cooked eggs, halved
parsley sprigs
1 cup Mayonnaise (page 409)

Tie the asparagus into a bundle. Bring a large pan of water to a boil. Add the sea salt and the asparagus, standing the bundle upright. Cook over a moderate heat for 14 minutes from the time the water returns to a boil. Rinse the asparagus in cold water and drain thoroughly.

Leave the asparagus to cool for 5 minutes. Untie the bundle and cut off the woody part of each stem. Arrange the asparagus on a serving plate.

Separately crush the yolks and the whites of the eggs. Garnish the asparagus with the chopped egg, placing the yolks in the center of the plate, surrounding with a ring of egg white and then a ring of parsley. Serve the Mayonnaise separately.

Green Bean Salad

Serves 6

¾ lb potatoes, fairly thinly sliced
1½ lb green beans
salt and pepper
2 shallots, chopped
juice of 1 lemon
1 tablespoon vinegar
3 tablespoons corn oil
3 slices bacon, cut into strips

Cook the potatoes in boiling salted water for 20 minutes. Meanwhile, cook the beans in boiling salted water for 15 minutes.

Drain the beans and potatoes. Arrange the beans in the center of a salad bowl and surround with the potato slices.

Make the dressing: season the shallots and sprinkle over the lemon juice. Add the vinegar and gradually beat in the oil until it is all incorporated. Pour the dressing over the salad.

Fry the bacon in a skillet in its own fat over a moderate heat. Drain on paper towels and sprinkle over the salad. Serve immediately.

RICE AND PASTA

Rice and pasta are among the most versatile of ingredients to keep in store. These filling ingredients can be served hot or cold, as accompaniments or as part of the main dish. Combined with the simplest of ingredients – herbs, spices, cheese, oil and nuts – they are quickly turned into a wide variety of supper dishes and snacks.

There are several different types of rice available in the markets and it is a good idea to try them so that you can decide which you prefer. Ordinary white long-grain rice is the most popular. To cook it, allow about $1\frac{3}{4}$ cups of water for each cup of rice. Bring the water to a boil, add the rice, stir once and cover the pan very tightly. Leave to simmer gently for about 12 to 15 minutes or until the grains are tender and all water has been absorbed. Fluff the rice before serving it.

Converted rice, which is partially cooked, takes about 3 to 5 minutes more cooking than ordinary rice. There are lots of other types of white rice available: preseasoned rice, where the grains are enclosed in a perforated boilable bag, ready to be lowered into boiling water for the stated time; canned, partially cooked rice is also available, ready to be heated before serving.

Basmati or bashmati and patna rices are flavorful varieties of long-grain white rice, much used in Indian dishes. They are prized for their dry, fluffy texture and grains that remain separate when cooked. The rice can be cooked in the same way as ordinary white rice. Brown rice retains the outer bran and germ that are removed to make white rice. Brown rice has more flavor and a nuttier texture that white rice and it requires longer cooking in more water. Use about 3 cups of water to 1 cup of rice and allow about 40 minutes cooking. Wild rice, which is really a cereal grain, is also available.

This chapter includes recipes for making your own pasta. This is not a difficult task and the result is really well worth the effort involved. If, however, you prefer to buy dried pasta, there are lots of different shapes available. Pasta which is freshly prepared should be cooked in boiling water for about 5 minutes – it should not be overcooked. Dried pasta requires longer cooking – about 12 to 15 minutes – in plenty of boiling salted water. A little oil can be added to the cooking water to prevent the pasta from sticking together and from boiling over during cooking. The drained pasta can be tossed with herbs and oil, butter or Parmesan cheese and served very simply. Alternatively, if it is to be served cold, it should be rinsed under cold water immediately it is drained, then left to drain thoroughly.

Baked stuffed pasta dishes are also particularly delicious and very popular for preparing in advance, then chilling or freezing until they are finally baked and served. There are lots of ideas to choose from in this chapter – many traditional dishes and some which will encourage you to experiment with new ingredients.

Ravioli in Three Colors

Serves 5

3½ cups flour
6 eggs
salt and pepper
¾ lb fresh bulk spinach
5 tablespoons Tomato Sauce
(page 391)
pinch of saffron powder
(optional)
2 tablespoons butter
½ lb lean boneless veal, chopped
5 oz Parma ham, chopped
1 onion, chopped
1 cup white wine
1 teaspoon chopped thyme *or* ½
teaspoon dried thyme
1 bay leaf
2 egg yolks

Begin by making the pasta: sift the flour into a bowl. Break 5 eggs into the flour, add a pinch of salt and, using your fingers, work the eggs into the flour to give a smooth dough. Shape into a ball and leave to stand for 20 minutes.

Cook the spinach in boiling salted water for 5 minutes, then drain thoroughly and finely chop.

Divide the dough into three equal portions. To make green pasta, add a few tablespoons chopped spinach to one portion of Pasta. Work in thoroughly and set aside.

To make red pasta, add the tomato sauce to the second portion of dough. Work in thoroughly to give a uniform color and set aside.

The last portion of dough can either be left plain or colored a pale yellow by adding a little saffron powder.

To make the filling: melt the butter in a pan and add the veal, ham and onion and fry for about 15 minutes.

When the meat and onion are golden brown stir in the white wine and add the thyme and bay leaf. Season with salt and pepper and simmer over a low heat for 1 hour.

Remove the bay leaf and, using a wooden spoon, stir in the remaining chopped spinach together with 2 egg yolks.

On a lightly floured board, roll out the pasta to a thickness of ⅛ inch and, using the rim of a small glass or a small pastry cutter, cut out rounds of each color. Place a little of the filling in the middle of each round. Beat the remaining egg and use to brush the edges of the pastry rounds. Fold the round in half and pinch the edges together to seal. Alternatively, top with a second round of pasta (to vary the shape) and pinch the edges together.

Cook the ravioli for 5 minutes in a large pan of boiling salted water. As they rise to the surface lift them out using a slotted spoon and drain.

Serve with butter, grated cheese or Tomato sauce (see page 391).

Spaghetti Ménagère

Serves 6

1¼ lb spaghetti
½ lb slab bacon, diced
½ lb cooked ham, cut into strips
3 garlic cloves, coarsely
   chopped
salt and pepper
6 tablespoons butter

Cook the spaghetti in a large pan of boiling salted water for 10 minutes or until just tender.

Meanwhile, cook the bacon in a skillet until the fat is rendered. Add the ham and garlic and cook gently for about 5 minutes. Season to taste. Drain off excess fat.

Drain the spaghetti and tip into a shallow dish. Add the contents of the skillet and dot with the butter.

Cannelloni au Gratin

Serves 4

4 cups flour
5 eggs
salt and pepper
1 cup grated Gruyère cheese
FILLING
3 tablespoons butter
1 onion, sliced
$\frac{3}{4}$ lb ground meat
$\frac{1}{4}$ lb Parma ham, chopped
$\frac{1}{4}$ lb cooked ham, chopped
5 tablespoons white wine
1 egg
SAUCE
2 tablespoons oil
1 onion, sliced
$\frac{1}{2}$ lb tomatoes, peeled
1 teaspoon sage

For the pasta, sift the flour into a bowl, break in 4 eggs, add a pinch of salt and, using your fingers, work the eggs into the flour until smooth.

Make the filling: melt the butter and soften the onion. Add the ground meat and all the ham. Season and fry gently for a few minutes. Add the wine and cook gently for 25 minutes. Remove the pan from the heat and work in the egg. Set aside. Make the tomato sauce: heat the oil and fry the onion, then add the tomatoes and sage. Season and simmer for 40 minutes.

Roll out the pasta to a thickness of $\frac{1}{8}$ inch and, using a pastry wheel, cut into equal rectangles. Cook for 10 minutes in a large pan of boiling salted water. Drain and arrange on a dish towel. Beat the remaining egg. Fill pairs of the pasta rectangles with the cooled meat filling, sealing with beaten egg.

Arrange the cannelloni in a greased ovenproof dish. Top with the sauce and grated cheese. Brown in a preheated 475° oven for 15 minutes. Serve at once.

Spaghetti with Seafood

Serves 6

1 pint clams
1 pint mussels, scrubbed
2 tablespoons peanut oil
2 garlic cloves, finely sliced
1½ teaspoons chopped chervil
¾ lb raw shrimp, peeled
salt and pepper
1¼ lb spaghetti

If any of the clams or mussels are open, tap them and discard if they do not close. Put them into a large pan of water and bring to a boil. Simmer for 5 to 6 minutes until the shells open. Discard any that do not open. Remove the fish from their shells and set aside. Strain the liquid contained in the shells and reserve.

Heat the oil in a pan and fry the garlic. Add the chervil and liquid from the clam and mussel shells. Reduce the liquid by half over a low heat, then add the mussels, clams and shrimp and season to taste. Leave the sauce to cook for another 5 minutes.

Meanwhile, cook the spaghetti in a large pan of boiling salted water for 10 minutes until just tender. Drain and transfer to a shallow serving dish. Pour over the seafood sauce and serve very hot.

Spaghetti with Garlic

Serves 4

1 lb spaghetti
2 tablespoons olive oil
5 garlic cloves, sliced
2 tablespoons chopped parsley
salt and pepper
parsley sprig for garnish

Cook the spaghetti in a large pan of boiling salted water for about 10 minutes or until just tender.

Heat the oil and fry the garlic until golden. Add the chopped parsley and fry for a few minutes over a low heat. Season.

Drain the cooked spaghetti and transfer to a shallow serving dish. Sprinkle with the fried garlic and parsley and serve very hot, garnished with a parsley sprig.

Multicolored Pie

Serves 6

¼ lb green noodles
¼ lb egg noodles
14 oz pasta twists
¼ lb tortellini
1½ quantities Basic Pie pastry
   (page 431)
2 thin slices cooked ham,
   chopped
salt and pepper
2 egg yolks, beaten
5 tablespoons Crème Fraîche
   (page 398)
½ cup grated Parmesan cheese
1 egg, beaten

Cook the two types of noodles and the pasts twists in a large pan of boiling salted water for 10 minutes or until just tender. Drain. Cook the tortellini in a pan of boiling salted water for about 5 minutes. Drain.

On a lightly floured board, roll out two-thirds of the pastry to a ¼ inch thickness and use to line a pie pan.

Arrange the pasta in the pastry case and add the ham. Season the egg yolks and pour over the pasta with the Crème fraîche. Sprinkle with the grated cheese. Roll out the rest of the pastry and use to cover the filling. Moisten the pastry edges and press together to seal. Make a hole in the center of the pie. Brush with beaten egg and bake in a preheated 400° oven for 20 minutes. Serve hot.

Fisherman's Noodles

Serves 6

1 quart mussels, scrubbed
1 lb noodles
1 tablespoon olive oil
¾ lb scallops
1 cup Crème Fraîche (page 398)
pinch of saffron powder
salt and pepper
1 cup grated Gruyère cheese

If any of the mussels are open, tap them and discard if they do not close. Put them into a large pan of water and bring to a boil. Simmer for 5 to 6 minutes until the shells open. Discard any that do not open. Remove the fish from their shells and set aside. Strain the liquid contained in the shells and reserve.

Cook the noodles in a large pan of boiling salted water for 8 minutes until just tender. Drain.

Heat the olive oil in a pan and cook the mussels and scallops for a few minutes. Add 3–4 tablespoons of the liquid from the mussel shells and cook over a moderate heat for 5 minutes to reduce.

Add the noodles to the pan and stir into the seafood. Add the Crème fraîche and saffron. Season with pepper and gently stir all the ingredients together.

Generously butter an ovenproof dish. Sprinkle with the Gruyère. Add the fish mixture and brown in a preheated 450° oven for 10 minutes. Serve straight from the dish.

Noodles with White Beans

Serves 6

2 cups dried navy beans, soaked
   overnight
2 celery stalks, diced
4 potatoes, cubed
$\frac{1}{4}$ lb slab bacon, chopped
salt and pepper
$\frac{3}{4}$ lb noodles

Drain the beans and put into a large saucepan with the celery. Cover with water and bring to a boil. Lower the heat and simmer for 1 hour until the beans are cooked.

Add the potatoes and bacon to the pan and season with salt and pepper. About 5 minutes after the liquid comes back to a boil, add the noodles. Cook for a further 15 minutes and serve immediately.

Pasta Twists with Olives

Serves 4

½ lb slab bacon, diced
2 tablespoons butter
1 tablespoon flour
1 (8-oz) can whole button
   mushrooms, drained with
   liquid reserved
1 cup green olives
salt and pepper
1 lb pasta twists

Fry the bacon in a saucepan over a moderate heat until golden brown. Drain off excess fat. Add the butter and melt it. Stir in the flour and add a few tablespoons mushroom liquid, stirring until the sauce thickens.

Add the mushrooms and olives, season to taste and simmer gently over a low heat for about 15 minutes.

Meanwhile, cook the pasta twists in a large pan of boiling salted water for 10 minutes until just tender. Drain and add to the mushroom sauce. Stir in and serve very hot.

Macaroni Timbale

Serves 6

2 large eggplants, cut
   lengthwise into thin slices
2 tablespoons oil
1 lb macaroni
1 (7-oz) can tuna in oil, drained
   and flaked
1 (8-oz) can peas, drained
salt and pepper

Sprinkle the eggplant slices with salt to draw out the bitter juices. Leave for 20 minutes, then rinse and dry. Heat the oil and fry the eggplants. Cook the macaroni in a large pan of boiling salted water for about 10 minutes until just tender. Drain.

Mix the tuna and peas together in a bowl. Add the macaroni, season to taste and mix well. Butter a deep ovenproof mold or baking dish and line the bottom and sides with the slices of eggplant. Fill with the macaroni mixture.

Bake the timbale in a preheated 400° oven for about 20 minutes. Turn the timbale out of the mold onto a serving plate.

Pasta and Chicken Timbale

Serves 4

5 tablespoons butter
$\frac{3}{4}$ lb skinless, boneless chicken
   breast, cooked and cut into
   thin strips
1 lb macaroni or pasta shells
2 tablespoons flour
1 cup hot chicken broth
salt and pepper
pinch of grated nutmeg
$\frac{2}{3}$ cup Crème Fraîche (page 398)
1 cup grated Gruyère cheese

Melt 2 tablespoons butter in a skillet and fry the chicken until golden brown.

Cook the pasta in a large pan of boiling salted water for about 12 minutes until just tender. Drain.

Melt the remaining butter in a small pan and stir in the flour. Cook for 1 to 2 minutes, stirring until smooth. Add the hot broth and stir for about 5 minutes until the sauce thickens. Season with salt, pepper and nutmeg. Remove the pan from the heat and stir in the Crème fraîche. Return the pan to a low heat, add half the grated cheese and allow to melt.

Butter a deep ovenproof mold or dish and fill with alternate layers of pasta, chicken and sauce, finishing with a layer of pasta and the remaining grated cheese. Brown in a preheated 425° oven for 15 minutes. Serve very hot.

Noodles and Bacon Timbale

Serves 6

1¼ lb noodles
½ lb slab bacon, chopped
2 tablespoons butter
salt and pepper
3 eggs, beaten

Cook the noodles in a large pan of boiling salted water for 10 minutes until just tender. Meanwhile, fry the bacon in a skillet. Drain and set aside.

Drain the noodles and return to the pan. Stir in the bacon and butter using a wooden spoon. Grease a soufflé dish or other deep ovenproof dish and transfer the noodle mixture to it. Season the eggs and pour over the noodles. Bake in a preheated 400° oven for about 15 minutes.

Remove the timbale from the oven and unmold onto a serving plate.

Homemade Ravioli

Serves 4

2½ cups flour
4 eggs
salt and pepper
1 tablespoon oil
5 oz slab bacon, finely diced
½ lb ground round
1½ teaspoons chopped chervil
pinch of grated nutmeg
Tomato Sauce (page 391) for
   serving

Begin by making the pasta: sift the flour into a bowl. Break the eggs into the flour, add a pinch of salt and the oil and, using your fingers, work the ingredients together to give a smooth dough. Leave to stand for at least 30 minutes.

Meanwhile, make the filling: put the bacon into a bowl. Add the ground round and chervil and season with nutmeg, salt and pepper. Mix thoroughly.

Halve the pasta dough and, on a lightly floured board, roll both pieces out to a thickness of ⅛ inch.

On one of the sheets put small spoonfuls of the meat filling, arranged at regular intervals. Cover with the second sheet of pasta and press firmly together with your fingers between the mounds of filling. Using a pastry wheel cut into individual ravioli.

Cook in boiling salted water for 8 minutes, and as the ravioli rise to the surface lift out of the pan using a slotted spoon.

Serve with Tomato sauce.

Macaroni au Gratin

Serves 4

1 tablespoon olive oil
1 onion, thinly sliced
1 (16-oz) can peeled tomatoes,
    drained and crushed
½ teaspoon dried thyme
1 teaspoon dried chervil
salt and pepper
1 lb macaroni
¾ cup grated Gruyère cheese

Heat the oil in a skillet and fry the onion until golden. Add the tomatoes, thyme and chervil. Season to taste and simmer gently over a low heat for about 15 minutes.

Meanwhile, cook the macaroni in a large pan of boiling salted water for about 10 minutes, until just tender. Drain.

Transfer the macaroni to a shallow buttered baking dish. Cover with the tomato sauce and sprinkle with the Gruyère. Brown in a preheated 425° oven for about 10 minutes and serve very hot.

Green Lasagne au Gratin

Serves 6

3 tablespoons oil
1 carrot, finely sliced
1 onion, finely sliced
1 celery stalk, finely sliced
½ lb ground beef
2 tablespoons white wine
salt and pepper
¾ lb tomatoes, peeled
2 cups Béchamel Sauce (page 384)
pinch of grated nutmeg
1¼ cups grated Gruyère cheese
1 lb green lasagne

Heat the oil and fry the carrot, onion and celery until golden brown. Add the meat and the wine and season to taste with salt and pepper. Cook over a high heat until the liquid has evaporated.

Add the tomatoes, adjust the seasoning and cook over a moderate heat for 30 minutes.

Season the Béchamel with nutmeg, salt and pepper and stir in 1 cup Grùyere.

Cook the lasagne in a large pan of boiling salted water for 10 minutes. Drain. Cover the bottom of a greased ovenproof dish with a layer of lasagne, allowing the pasta to overhang the length of the dish by about 2 inches. Add a layer of the meat and tomato sauce and then a layer of Béchamel sauce. Continue layering in this way until all the ingredients have been used. Sprinkle the rest of the Gruyère on top. Fold over the lasagne overhang and brown in a preheated 450° oven for 15 minutes.

Macaroni with Roquefort

Serves 6

6 tablespoons butter
1 tablespoon chopped parsley
1½ cups crumbled Roquefort
   cheese
salt and pepper
1 lb macaroni
1 cup grated Emmental cheese

Melt ¼ cup butter over a low heat in a skillet and fry the parsley. When it begins to color remove the pan from the heat and add the Roquefort. Season to taste.

Cook the macaroni in a large pan of boiling salted water for about 12 minutes until just tender.

Butter a shallow baking dish or soufflé dish and fill with alternate layers of macaroni and the Roquefort mixture until all the ingredients are used. Sprinkle with the grated Emmental cheese and dot with the remaining butter. Brown in a preheated 450° oven for about 12 minutes.

Kidneys in a Nest

Serves 4

1 lb noodles
5 tablespoons butter
10 pearl onions
½ lb slab bacon, diced
8 lamb kidneys, skinned and
   halved
salt and pepper

Cook the noodles in a large pan of boiling salted water for 7 minutes until just tender. Drain carefully and transfer to a buttered 1½-quart ring mold. Dot with 2 tablespoons butter and bake in a preheated 375° oven for 15 minutes.

Melt the remaining butter in a skillet and fry the onions whole with the bacon. Add the kidneys to the pan and fry for a few minutes, turning frequently. Season to taste. Cook over a moderate heat for a further 5 minutes.

Remove the ring mold from the oven and turn out onto a serving plate. Arrange the kidney mixture in the center and serve very hot.

Spaghetti with Walnuts

Serves 6

2½ cups walnut halves
5 garlic cloves, chopped
5 tablespoons olive oil
1 lb spaghetti
salt and pepper
pinch of grated nutmeg
½ cup grated Parmesan cheese

Reserve one-quarter of the walnut halves and finely chop the remainder. Put the garlic and chopped nuts into a bowl and crush with a pestle or a wooden spoon.

Heat the oil in a skillet and fry the garlic and walnut mixture for a few minutes over a low heat.

Cook the spaghetti in a large pan of boiling salted water for about 10 minutes until just tender. Drain, transfer to a shallow serving dish and top with the nut and garlic mixture. Season with pepper and nutmeg and sprinkle with grated cheese.

Stir in the whole nuts, keeping a few to garnish the top. Serve immediately.

Spaghetti with Anchovies

Serves 6

1 tablespoon olive oil
2 garlic cloves, chopped
1 bouquet garni
2 tablespoons capers
1 (16-oz) can peeled tomatoes, drained
2 (2-oz) cans anchovies in oil, drained
salt and pepper
1¼ lb spaghetti
½ cup ripe olives
a few sprigs chervil or parsley (optional)

Heat the oil in a skillet and fry the garlic until golden. Add the bouquet garni, half the capers and the tomatoes.

Chop a quarter of the anchovies and add to the pan. Season with pepper, stir with a wooden spoon and cook over a low heat until the sauce is quite thick. Discard the bouquet garni. Wrap the remaining anchovies around the rest of the capers. Set aside.

Cook the spaghetti in a large pan of boiling salted water for about 10 minutes until just tender. Drain and transfer to a serving dish.

Pour the tomato sauce into the center. Garnish with the anchovy fillets and capers, the olives and a few sprigs of chervil.

Macaroni Hotpot

Serves 4

1 lb bacon, chopped coarsely
1¼ cups hot meat or vegetable
  broth
salt and pepper
1 lb elbow macaroni
2 tablespoons butter
parsley for garnish

Blanch the bacon to remove some of the salt: put into boiling water for 10 minutes. Drain on paper towels.

Cook the bacon in a flameproof casserole until golden. Drain off excess fat, then add the broth. Season to taste and simmer over a moderate heat for 5 minutes.

Cook the macaroni in a large pan of boiling salted water for 5 minutes, until just tender. Drain carefully and transfer to the casserole. Add the butter. Stir to mix and simmer for a further 10 minutes, stirring occasionally. Garnish with a sprig of parsley, if desired.

Tagliatelle in Cream

Serves 4

¼ cup butter
5 oz cooked ham, diced
¾ lb button mushrooms,
   quartered
salt and pepper
1 tablespoon flour
2 tablespoons Crème Fraîche
   (page 398)
¼ cup white wine
1 lb plain or crinkly tagliatelle

Melt half the butter in a skillet and fry the ham.

Put the mushrooms into a saucepan with the rest of the butter and cook over a moderate heat for a few minutes until some of their liquid has evaporated. Season to taste and sprinkle over the flour. Add the ham, Crème fraîche and wine. Cover the pan, lower the heat and simmer for 15 minutes.

Meanwhile, cook the tagliatelle in a large pan of boiling salted water for about 10 minutes until just tender. Drain and transfer to a serving dish. Pour over the mushroom sauce and serve at once.

Two-Cheese Rigatoni

Serves 4

5 oz Danish blue or blue Bresse
  cheese, rinded and diced
¼ lb Port-Salut cheese, rinded
  and diced
2 tablespoons Crème Fraîche
  (page 398)
2 tablespoons cognac
salt and pepper
1 lb rigatoni

Put both cheeses into a pan with half the Crème fraîche, and stir constantly with a wooden spoon over a low heat until the mixture is creamy. Stir in the cognac and season to taste. Keep hot in a preheated 275° oven, stirring from time to time.

Meanwhile, cook the rigatoni in a large pan of boiling salted water for about 10 minutes until just tender. Drain and return to the saucepan. Add the cheese sauce and the remaining Crème fraîche and stir in gently until the pasta is coated. Serve very hot.

Pasta Bows with Pesto Sauce

Serves 4

2 cups fresh basil leaves *or* $\frac{1}{3}$
  cup dried basil
2 garlic cloves, chopped
2 tablespoons pine nuts
5 tablespoons olive oil
2 tablespoons grated Parmesan
  cheese
salt
1 lb pasta bows
basil leaves for garnish

With a pestle and mortar, thoroughly crush the basil, garlic and pine nuts. Add the oil gradually, a drop at a time at first, and then more quickly, stirring constantly. When the mixture is smooth, work in a little grated cheese. Season to taste.

Cook the pasta bows in a large pan of boiling salted water for about 10 minutes or until just tender. Drain, reserving about 1 cup of the cooking water.

Transfer the bows to a shallow serving dish and pour the sauce into the center. Add a little of the cooking water, mix in quickly over a low heat and serve very hot garnished with basil leaves.

Spinach Gnocchi

Serves 8

1 lb fresh bulk spinach
½ cup Crème fraîche (page 398)
salt and pepper
double quantity Gnocchi
   Dough (right)
½ cup butter
2 cups grated Parmesan cheese

Cook the spinach in a pan of boiling salted water for 10 minutes. Drain thoroughly, pressing the spinach to remove all excess water. Chop and put into a bowl.

Add the Crème fraîche, season to taste and mix well. Work the chopped spinach into the gnocchi dough. Cook the gnocchi in a large pan of boiling salted water (see right) and serve with the butter and Parmesan, or with a Tomato Sauce (see page 383) if wished.

Gnocchi with Meat Sauce

Serves 4

¼ cup butter
½ lb ground beef
1 onion, sliced
2 tablespoons flour
1¼ cups milk
salt and pepper
pinch of grated nutmeg
GNOCCHI
½ cup butter, chopped
⅓ cup water
pinch of salt
1 cup flour
4 eggs

For the gnocchi: melt the butter with the water and salt. Remove the pan from the heat and tip in the flour. Mix thoroughly. Stir the mixture over a low heat until it comes away from the sides of the pan. Off the heat, add the eggs, one by one, beating each in well before adding the next. Leave for about 2 hours.

In a skillet, melt 2 tablespoons butter and fry the beef and onion for about 10 minutes. Melt the rest of the butter in a saucepan and stir in the flour. Cook, stirring, for 1 to 2 minutes until smooth. Off the heat, gradually add the milk. Return to the heat and stir for about 5 minutes until the sauce thickens. Season, add nutmeg and stir in the meat.

Cook the gnocchi in a large pan of boiling salted water: shape teaspoons of the dough into balls and drop into the boiling water. As they rise to the surface, remove with a slotted spoon and drain. Arrange in a serving dish and top with the meat sauce. Serve very hot.

Stuffed Cabbage

Serves 4

1 head green cabbage
1 tablespoon vinegar
$\frac{1}{2}$ cup long-grain rice
3 cups boiling water
2 tablespoons peanut oil
1 cup finely chopped cooked
    boneless veal or chicken
1 egg
1 (8-oz) can peas, drained
salt and pepper
pinch of grated nutmeg
3 tablespoons butter, melted
Tomato Sauce (page 391) for
    serving

Rinse the cabbage in cold water with the vinegar added. Cook for 10 minutes in a pan of boiling salted water. Drain and gently pull back the outside leaves. Remove the heart.

Cook the rice in the boiling water with salt to taste for 12 minutes until just tender.

Meanwhile, heat the oil in a skillet and fry the meat until browned.

Drain the rice, if necessary, and transfer to a bowl. Work in the egg. Add the meat and peas and season with salt, pepper and nutmeg. Mix thoroughly and fill the center of the cabbage with the mixture. Reclose the leaves over the stuffing, and tie with fine string. Place the stuffed cabbage in a deep round baking dish. Pour the butter over the cabbage and bake in a preheated 375° oven for 20 minutes.

Serve with Tomato sauce.

Veal Olives with Rice Stuffing

Serves 4

$\frac{1}{2}$ cup long-grain rice
3 cups boiling water
$\frac{1}{4}$ cup butter
1 cup finely sliced button
    mushrooms
salt and pepper
4 veal cutlets (about 5 oz each)
2–3 tablespoons flour
2 tomatoes, quartered
1 teaspoon chopped thyme or $\frac{1}{2}$
    teaspoon dried thyme
1 carrot, sliced
1 onion, sliced

Cook the rice in the boiling water with salt to taste for about 15 minutes until just tender. Drain if necessary.

Melt half the butter in a pan and gently fry the mushrooms. When they begin to brown, transfer to a bowl. Add the rice and mix with the mushrooms. Season to taste. Spread the veal cutlets on a work surface and cover with the rice stuffing. Roll up and secure with fine string. Lightly roll in the flour to coat.

Heat the remaining butter and brown the veal olives all over. Add the tomatoes, thyme, carrot and onion. Season to taste and cook the veal olives, covered, for about 25 minutes over a moderate heat, basting with the cooking juices from time to time.

Rice with Peas

Serves 4

¼ cup butter
¾ lb pearl onions or scallions
   (white part only)
1½ lb peas, shelled
2 cups hot chicken broth
1 cup long-grain rice
salt and pepper
2 cups water
5 tablespoons Crème Fraîche
   (page 398)

Melt the butter in a pan and fry the onions or scallions for a few minutes. Add the peas and stir in the broth. Cook over a low heat for 15 minutes, stirring from time to time.

Sprinkle the rice into the pan, stir in and cook until it has absorbed the broth.

Meanwhile, salt the water and bring to a boil. Add to the rice when all the broth has been absorbed. Cover the pan and simmer for 15 minutes until the water is absorbed. Taste and adjust the seasoning. Just before serving, stir in the Crème fraîche and transfer to a serving dish.

Stuffed Grape Leaves

Serves 8

16 grape leaves
1 cup long-grain rice
6 cups boiling water
¼ cup peanut oil
6 scallions, finely sliced
½ lb cooked boneless veal,
    ground (about 1 cup)
salt and pepper
1½ cups chicken broth

Soak the grape leaves in cold water for 20 minutes. Meanwhile, cook the rice in the boiling water with salt to taste for 15 minutes. Drain if necessary.

Heat the oil in a pan and fry the onions over a low heat. Add the veal and rice. Season to taste, remove from the heat and stir thoroughly.

Drain and dry the grape leaves. Spread them out and place a little of the rice stuffing in the center of each. Fold in the outside edges and roll up, securing with fine string.

Arrange the stuffed grape leaves side by side in an ovenproof dish and pour over the broth. Cook in a preheated 350° oven for about 45 minutes, turning the rolls from time to time.

Chicken with Rice

Serves 4 to 6

3 tablespoons peanut oil
1 (3½-lb) chicken, cut into large
  pieces
1 green pepper
1 onion, chopped
½ lb carrots, chopped
½ cup long-grain rice
1 quart hot chicken broth
1 cup raisins
1 teaspoon saffron powder
salt and pepper

Heat the oil in a pan and brown the chicken pieces all over.

Remove stalk from the pepper, cut the pepper in half and remove the seeds and pith, then dice the pepper.

Add the pepper, onion and carrots to the chicken and stir in with a wooden spoon. Fry for a few minutes.

Sprinkle the rice into the pan and add the broth with the raisins and saffron. Season to taste and stir.

Simmer over a low heat until all the liquid has been absorbed. Serve straight from the pan.

Rice Ring with Eggplant

Serves 6

4 eggplants
$\frac{1}{2}$ lb slab bacon, chopped
$1\frac{1}{2}$ cups long-grain rice
$2\frac{1}{4}$ quarts boiling water
2 tablespoons butter
salt and pepper
Tomato Sauce (page 391) for
   serving

Cut 2 eggplants into small cubes and finely slice the others lengthwise. Cook in boiling salted water for 10 minutes and drain.

Fry the bacon until golden brown. Drain and set aside. Cook the rice in the boiling water with salt to taste for 15 minutes. Drain if necessary. Transfer to a bowl and add the bacon, butter and diced eggplant. Gently stir together and season to taste.

Butter a $1\frac{1}{2}$-quart ovenproof ring mold and arrange the eggplant slices at intervals around the bottom, reserving any small pieces. Fill the mold with the rice mixture and press down gently. Bake in a preheated 375° oven for 20 minutes. Serve with Tomato sauce and the reserved eggplant.

Tomatoes with Rice Stuffing

Serves 4

8 tomatoes
1 cup long-grain rice
1½ quarts boiling water
3 garlic cloves, finely chopped
1 teaspoon chopped thyme *or* ½
    teaspoon dried thyme
3 tablespons butter
salt and pepper
2 tablespoons olive oil
parsley sprigs for garnish
    (optional)

Cut a lid from the top of each tomato and reserve. Using a small spoon, scoop out the insides of the tomatoes. Lightly salt the insides and turn upside down on a plate to drain.

Meanwhile, cook the rice in the boiling water with salt to taste for 15 minutes until just tender. Drain if necessary, rinse and drain again. Transfer to a bowl. Stir in the garlic and thyme with the butter. Season to taste.

Fill the tomatoes with the rice stuffing and arrange in an ovenproof dish. Replace the lids and sprinkle each with a few drops oil. Bake in a preheated 375° oven for 30 minutes. Serve hot garnished with a parsley sprig, if desired.

Rice with Almonds

Serves 6

1½ cups long-grain rice
2¼ quarts boiling water
2 tablespoons peanut oil
3 onions, finely sliced
1 lb tomatoes, peeled and
    chopped
salt and pepper
1½ cups blanched almonds
1 tablespoon butter

Cook the rice in the boiling water with salt to taste for 15 minutes until just tender.

Meanwhile, heat the oil in a skillet and fry the onions for a few minutes. When they begin to brown, add the tomatoes. Season to taste and simmer for 20 minutes over a low heat.

Thoroughly grease a 1½-quart ring mold. Drain the rice if necessary. Cover the bottom of the mold with a layer of rice. Spoon in the tomato sauce, reserving a few tablespoons. Spread 1 cup almonds over the sauce and finish with a layer of rice. Bake in a preheated 375° oven for about 15 minutes.

Melt the butter in a skillet and fry the remaining almonds until golden brown.

Remove the rice ring from the oven, unmold onto a serving plate and garnish with the remaining sauce and the browned almonds.

Tomato Rice

Serves 4

¼ cup olive oil
3 onions, finely sliced
2 garlic cloves, finely sliced
1½ lb tomatoes, peeled and
    quartered
1¼ cups long-grain rice
2½ cups hot beef broth
salt and pepper
pinch of saffron powder
2 teaspoons chopped parsley

Heat half the oil in a pan and fry the onions and garlic. When golden brown, add the tomatoes. Stir with a wooden spoon and simmer over a low heat for about 15 minutes.

Heat the remaining oil in another pan, sprinkle in the rice and stir with a wooden spoon until transparent. Add the tomatoes, onion, garlic and broth. Season with salt, pepper and saffron and add the parsley. Cook over a low heat for about 20 minutes. Transfer to a serving dish and serve very hot.

Fried Rice Cakes

Serves 4

2 cups long-grain rice
3 quarts boiling water
salt
½ cup butter

Cook the rice in the boiling water with salt to taste for about 15 minutes until just tender. Drain if necessary, rinse in cold water and drain again.

Melt 1 tablespoon butter in a skillet and add one-quarter of the rice. Flatten the rice using a spatula to form a flat cake. Cook over a high heat checking that the rice browns without sticking to the pan. The outside of the cake should be crisp and golden.

Turn the cake onto a plate. Melt another 1 tablespoon butter in the skillet and fry the cake on the other side. Cook for a few minutes until brown.

In the same way make three more rice cakes and serve very hot.

Rice cakes are an excellent accompaniment for meat cooked in a sauce, or for poached fish.

Rice and Mushroom Timbale

Serves 3

2 tablespoons peanut oil
$\frac{2}{3}$ cup long-grain rice
1 quart hot meat or vegetable
 broth
salt and pepper
2 tablespoons butter
5 oz button mushrooms
Tomato Sauce (page 391)
 optional

Heat the oil in a large pan, sprinkle in the rice and fry for a few minutes, stirring constantly until transparent.

Add the broth to the pan. Season and cook over a moderate heat for 12–15 minutes. Meanwhile, melt 2 tablespoons butter in a skillet and fry the mushrooms until golden. When the rice is cooked, drain if necessary and stir in the mushrooms.

Grease a deep ovenproof mold (soufflé dish or charlotte mold) and fill with the rice and mushroom mixture. Bake in a preheated 375° oven for about 15 minutes. To serve, unmold the timbale onto a serving plate and, if wished, top with Tomato sauce.

Chicken Pieces with Mushroom Pilaf

Serves 4

3 tablespoons olive oil
2 onions, finely sliced
1½ lb chicken pieces
1¼ cups long-grain rice
2½ cups chicken broth
1 tablespoon curry powder
salt and pepper
2 tablespoons butter
½ lb button mushrooms, finely
   sliced

Heat the oil in a large pan and brown the onions over a high heat for a few minutes. Add the chicken pieces and brown all over, turning them from time to time.

Sprinkle the rice into the pan and stir until transparent. Add the broth and curry powder. Season to taste and cook over a moderate heat for about 20 minutes until all the liquid has been absorbed.

Melt the butter in a skillet and fry the mushrooms for about 1 minutes. Add to the rice mixture.

When all the liquid has been absorbed check that the rice is cooked. Cook for a few minutes longer if necessary. Serve straight from the pan.

Rice Ring with Tuna

Serves 6

2 tablespoons olive oil
1½ lb fresh boneless tuna, cut
   into 2-inch cubes
1 onion, finely sliced
2 lb tomatoes, quartered
3 tablespoons dry white wine
1 bouquet garni
salt and pepper
1¼ cups long-grain rice
2 quarts boiling water
1 tomato, sliced, for garnish
1 teaspoon chopped thyme or
   rosemary for garnish

Heat the oil in a large pan and seal the tuna all over, turning it from time to time. Add the onion, tomatoes, white wine and bouquet garni. Season to taste and simmer over a low heat for about 35 minutes.

Meanwhile, cook the rice in the boiling water with salt to taste for about 15 minutes until just tender. Drain if necessary, rinse in cold water and drain again.

Press the rice into a greased 1½-quart ring mold and keep hot in a preheated 225° oven until the tuna is cooked, about 10 minutes.

Meanwhile, broil the sliced tomatoes with a sprinkling of thyme or rosemary. Remove the rice ring from the oven and unmold onto a serving plate. Remove the bouquet garni from the tuna and pour the fish in tomato sauce into the center of the rice ring. Garnish the dish with the broiled sliced tomatoes.

Rice with Pumpkin

Serves 6

1 lb pumpkin, peeled, seeded
   and cut into large cubes
2 onions, finely sliced
¼ lb slab bacon, diced
1 bay leaf
salt and pepper
2 cups long-grain rice
3 quarts boiling water
2 eggs, separated
½ cup grated Gruyère cheese
¼ cup butter

Cook the pumpkin and onions in a large pan of boiling salted water for about 10 minutes. Drain. Cook the bacon in a skillet. Add the onion, pumpkin and bay leaf and season to taste. Cook gently over a low heat.

Meanwhile, cook the rice in the boiling water with salt to taste for about 15 minutes until just tender. Drain if necessary.

Remove the bay leaf from the pumpkin mixture and drain off excess fat. Add the egg yolks. Add 2 tablespoons grated cheese and stir until the cheese has melted. Add the rice, the remaining grated cheese and the butter. Season with pepper and mix gently. Serve very hot.

Spicy Rice Ring

Serves 6

¼ lb slab bacon, diced
4 slices cooked ham, 2
  shredded, 2 left whole
1¼ cups long-grain rice
2½ cups hot chicken or
  vegetable broth
⅔ cup ripe olives
1 cucumber
3 tomatoes, peeled and chopped
pinch of saffron powder
2 teaspoons curry powder
salt and pepper

Fry the bacon in a saucepan until the fat is beginning to render. Add the shredded ham. Sprinkle in the rice and stir with a wooden spoon until transparent. Stir in the broth.

Pit and chop a few of the olives. Peel half the cucumber and cut into slices. Add the chopped olives and tomatoes to the pan.

Season with the saffron, curry powder, salt and pepper and stir in. Cover and cook over a moderate heat for 20 minutes.

Butter a 1½-quart ring mold and fill with the rice mixture. Bake in a preheated 375° oven for about 15 minutes. Unmold onto a plate. Garnish with the remaining ham slices, olives and unpeeled sliced cucumber.

— Dressings and Sauces —

It is often the condiments and accompaniments which make or break the meal and a good sauce will retrieve the plainest of broiled steaks, fish fillets or chops from being labeled tasteless. The cook who has a few sauce recipes tucked up his or her sleeve will almost always be able to turn a simple meal into a roaring success.

This chapter offers a broad selection of recipes for sauces both hot and cold, savory and sweet. There are dressings ranging from the basic to the unusual, ready to bring a simple salad to life, or turn a couple of hard-cooked eggs into an exciting first course. Many of the pictures offer ideas for serving the sauces by showing simple foods which they will complement.

There are a few basic techniques to master, and then you will find sauce-making a simple task. Many hot sauces rely on the preparation of a *roux*: a mixture of fat and flour, cooked for a few minutes to make a thin paste, then combined with liquid which is poured into the pan as the sauce is stirred continuously. This technique is useful for basic milk and stock-based sauces – Béchamel sauce or gravy, for example. Another method of thickening sauces is by adding a *beurre manié*: this is a mixture of flour and butter, where the flour is beaten into the softened butter until a smooth, very thick paste is formed. Small pieces of this are then added to the simmering sauce which is whisked continuously until the butter melts and the flour is incorporated into the liquid. The sauce should be simmered for a few minutes longer until the flour thickening is cooked.

Other methods of thickening sauces include the addition of egg yolks. This method is more difficult and there is a danger of the sauce curdling if it is cooked over too high a heat or for too long. Mayonnaise-type sauces are thickened by adding oil to beaten egg yolks – this is referred to as a *liaison*. For success, the ingredients should all be at the same temperature before use. The eggs should be thoroughly beaten with the seasonings, then the oil added very slowly at first, in a steady stream later as the mixture thickens. Finally, lemon juice is added to both stabilize and flavor the mixture. This basic mayonnaise forms the starting point for many familiar sauces.

Modern kitchen gadgetry certainly has a useful role to play in the preparation of sauces and dressings. Turn to your food processor or blender whenever you prepare a mayonnaise, for example. Other speedy methods of preparation include one-stage sauces, where all the ingredients are put into a pan and whisked vigorously over the heat until they boil and thicken (for sauces which would otherwise be prepared by the roux method). Microwave ovens are also very useful for sauce-making and it is certainly worth following the manufacturer's instructions and experimenting with this cooking method.

For fruit sauces, purées and those dressings which require chopped ingredients, then there is no real substitute for the blender or food processor. For more conventional methods, a good heavy-based saucepan, wooden spoon and whisk are probably the cook's best friend.

Cherry Sauce

Serves 4

1 lb cherries
2 tablespoons sugar
juice of ½ lemon
1 pinch freshly grated nutmeg
1 pinch cayenne

Wash the cherries and remove the stalks and the pits. Place three-quarters of the cherries in a saucepan and add the sugar and lemon juice. Simmer over a low heat for 10 minutes. Purée this mixture in a blender or food processor, then sieve or pass through a vegetable mill to remove the cherry skins. Pour the juice obtained back into the saucepan and season with the nutmeg and cayenne. Add the remaining whole cherries and cook the sauce gently for a further 5 minutes.

Serve the sauce from a warmed sauceboat with game, pork or oily fish, such as mackerel or herring.

Choron Sauce

Serves 4

2 shallots, chopped
5 tarragon leaves, chopped *or* ½
    teaspoon dried tarragon
3 tablespoons wine vinegar
2 egg yolks
2 tablespoons water
salt and pepper
½ cup butter, softened
1 teaspoon tomato paste

Boil the shallots and tarragon in a heavy-bottomed saucepan with the wine vinegar until the vinegar has almost completely evaporated. Leave to cool.

Away from the heat, add the egg yolks and water. Mix well and season. Return the saucepan to a very low heat and whisk vigorously until the mixture is of a mousse-like consistency.

Turn off the heat and add the butter a little at a time and then add the tomato paste, stirring constantly to obtain a smooth consistency. Taste and adjust the seasoning. Choron sauce is an excellent accompaniment to broiled or fried steaks, poached or hard-cooked eggs or fried or broiled fish. Serve hot or warm in a sauceboat.

Onion Sauce

Serves 4

½ lb onions, chopped
¼ cup butter
1 tablespoon flour
2 cups milk
salt and pepper
2 tablespoons Crème Fraîche
　(page 398)

Blanch the onions by immersing them in a saucepan of boiling salted water for 5 minutes. Drain well and brown in a saucepan in half the butter. Cover and stew for 10 minutes over a low heat.

Meanwhile, prepare a béchamel sauce. Melt the remaining butter in a saucepan over a low heat. Add the flour and stir with a wooden spoon until smooth. Cook gently for 1–2 minutes. Pour in the milk little by little, continuing to stir until the sauce thickens. Add the onions to the sauce, season with salt and pepper to taste and simmer for 10 minutes.

Just before serving remove the sauce from the heat and add the cream, stirring it in carefully. Taste and adjust the seasoning.

Onion sauce is a perfect accompaniment for veal chops or cutlets, poultry, artichoke hearts, and hard-cooked or poached eggs.

Rémoulade Sauce

Serves 4

1 teaspoon strong mustard
1 yolk of a hard-cooked egg
salt and pepper
$\frac{2}{3}$ cup peanut oil
1 teaspoon vinegar
1 tablespoon capers
1 onion
1 bunch fresh herbs (for
   example chives, parsley,
   chervil)
2 gherkins

Mix together in a bowl the mustard and the hard-cooked egg yolk. Season and work to a paste. Add the oil little by little, whisking as you do so. Once the mixture has a smooth consistency, pour in the vinegar and mix gently for a little while longer.

Drain the capers thoroughly. Finely chop the onion and the herbs. Dice the gherkins and add all these to the sauce, mixing them in gently with a wooden spoon.

Taste and adjust the seasoning, adding extra mustard, salt and pepper as required. Pour the sauce into a sauceboat.

Rémoulade sauce is excellent for bringing out the flavor of cold cuts and fish. It is also a perfect accompaniment for some vegetables, particularly celery.

Béchamel Sauce

Serves 4

2 tablespoons butter
2 tablespoons flour
1½ cups cold or lukewarm milk
salt and pepper

It was Louis de Bechameil who, under Louis XV, invented this sauce which has now become important in the preparation of so many dishes.

Melt the butter in a heavy-bottomed saucepan over a low heat. Add the flour and stir with a wooden spoon until the mixture becomes white and foamy.

If using warm milk pour it in all at once off the heat. If using cold milk add it little by little over the heat. Some people say it is more difficult to avoid lumps if you pour the milk in a little at a time, but this is a personal matter. Stir well, return to a medium heat and stir continuously until the sauce thickens. Season to taste.

If the sauce is too thick you can add more milk while still stirring. Serve the sauce hot as an accompaniment to poached fish or vegetables. Béchamel sauce forms the basis for many other sauces such as Cheese or Mornay sauce.

Cheese Sauce

Serves 4

3 tablespoons butter
2 tablespoons flour
2 cups milk
salt and pepper
½ cup grated Gruyère cheese
1 egg yolk

Mornay sauce is simply a Béchamel sauce with cheese. Its origin is attributed to the famous dandy, Morny, a duke and half-brother to Napoleon III.

Melt the butter in a heavy-bottomed saucepan over a gentle heat. Add the flour and whisk until the mixture foams lightly. Pour in the milk all at once and bring to a boil, whisking continually to obtain a smooth cream. Season and simmer over a low heat for 10 minutes, stirring from time to time to prevent the sauce sticking. Remove from the heat and stir in the cheese and the egg yolk. Blend well, then taste and adjust the seasoning.

The flavor of the sauce can be varied by adding 2 or 3 pinches of grated nutmeg. Mornay sauce goes well with white meat and fish, and also with vegetables (e.g. asparagus). It is also excellent for gratin dishes.

Shrimp Sauce

Serves 6

½ cup butter
3 tablespoons flour
3 cups fish broth
salt and pepper
¼ teaspoon paprika
½ lb cooked peeled shrimp
juice of 1 lemon

Melt 3 tablespoons of butter in a heavy-bottomed saucepan. Add the flour and stir with a wooden spoon until the mixture is foamy. Allow to brown a little and then remove from the heat.

Pour the fish broth over the cooked roux. Whisk this sauce until smooth and then leave it to cook for 15 minutes over a gentle heat, stirring from time to time. Season with salt, pepper and a few pinches of paprika.

Mash the shrimp with the remaining butter and the lemon juice. Remove the sauce from the heat and add the shrimp mixture a little at a time, stirring constantly to obtain a smooth, creamy consistency. Taste and adjust the seasoning.

Serve immediately in a warmed sauceboat. Shrimp sauce is a good accompaniment for most fish dishes. It can also be served cold, sprinkled with paprika as an unusual salad dressing.

Chaudfroid Sauce

Serves 4

3 tablespoons butter
3 tablespoons flour
2 cups chicken broth
salt and pepper
1 pinch cayenne

Melt the butter over a low heat in a small saucepan and stir in the flour. Add the broth and bring to a boil, stirring constantly. Season to taste with salt, pepper and cayenne.

Once it has come to a boil, lower the heat and leave the sauce to simmer for 20 minutes, stirring from time to time to prevent sticking. Remove from the heat and leave to cool for a while.

This sauce is served warm or cold as an accompaniment to poultry, shellfish and fish. It is often used, mixed with gelatin to coat a cold dish.

Mushroom and Wine Sauce

Serves 4

¼ lb mushrooms
¼ cup butter
¼ lb cooked ham
1 bouquet garni
3 tablespoons flour
⅔ cup dry white wine
2½ cups chicken broth
1 truffle
⅔ cup Madeira
salt and pepper

Wipe and thinly slice the mushrooms. Brown them in a wide saucepan in the butter, remove from the pan and keep them warm.

Finely chop the ham and add it to the butter you fried the mushrooms in. Add the bouquet garni. Once the ham is golden, sprinkle it with flour, stir well with a wooden spoon and leave it to brown. Add the wine and broth and bring to a boil, stirring all the time. Chop the truffle and add it to the pan. Let the sauce simmer for 20 minutes, stirring from time to time to prevent sticking.

Remove the bouquet garni and add the mushrooms and then the Madeira. Cook for a further 3 minutes. Taste and adjust the seasoning.

Variation
This is a simpler and cheaper version of mushroom sauce. Wash ¼ lb of mushrooms as above, cut them into strips and sauté them in 3 tablespoons of butter. Add 2 chopped shallots and cook over a low heat for 2 or 3 minutes without browning them. Sprinkle with 1 tablespoon of flour and mix well with a wooden spoon to obtain a smooth, creamy mixture. Pour in 1¼ cups broth and ⅔ cup dry white wine. Add a bouquet garni and 1 tablespoon of tomato paste. Season and stir until it comes to a boil.

Cover and cook over a low heat for 20 minutes. Serve in a warmed sauceboat once you have removed the bouquet garni. This sauce is used to accompany white meat, chicken or rabbit.

Take care with sauces that contain white wine. They must be left to simmer for at least 20 minutes to reduce the acidity of the wine.

Red Wine Sauce

Serves 4

2 cups red wine
3 shallots, chopped
1 bouquet garni
$\frac{1}{2}$ cup butter
1 tablespoon flour
salt
1 pinch cayenne

Boil the red wine, finely chopped shallots and the bouquet garni in a heavy-bottomed saucepan for 10 minutes over a medium heat to reduce and concentrate the flavor.

Meanwhile, knead together in a bowl 2 tablespoons of the butter and the flour to form a small ball of paste.

Once the wine has reduced by half, strain it. Return it to the heat, season with salt and bring back to a boil. Mix the paste with 2 tablespoons of the wine. Pour into the saucepan, stirring continuously with a wooden spoon to obtain a smooth, homogeneous mixture. Leave to simmer over a very gentle heat until the sauce thickens.

Remove the pan from the heat and whisk in the remaining butter a little at a time. Season with a pinch of cayenne.

This sauce should be made just before it is required and used to garnish eggs, red meat and poultry.

Tomato Sauce

Serves 4

1 lb tomatoes
1 carrot
2 tablespoons olive oil
2 onions, chopped
1 teaspoon chopped fresh
    parsley
1 sprig of fresh thyme *or* pinch
    dried thyme
1 bay leaf
2 teaspoons flour
2 cloves garlic, crushed
1 tablespoon butter
1 teaspoon sugar
salt and pepper

Peel the tomatoes, halve them and remove the seeds.

Cut the carrot into thin strips and fry in a flameproof casserole in the oil along with the onion, parsley, thyme and bay leaf. Leave to soften for a few minutes.

Sprinkle with the flour and then add the garlic and tomatoes. Mix with a wooden spoon. Add a little water to moisten the mixture, cover and cook for 30 minutes over a low heat.

Strain the sauce through a fine sieve, pressing the mixture through to obtain a smooth purée. Return to a low heat and cook for 10 minutes, adding the butter and the sugar which will reduce the acidity of the tomatoes. Season to taste. If the sauce is too thick you can thin it with a little hot water.

This sauce can be served with vegetables, boiled meats and fish, but is most often served with pasta and rice dishes.

Suprême Sauce

Serves 4

3 tablespoons butter
2 tablespoons flour
2 cups chicken broth
1 cup finely chopped button
  mushrooms
salt and pepper
2 egg yolks
5 tablespoons Crème Fraîche
  (page 398)
2 teaspoons lemon juice

Heat the butter in a heavy-bottomed saucepan over a gentle heat. Add the flour and stir well using a wooden spoon until the mixture is pale and foamy.

Add the broth and the mushrooms. Season to taste. Stir until the sauce comes to a boil and leave to reduce for 20 minutes over a very low heat. Strain the sauce and discard the mushrooms, if desired.

Whisk together in a bowl the egg yolks, cream and lemon juice. Add this mixture to the sauce, off the heat. Mix well and return to a low heat to cook for 5 minutes. Do not boil.

Suprême sauce is traditionally used to accompany chicken, but can also be served with eggs and boiled vegetables.

Anchovy Butter with Capers

Serves 4

1 (2-oz) can anchovies
½ lb (2 sticks) butter
pepper
2 tablespoons capers, chopped

Pound the anchovies to a purée using a pestle and mortar or mash finely with a fork. Then gradually incorporate the butter, which should be soft (remember to take it out of the refrigerator in advance). You can speed up this process by working the anchovies and the butter in a food processor or blender. The mixture should be of a smooth consistency. Season with pepper and mix in the capers.

Anchovy butter can be used spread on lightly broiled canapés eaten as an hors d'oeuvre or first course, or it can be served to accompany broiled fish or meat, as well as poached eggs, in the same way as anchovy sauce.

Roquefort Sauce

Serves 4

2 tablespoons flour
3 tablespoons butter
3 oz Roquefort cheese
salt and pepper
$1\frac{1}{4}$ cups clear meat juices from a
  roast or good broth

Mix together in a bowl the flour and the butter. Work in the cheese with a fork until you have a smooth consistency. Season to taste with salt and pepper.

Bring the meat juices or broth to a boil in a saucepan and then add the Roquefort mixture a little at a time, stirring constantly with a wooden spoon. Once it has come back to a boil, lower the heat and whisk so that no lumps form. Cook over a gentle heat for 15 minutes, stirring from time to time. If the sauce becomes too thick, you can thin it by adding a little water.

Roquefort sauce can be used to accompany roast lamb or spit or oven-roasted veal dishes. It can also be used to garnish potatoes. In addition, it goes well with all kinds of vegetable salads (green salad, green bean salad and potato salad).

Walnut Sauce

Serves 4

½ cup broken walnuts
1 oz Roquefort cheese
salt and pepper
1 teaspoon lemon juice
½ cup olive oil

Grind the nuts in a pestle and mortar, blender or food processor. Mash the cheese and mix it with the walnuts in a bowl. Season with just a little salt and some pepper and mix well. Add the lemon juice, stir and then pour in the oil, a drop at a time to begin with, and then once the sauce begins to thicken, pour in the oil a little more quickly, whisking it vigorously as when making a mayonnaise. Taste and adjust the seasoning.

Walnut sauce goes very well with red meat dishes, whether hot (kabobs, broiled meats or fondue etc.) or cold (roast beef or roast lamb). It is also good with endive salad and is also an excellent flavoring for pasta or rice.

Deviled Sauce

Serves 4

$1\frac{1}{2}$ cups white wine
salt and pepper
$\frac{1}{3}$ cup vinegar
4 shallots, chopped
1 sprig of thyme
1 bay leaf
$\frac{1}{4}$ cup butter
3 tablespoons flour
2 cups chicken or beef broth
pinch cayenne
2 tablespoons chopped parsley

Put the wine in a saucepan and season with salt and pepper. Add the vinegar, shallots, thyme and bay leaf. Boil until reduced to approximately $\frac{2}{3}$ cup. Strain.

Meanwhile melt half the butter in a saucepan over a low heat. Add the flour and stir with a wooden spoon until the mixture is golden and frothy. Add the broth and bring to a boil, whisking constantly to obtain to smooth consistency. Simmer gently for 15 minutes. Add cayenne to taste.

Add the strained wine mixture, mix well and cook for a further 5 minutes. Remove from the heat and add the remaining butter, in small pieces and the chopped parsley.

Deviled Sauce should be served hot. It is excellent for bringing out the flavor of poultry, broiled meat and fish.

Armoricaine Sauce

Serves 4

2 tablespoons butter
1 onion, chopped
2 shallots, chopped
1 tablespoon chopped parsley
1 teaspoon fresh tarragon leaves
  or ½ teaspoon dried tarragon
2 tablespoons brandy
⅔ cup dry white wine
2 cups fish broth
2 tablespoons tomato paste
1 clove garlic, crushed
salt and pepper
pinch of cayenne
¼ cup Crème Fraîche (page 398)
2 tablespoons flour

Melt the butter in a heavy-bottomed saucepan and fry the onion, shallots, parsley and tarragon until soft but not browned. Pour over the brandy, bring to a boil and flambé over the heat. Add the white wine, the fish broth, the tomato paste, garlic, salt, pepper and cayenne. Do not cover, but leave to boil for 5 minutes.

Meanwhile, mix together the crème fraîche and flour in a bowl. Add this to the sauce a little at a time, whisking it as you do so. Simmer for 3 minutes. Taste and adjust the seasoning.

Serve the sauce from a warmed sauceboat as an accompaniment for fish or shellfish.

Garlic Mayonnaise

Serves 4

8 cloves garlic
1 egg yolk
salt
1 cup olive oil
juice of 1 lemon
1 tablespoon lukewarm water

Aïoli is a mayonnaise highly flavored with garlic, and this classic Provençal sauce has also given its name to the dish it accompanies which is made with boiled salted cod, boiled vegetables and small shellfish.

Peel the cloves of garlic and crush them, if possible in a pestle and mortar. Place in a bowl, add the egg yolk and salt and mix well. Pour in the oil, a drop at a time to begin with and then in a steady stream, whisking it constantly until you obtain a thick and creamy sauce.

When you have added about 4 tablespoons of oil, add the lemon juice and lukewarm water so that the sauce does not curdle. Once all the oil has been absorbed, taste and adjust the seasoning.

Serve the Aïoli in a bowl surrounded by the chosen accompaniments. Aïoli can also be served with potato salad or hot baked potatoes.

Variation

Another sauce from the South of France based on garlic and pepper is Spicy Provençal Sauce. The perfect accompaniment for Bouillabaisse and other fish soups, it is also used to garnish small croûtons served as canapés. To prepare this sauce, soak $\frac{1}{4}$ cup soft bread crumbs in $\frac{1}{2}$ cup of lukewarm milk. Once the bread has soaked up the milk, press it a little. Crush 3 cloves of garlic and a small seeded and chopped hot red pepper using a pestle and mortar. Add the soaked bread crumbs and mix it all together. Pour in $\frac{1}{2}$ cup of oil, a drop at a time, stirring constantly with a wooden spoon so that the mixture becomes the same consistency as mayonnaise. Season and add about $\frac{1}{2}$ teaspoon powdered saffron. You can also make this spicy sauce in a blender or food processor. At the last minute, instead of adding saffron you can add a tablespoon of tomato paste.

Crème Fraîche

This is a cream which has a special culture added in order to give a slight tang. An alternative can be prepared by mixing 1 tablespoon buttermilk into 2 cups whipping cream, then leaving it in a warm place for 2–3 hours. For a quick substitute, enliven whipping cream with just a little lemon juice.

Mustard Sauce

Serves 4

¼ cup butter
3 tablespoons flour
2 cups chicken broth
salt and pepper
2 tablespoons strong mustard

Melt the butter in a saucepan over a gentle heat and add the flour. Stir with a wooden spoon until the mixture is of a smooth consistency. Add the broth, season and bring to a boil, stirring until the sauce thickens. Remove the pan from the heat and add the mustard.

Mustard sauce goes well with rabbit and certain fish dishes and veal and lamb kidneys and sweetbreads. It is also served with various vegetables such as mushrooms.

Variation

There is a variation on this sauce which is even quicker to prepare. Mix together ⅔ cup Crème fraîche (page 398), 2 tablespoons of mustard and the juice of half a lemon and pour over your meat or fish dish just before the end of the cooking time so that the sauce is warmed up a little.

Burgundy Sauce

Serves 4

2½ cups red wine
3 shallots, finely chopped
1 bouquet garni
2 tablespoons butter
1 tablespoon flour
salt and pepper
pinch of cayenne
8 mushrooms, thinly sliced

Gently boil the wine, shallots and bouquet garni in a heavy-bottomed saucepan for about 10 minutes. Strain the liquid through a fine sieve.

In another saucepan, melt the butter over a gentle heat, add the flour and stir with a wooden spoon until the mixture is golden. Add the red wine and season to taste with salt, pepper and cayenne. Bring to a boil, stirring constantly to obtain a sauce of a smooth consistency. Cook for 5 minutes over a gentle heat. Add the mushrooms to the sauce and simmer for a further 10 minutes.

Serve this sauce in a warmed sauceboat. It is a perfect accompaniment for poached or hard-cooked eggs, freshwater fish and red meat.

Tartare Sauce

Serves 4

1 egg yolk
1 teaspoon vinegar
1 teaspoon strong mustard
salt and pepper
1 cup sunflower oil
1 onion, finely chopped
1 tablespoon chopped fresh
 mixed herbs (for example
 parsley, chives, chervil,
 tarragon)
5 gherkins, chopped
2 teaspoons capers

Whisk the egg yolk in a bowl with the vinegar, mustard, a pinch of pepper and $\frac{1}{2}$ teaspoon of salt. Once the mixture is of a smooth consistency, add the oil, a drop at a time to begin with, and then in a thin stream until the sauce begins to thicken. Whisk constantly at this stage to prevent curdling.

Add the onion, herbs, the gherkins and the capers. Taste the sauce, which should be spicy, and adjust the seasoning, ensuring that there is the correct amount of pepper.

Tartare sauce is a spicy mayonnaise. It is served cold, traditionally with fish dishes, although it also goes well with cold meats.

Béarnaise Sauce

Serves 4

⅔ cup vinegar
½ clove garlic, crushed
1 tablespoon chopped fresh
   herbs (for example parsley,
   chives, thyme, chervil)
2 shallots, chopped
2 egg yolks
salt
½ cup butter

Place the vinegar, crushed garlic, half the herbs and the shallots in a saucepan and reduce over a low heat until the vinegar has almost completely evaporated. Leave to cool. Add to the egg yolks in a bowl and whisk the ingredients, while adding 2 or 3 tablespoons of water to obtain a creamy mixture. Season with salt.

Cook this mixture in a bain-marie or double boiler, or place the bowl over simmering water and add the butter a little at a time, stirring constantly until the sauce becomes the consistency of a mayonnaise. Fresh, good quality butter will give the sauce a better flavor. Once the butter has been completely absorbed, remove the saucepan from the heat, taste the sauce and adjust the seasoning.

Serve the sauce in a sauceboat, sprinkled with the remaining herbs and use to accompany broiled meat or fish.

Maître d'Hôtel Butter

Serves 4

¼ cup softened butter
juice of ½ lemon
2 tablespoons chopped parsley
salt and pepper

Mash the butter in a dish with a fork until smooth and creamy. Add the lemon juice and parsley and season to taste with salt and pepper. Work with the fork until smooth again. Pack into a small pot and smooth the top. Alternatively, form into a roll, wrap in foil and chill in the refrigerator. Cut slices from the roll, as required.

Maître d'hôtel butter can also be served hot by simply melting the butter and makes the perfect accompaniment for all hot poached fish.

Variations

Beurre noir   This literally means black butter and can be prepared to accompany fish such as skate, boiled vegetables or variety meats. To make this, melt ½ cup butter in a skillet over a medium heat. Once it is frothy, add 1 tablespoon of chopped parsley, and 1 teaspoon of capers. Lower the heat so that the butter turns a light brown without burning. Once the butter has darkened, turn off the heat and quickly add 2 tablespoons of wine vinegar. Mix well and serve immediately.

Noisette butter   This is a variation on Beurre noir. Cooking is stopped at the moment the butter becomes a light hazelnut color. Lighter than beurre noir, it is, however, used in the same way.

Tarragon butter   Butter can be flavored in many different ways. The butter should be soft and worked into a smooth paste with a fork, as described above. Choose good quality butter. Add 3 tablespoons of chopped fresh tarragon to ½ cup soft, seasoned butter.

Garlic butter   Peel 6 cloves of garlic and cook for 8 minutes in a small saucepan of boiling water. Drain well, then add to ½ cup of soft butter.

Mustard butter   Add 2 tablespoons of strong mustard to ½ cup of soft butter. Mustard butter goes very well with beef, veal and pork.

Herb butter   Mix ½ cup of soft butter with 1 tablespoon of chopped chives, 1 tablespoon of chopped parsley and 1 of chopped chervil. Add salt to taste.

Mousseline Sauce

Serves 6

2 tablespoons Crème Fraîche
  (page 398)
3 tablespoons ice water
3 egg yolks
juice of $\frac{1}{2}$ lemon
salt and pepper
$\frac{1}{2}$ lb (2 sticks) butter, softened
$\frac{1}{3}$ cup vinegar

Whip together gently the crème fraîche and 1 tablespoon of the ice water in a bowl. As soon as the cream starts to increase in volume, whip it more quickly so that it attains the consistency of beaten egg whites.

Beat the egg yolks with the remaining ice water and a few drops of lemon juice in a heavy pan over a low heat or in a bowl over a pan of simmering water. Season and remove from the heat as soon as the mixture becomes creamy.

Add the butter, which should be soft, a little at a time, stirring constantly with a wooden spoon. Then add the vinegar and the remaining lemon juice. When the sauce looks like mayonnaise, taste and adjust the seasoning. Finally add the whipped cream to the sauce, folding it in gently. Pour into a sauceboat and serve immediately.

Mousseline sauce is a good accompaniment for poached fish, eggs and delicate-flavored vegetables.

Madeira Sauce

Serves 4

3 onions, chopped
$\frac{1}{4}$ cup butter
2 tablespoons flour
$\frac{2}{3}$ cup dry white wine
2 cups beef broth
salt and pepper
1 bouquet garni
$\frac{1}{3}$ cup Madeira

Fry the onions in the butter in a saucepan over a low heat. Once they are browned, add the flour and mix well using a wooden spoon. As soon as the mixture becomes a light brown, gradually add the white wine and the broth. Season and add the bouquet garni. Bring to a boil, stirring constantly, and cook over a gentle heat for 20 minutes.

Strain the sauce. Cook for a further 5 minutes, then add the Madeira at the last minute, stirring it in well. Taste and adjust the seasoning.

Ideally this sauce should be quite thin. If it becomes too thick, add a mixture of Madeira and broth. It should be served hot with broiled or roast meat. It also makes an unusual supper dish poured over hard-cooked eggs.

Barbecue Sauce

Serves 6

2 tablespoons olive oil
2 onions, chopped
1 lb tomatoes, peeled and
    quartered
2 cloves garlic, crushed
2 tablespoons vinegar
½ teaspoon celery salt
salt and pepper

Heat the oil in a heavy saucepan or flameproof casserole and fry the onions over a gentle heat until soft but not browned. Add the tomatoes, the garlic, vinegar and celery salt. Stir well with a wooden spatula. Cover and simmer for 25 minutes over a low heat, stirring from time to time to prevent the sauce sticking. If, after the end of the cooking time, the sauce is too liquid, take off the lid and cook for a further 5 minutes. If, on the other hand, the sauce seems too thick and looks as though it might burn, add a little water. Add salt and pepper to taste.

Barbecue sauce is not usually strained, but if you would prefer a smoother sauce, purée it in a blender or food processor and sieve or pass through a vegetable mill. Barbecue sauce can be served hot or cold with brochettes, meat dishes or grilled fish.

Mayonnaise

Serves 4

1 egg yolk
salt and pepper
1 tablespoon strong mustard
1 cup peanut or olive oil
1 tablespoon vinegar

Whisk the egg yolk, salt, pepper and mustard together until smooth. Add the oil a drop at a time, whisking continuously. Once the sauce begins to thicken, add the oil in a thin stream. Whisk in the vinegar which stabilizes the sauce. (The juice of a lemon can be used instead, if desired.) Taste and adjust the seasoning.

It is often thought difficult to prepare a good mayonnaise, but it need not be if you take the following precautions: do not exceed the correct amount of oil and use a fresh egg that has not been in the refrigerator for a long time, or an egg you have taken out of the refrigerator well in advance. Ideally the oil and the egg should be the same temperature. Mayonnaise can easily be made in a blender, following the instructions above, adding the oil through the hole in the lid a drop at a time.

Mayonnaise is the perfect accompaniment for cold fish cooked in court bouillon and cold roast meats, as well as for many hors-d'oeuvre and salads.

Curry Sauce

Serves 4

1 onion, chopped
2 tablespoons butter
1 tablespoon flour
2 teaspoons curry powder
2 cups chicken broth
salt and pepper
2 tablespoons Crème Fraîche
   (page 398)

Fry the onion in the butter in a heavy-bottomed saucepan until soft but not brown. Sprinkle in the flour and curry powder and stir with a wooden spoon until smooth. Stir in the broth, a little at a time. Season and bring the mixture to a boil over a medium heat, stirring constantly until the sauce thickens. Simmer for 15 minutes over a gentle heat, stirring from time to time. At the end of the cooking time, add the crème fraîche and mix in gently. Taste and adjust the seasoning.

Serve Curry sauce very hot with boiled chicken and rice, or with other meat (it is particularly good with lamb). It also goes well with hard-cooked or poached eggs.

Variations
You can make Curry sauce with 2 shallots instead of the onion, but it is then preferable to strain the sauce at the end of the cooking time to remove the shallots. You can also add, at the same time as the broth, $\frac{1}{3}$ cup dry white wine.

Cook's tip
To avoid a skin forming on a sauce, place a pat of butter on a fork and rub gently over the sauce to form a layer of butter. Reheat the sauce gently, stirring to incorporate the extra butter.

Vinaigrette Dressing

6 tablespoons olive oil
2 tablespoons wine vinegar
$\frac{1}{2}$ teaspoon Dijon-style mustard
$\frac{1}{2}$ teaspoon sugar
salt and pepper

Put all the ingredients in a screw-topped jar and shake thoroughly until the dressing is well combined. Use as required. The dressing can be stored in the refrigerator for several weeks.

Mint Sauce

Serves 4

$\frac{1}{4}$ cup water
2 tablespoons sugar
1 handful fresh mint leaves
salt
$\frac{1}{3}$ cup cider vinegar

Bring the water to a boil and add the sugar. Stir well until dissolved and remove from the heat.

Wash the mint leaves, shake them and chop them finely. Put them in a bowl with a pinch of salt. Add the vinegar and sugar syrup and leave to cool.

If possible, leave the sauce to stand for at least 30 minutes before serving for the flavors to develop. Mint sauce is excellent with all cuts of lamb. You can also serve Mint sauce with meatballs or fried croquettes.

Meat Sauce

Serves 4

2 tablespoons butter
1 onion, chopped
1 carrot, diced
2 stalks celery, chopped
1 slice of cooked ham
½ lb ground beef
salt and pepper
1 tablespoon flour
2 cups beef broth
¾ lb tomatoes, peeled

Heat the butter in a saucepan and fry the onion, carrot and celery until beginning to soften. Chop the ham and add it to the contents of the saucepan along with the beef and seasoning. Cook over moderate heat until the beef is browned, stirring to break up the lumps. Sprinkle over the flour, mix them together and leave to brown for a few minutes.

Add the broth and the tomatoes. Cover the saucepan, and simmer the sauce for 30 minutes over a gentle heat. Taste and adjust the seasoning.

This sauce is especially good with pasta or boiled rice and various gratin dishes.

Aurora Sauce

Serves 4

2 tablespoons butter
1 tablespoon flour
2 cups milk
1 tablespoon tomato paste
salt and pepper

Aurora sauce is a béchamel sauce flavored with tomato, and it is the tomato that gives it its pink color. This led to its name, Aurora sauce from the French word "*aurore*," meaning dawn.

Melt the butter in a heavy-bottomed saucepan over a gentle heat. Add the flour and mix well using a wooden spoon until the mixture becomes frothy.

Pour in the milk a little at a time, stirring constantly, until the sauce thickens. Cook for 10 minutes over a very gentle heat. At the end of the cooking time, add the tomato paste, stirring until you obtain a smooth consistency. Season to taste.

Serve the sauce in a warmed sauceboat to accompany poached or hard-cooked eggs, poached fish, white meat and vegetables such as cauliflower.

DESSERTS

If there is any way in which to make sure that a special meal leaves a lasting good impression, then it is by serving a spectacular dessert. This too, is the area in which most people are likely to experiment – the main course may be a well-tried favorite, served many times before, but often the dessert is a brand new recipe, attempted once only.

The same guidelines for menu planning apply here as well as in the very first chapter of the book. Even if the meal consists of the most spectacular dishes, if they are not selected to complement each other, then they are totally wasted. Think about the dessert course alongside the appetizer and the main dishes – will it clash dreadfully in flavor, texture or in content? If the first course is light and creamy, a mousse-like creation, then avoid serving a dessert which is similar in texture. Fruits may well be included in another course of the meal, combined with savory ingredients in a sauce, stuffing or salad, in which case they should be avoided for the dessert. If the weather is cool or the main course cold, then you may like to offer a hot dessert. These are just a few of the things to keep in mind before you plan the menu.

It is sometimes a good idea to offer more than one dessert; for example, some individual soufflés can be prepared along with a more substantial hot pudding. People have different ideas about the dessert – some save a space for the sweet dishes, others prefer a light fruit salad as a substitute to the richer alternatives. If you know your guests' tastes, then you can plan the

meal accordingly but if you are not sure, you may like to make a couple of dishes.

If you plan to serve a cheese course, then decide whether this is to be offered Continental-style before the dessert, between the main dish and the sweet, or at the end of the meal, just before the coffee. It really is a matter of personal preference, but it can be nice to finish eating savory food before the dessert.

In addition to desserts, you will find recipes for cookies included in this chapter. It is always a good idea to offer some crisp, light cookies with the dessert if it is a creamy one. You might like to serve a pitcher of cream with the dessert too. If you are trying to count the calories or if you are just trying to keep a firm hold on the healthy aspect of your diet, then there are ways in which the sweet course can be kept free from too much sugar, too much cream and lots of very rich mixtures without being banned completely.

Plain yogurt can be combined with fresh fruits, nuts and a little sugar or honey in a exciting and colorful chilled sundae. Fresh fruit salads can be served unsweetened given that the combination of fruits is one which already has sweeter ingredients – like figs, mangos and peaches – with the tart ones.

So even if you don't want to indulge yourself but feel you ought to prepare a dessert for others, try offering an alternative. Use your imagination and perhaps take up these suggestions to make the last course of the meal a luscious yet appropriate offering.

Almond Tuiles

Makes 15 cookies

3 egg whites
$\frac{2}{3}$ cup sugar
pinch of salt
3 tablespoons butter
$\frac{1}{3}$ cup flour
$1\frac{1}{4}$ cups flaked almonds

In a large bowl, mix the egg whites, the sugar and the pinch of salt with a wooden spoon just enough to amalgamate them. In a small saucepan, melt the butter. Add the flour to the egg white mixture and mix well, then add the butter. Mix everything with a wooden spoon to a quite smooth paste. Finally, mix in the almonds.

Cover a baking sheet with wax paper or baking parchment or, failing this, butter it generously. Place small heaps of the paste on it and flatten them well, leaving plenty of space for the cookies to spread. Bake in a preheated 375° oven for about 10 minutes. As soon as they are golden, loosen the cookies with a knife and place them on a rolling pin for a few seconds so that they harden and assume their characteristic curved shape. Bake the remaining mixture in the same way. Once they have cooled, keep in an airtight tin for up to a week.

Rocks

Makes 15 cookies

3 egg whites
small pinch of salt
$\frac{1}{4}$ cup water
1 cup sugar
$2\frac{2}{3}$ cups shredded coconut

Beat the egg whites with the salt until they form very stiff peaks. In a saucepan bring the water and the sugar to a boil over a gentle heat until small crystals are obtained. Pour the boiling syrup gradually over the whites, beating gently all the time until the mixture is both smooth and even. Gradually fold in the coconut.

Butter and flour a baking sheet. Using a spoon, shape mounds of mixture, well apart, on the sheet. Bake in a preheated 375° oven for 20 minutes, then turn up the oven temperature to 450° and bake for a further 5 minutes, watching to see that the cookies become quite golden but not too brown. After cooking, leave them to cool on a wire rack. Keep in an airtight tin.

Fig Cake

1h 45m

Serves 6

12 dried figs
$\frac{2}{3}$ cup raisins
$\frac{1}{4}$ cup rum
3 eggs
1 tablespoon brown sugar
$\frac{1}{4}$ cup runny honey
6 tablespoons butter, melted
2 packages active dry yeast
3 cups + 2 tablepoons flour
$1\frac{1}{2}$–$1\frac{3}{4}$ cups milk

Put 8 figs and the raisins to soak in the rum for at least 1 hour before beginning the cake. Reserve the other figs for decoration.

In a large bowl, beat the eggs and the sugar until pale and creamy. Add the honey. Fold in the butter. Mix the yeast with 2 cups of the flour and add it in small quantities to the mixture in the bowl. Beat to a smooth paste, then add the milk.

Drain the figs and the raisins reserving the rum. Chop the figs and coat them in the remaining flour. Add to the cake batter with the raisins. According to the consistency of the mixture, add 1–2 tablespoons of the rum used for soaking.

Butter and flour a 9 × 5 × 3 inch loaf pan. Pour the batter into it. Leave to rise in a warm place until the mixture is just below the top of the tin. Bake in a preheated 375° oven for 1 hour or until golden and firm to the touch. Leave to cool in the pan before unmolding. Decorate with the reserved figs.

Apple Roll

Serves 8

2½ cups flour
1 tablespoon oil
2 eggs
pinch of salt
½ cup water
1½ lb apples, peeled and diced
1 cup walnut halves
grated rind of ½ lemon
⅔ cup raisins soaked in 3
    tablespoons rum
½ cup sugar
⅔ cup butter, softened
1 cup soft bread crumbs
DECORATION
1 tablespoon confectioners'
    sugar
6 walnut halves

Pour the flour into a bowl and make a well in the center. Add the oil, one egg, the salt and water. Mix into a ball of smooth dough. Wrap loosely and leave to rest for 1 hour in a cool place.

Place the apples in a bowl. Add the walnuts, lemon rind, drained raisins and all but 1 tablespoon of the sugar. Mix well.

On a floured cloth, roll out the pastry to a ⅛-inch thick rectangle. Spread with 6 tablespoons butter. Sprinkle with the bread crumbs, leaving a 2-inch border, then spread the apple mixture over. Use the cloth to roll up the pastry, enclosing the filling in it. Seal the edges.

Put the roll on a buttered and floured baking sheet. Beat the remaining egg, sugar and butter, melted, together. Brush the cake with one-third of this. Bake in a preheated 375° oven for 40 minutes. During cooking glaze twice.

Cool on a wire rack. Serve as shown.

Crêpes Suzette

Serves 6

2 cups flour
1 cup sugar
3 eggs
2 cups milk
1 cup butter
pinch of salt
few drops of vanilla
grated rind and juice of 2
    oranges
½ cup Grand Marnier

Place the flour and 6 tablespoons of the sugar in a bowl and make a well in the center. Add the eggs and beat until smooth. Gradually stir in the milk.

Melt 6 tablespoons of the butter in a saucepan and blend it with the batter. Finally add the salt and the vanilla. Leave the batter to stand for 1 hour.

Before cooking each crêpe, grease the skillet or crêpe pan with some of the remaining butter or a little oil. Pour a ladleful of batter into the pan and tilt it in order to coat the bottom evenly. Cook the crêpe for 1 minute on either side over a moderate heat.

Fold each crêpe in four and arrange them in a serving dish; cover with a sheet of aluminum foil. Heat the rest of the butter and sugar, the orange rind and juice and 3 tablespoons of Grand Marnier to make a syrup. Heat the rest of the Grand Marnier separately. To serve, pour the syrup over the crêpes, then add the warm Grand Marnier and flame the dish at the table.

Kings' Cake

Serves 8

- ½ cup ground almonds
- ½ cup confectioners' sugar
- ¼ cup butter, softened
- 2 tablespoons flour
- ¼ cup granulated sugar
- ⅛ teaspoon vanilla
- 1 tablespoon rum
- 1 cup confectioner's custard (page 429)
- 1 (14-oz) package frozen puff pastry, thawed
- 1 egg yolk, beaten

Place the ground almonds, confectioners' sugar and butter together in a bowl. Mix with a wooden spoon until smooth. Add the flour, granulated sugar, vanilla and rum and mix well. Mix this almond cream with the confectioner's custard. Roll out the puff pastry to ⅛ inch thick, then cut out two rounds, each measuring 10 inches in diameter.

Using a pastry brush, brush the edge of one of the rounds of pastry to a width of 1 inch with some of the egg yolk and place on a baking sheet. Fill the center space marked out in this way with almond cream. Cover with the second round of pastry and seal the edges of the two rounds by pinching them together. Chill for 30 minutes.

Glaze the cake with the rest of the egg yolk, flute the edges and make several decorative incisions in the pastry. Bake in a preheated 400° oven for 40 minutes or until golden.

Floating Islands

Serves 4

2 cups milk
1 cup sugar
few drops of vanilla
4 large eggs, separated
2–3 tablespoons water

Heat the milk in a saucepan with 2 tablespoons of the sugar and the vanilla. Beat the egg whites into stiff peaks and fold in 6 tablespoons of the sugar, in two stages, mixing very gently. Place this meringue mixture, a tablespoonful at a time, in the hot milk. Poach the meringues for about 2 minutes turning them over carefully. Take them out of the milk and drain them, one after the other, in a sieve.

In a large bowl, beat the egg yolks with a fork. Gradually add the milk used for poaching, stirring all the time. Pour the mixture into a saucepan or place the bowl over a pan of simmering water. Cook over a very gentle heat stirring all the time until the custard thickens. Do not allow to boil. Leave the custard to cool, then pour it into a shallow bowl. Arrange the meringue "islands" on it.

Dissolve the remaining sugar in the water over a low heat. Increase the heat and allow the syrup to boil until golden. Trickle this caramel over, cool and serve.

Strawberry Tart

Serves 6

$\frac{1}{2}$ cup butter, softened
$\frac{1}{2}$ cup granulated sugar
1 egg
$\frac{1}{4}$ cup ground almonds
2 cups flour
1 cup confectioner's custard
  (page 429)
$2\frac{1}{2}$ pints strawberries
1 tablespoon strawberry jam
1 tablespoon confectioners'
  sugar for decoration

The rich flan pastry should be prepared the day before: cream together the butter and the granulated sugar in a large bowl, then work in the egg and the ground almonds. Add the flour and mix thoroughly – the pastry must be evenly blended. Add a little ice water if necessary to bind. Cover the pastry with plastic wrap and leave overnight in the refrigerator.

Next day prepare the confectioner's custard. Take the pastry out of the refrigerator and, on a floured worktop, roll it out to a thickness of $\frac{1}{4}$ inch. Line an 8-inch quiche or tart pan with the pastry and prick it with a fork. Fill the inside of the pastry case with the confectioner's custard. Bake in a preheated 425° oven for 25 minutes. During this time, wash, hull and wipe the strawberries. Remove the tart from the oven and allow to cool.

Arrange the strawberries on the confectioner's custard. Mix the jam with a little lukewarm water and brush the tart with this syrup. Sprinkle the confectioners' sugar over the pastry edge.

French-Style Waffles

For 6 waffles

2 cups milk
½ cup butter
pinch of salt
2 cups flour
4 eggs
½ cup Crème Fraîche (page 398)
confectioners' sugar for
    sprinkling

In a saucepan, boil half the milk with the butter and the salt. Remove from the heat and add the flour, stirring with a wooden spoon. Mix everything over a moderate heat for a few seconds until it becomes very liquid. Pour this mixture into a bowl. Add the eggs, one at a time, beating continuously.

In another saucepan, heat the rest of the milk, then add the crème fraîche and mix carefully. Blend this second mixture with the first, stirring gently.

Heat the waffle-iron for 3 minutes. Butter it lightly. Pour in a little batter and cook the waffle until the steaming stops. Sprinkle the waffles with confectioners' sugar and serve them hot or lukewarm. The waffles may simply be sprinkled with freshly squeezed lemon juice or served with jam or fresh or stewed fruit and cream.

French Toast

Serves 6

4 eggs
2 cups milk
⅔ cup sugar
12 1-inch-thick slices stale
    bread
½ cup butter
1 tablespoon ground cinnamon
½ cup rum

Beat the eggs in a large bowl as for an omelette. Add the milk and ½ cup of the sugar and whisk everything to mix thoroughly. Spread the bread slices with half the butter.

In a skillet, heat half of the remaining butter over a moderate heat. Dip the slices of buttered bread into the egg and milk mixture and add to the pan. Brown the slices lightly on both sides in the hot butter. Repeat this operation for all the slices, adding the remaining butter to the pan as necessary.

Arrange the French toasts in a serving dish. Sprinkle with a mixture of the remaining sugar and the ground cinnamon. Heat the rum in a small saucepan, pour over the French toast and flame it in front of your guests just before serving.

Note: French toast is popular with children. Instead of leaving the slices of bread whole, you can cut them into little pieces and omit the rum.

Flambé Bananas

Serves 4

4 bananas, not too ripe
$\frac{1}{4}$ cup butter
$\frac{1}{4}$ cup sugar
$\frac{1}{2}$ cup rum
1 tablespoon red currant jelly
  (optional)

Peel the bananas and cut them in half lengthwise. Heat the butter and the sugar in a skillet over a moderate heat. When the sugar begins to color, add the bananas. Reduce the heat a little and leave the bananas to cook for 2 minutes on each side, turning them over carefully so as not to break them.

Bring the rum to a boil in a small saucepan over a gentle heat. Arrange the bananas on a warmed serving dish. Sprinkle them with the mixture from the skillet and the boiling rum just before serving. Flame the dish at the table in front of your guests. Serve with red currant jelly, if liked.

Cherry Clafoutis

Serves 6

2½ pints cherries
1¼ cups milk
2 cups flour
1 cup sugar
pinch of salt
6 eggs
¼ cup butter

Rinse and stalk the cherries but do not remove the pits as they will retain more flavor like this.

Warm the milk in a saucepan. Mix the flour, the sugar and the salt in a bowl and beat in the eggs. When the mixture is quite smooth, add the warm milk a spoonful at a time, stirring until the batter has the consistency of a thick cream.

Generously butter an ovenproof dish or pan and cover the bottom with a thin layer of the batter. Put the dish over a moderate heat for 3 minutes so that the batter solidifies and forms a crust. Remove the dish from the heat. Quickly arrange the cherries in the pan and pour in the rest of the batter. Bake in a preheated 425° oven for 45 minutes. Serve the clafoutis still warm.

Chantilly Cups

Serves 4

1 quart Crème Fraîche (page 398)
¾ cup sugar
1 teaspoon vanilla
2 pints red currants

First make the Chantilly cream: Whip the crème fraîche with a few tablespoons of iced water until thick. Add the sugar, a spoonful at a time, whipping the cream continuously. Mix in the vanilla. Once thickened, the cream should be firm and very white. Chill the cream.

Carefully wash the red currants and strip them from the stalks, reserving several small bunches for decoration. Mix the cream with the red currants and divide this mixture between sundae glasses. Decorate with the reserved bunches of red currants. Serve chilled.

Nectarines with Custard Cream

Serves 4

CONFECTIONER'S CUSTARD
1 quart milk
1 vanilla bean
6 egg yolks
½ cup sugar

POACHED FRUIT
2 lb nectarines
6 tablespoons red currant jelly, warmed
1 cup flaked almonds

First make the confectioners' custard. Bring the milk to a boil with the vanilla bean split in half lengthwise. Meanwhile, beat the egg yolks with the sugar in a large bowl until pale and creamy. Add the milk a little at a time, removing the vanilla bean, and mix carefully. Pour this custard back into the saucepan and warm it over a gentle heat, stirring all the time with a wooden spoon, and taking care that it does not boil. When the cream coats the back of a spoon, remove it from the heat and allow it to cool.

Poach the nectarines in boiling water for 3 minutes, then leave them to cool slightly before peeling them. Cut them in half and take out their pits.

Pour the custard into a deep dish and place the nectarine halves on top. Brush the fruit with red currant jelly. Quickly toast the shredded almonds in a skillet or under the broiler and sprinkle them over the nectarines. Serve cold.

Pear Tart

Serves 6

BASIC PIE PASTRY
2 cups flour
pinch of salt
$\frac{1}{2}$ cup butter or margarine
$\frac{1}{3}$ cup ice water
FILLING
4 firm pears (about 2 lb)
2 eggs
$1\frac{1}{4}$ cups milk
3 tablespoons sugar

First make the pastry: sift the flour and salt into a bowl and rub in the butter. Add enough ice water to mix to a short dough. Flour a work surface and roll out the pastry until it is about $\frac{1}{4}$ inch thick. Use to line an 8-inch loose-bottomed quiche or flan dish and prick the bottom all over. Bake blind in a preheated 375° oven for 25 minutes.

Peel the pears, halve them and remove their cores. Arrange the halves in the pastry case. Mix the eggs, milk and the sugar together and pour this mixture over the pears. Bake the tart for a further 25 to 30 minutes or until the filling is cooked. Cool before serving.

Coffee Layer Cake

Serves 8

1 quantity Genoese Sponge
    Cake Batter (page 448)
1 egg
$2\frac{1}{2}$ cups confectioners' sugar
$\frac{1}{2}$ cup butter, softened
$\frac{1}{4}$ cup coffee flavoring
$\frac{1}{2}$ cup granulated sugar
2 tablespoons rum
2 tablespoons water
1 cup Crème Fraîche (page 398)

Pour the cake batter into an 8-inch cake pan. Bake in a preheated 375° oven for 40–45 minutes or until well risen and golden. Unmold onto a wire rack to cool. When cool, cut the cake into three layers using a knife with a serrated edge.

In a bowl placed over a pan of simmering water, warm the egg and 1 cup of the confectioners' sugar. Whisk until the mixture is pale and creamy. Add the softened butter and beat vigorously. Blend in 2 tablespoons of the coffee flavoring. Remove this buttercream from the heat.

Make a syrup with the granulated sugar, the rum and water. Soak the cake layers with it and place the bottom layer on a plate. Spread over half the buttercream. Cover with the second cake layer and spread with the remaining buttercream. Put the top cake layer in place.

Warm the crème fraîche and the remaining confectioners' sugar together over a very low heat for about 5 minutes. Stir in the remaining coffee flavoring. Cover the top and sides of the cake with this icing. Decorate with coffee-bean shaped candies, if obtainable.

French Prune Tart

Serves 6

1 quantity Basic Pie Pastry
  (page 431)
1 cup sugar
$\frac{1}{2}$ cup water
$\frac{1}{2}$ lb (about 2 cups) prunes,
  soaked overnight if necessary
3 eggs
1 cup Crème Fraîche (page 398)

Roll out the pastry to a thickness of $\frac{1}{4}$–$\frac{1}{2}$ inch and use to line an 8-inch quiche or tart pan. Prick it with a fork and line it with parchment paper and a handful of dried beans. Bake "blind" in a preheated 375° oven for 7 or 8 minutes. The pastry must be just dry.

Meanwhile, dissolve half of the sugar in the water in a saucepan over a moderate heat. When the syrup has come to a boil, poach the prunes in it for about 15 minutes or until soft. Drain and pit the prunes. Arrange in the pastry case. Mix the eggs with rest of the sugar. Add the crème fraîche and beat the mixture lightly. Pour it over the prunes. Return the tart to the oven and bake for 30 minutes or until the filling is set and lightly browned. Serve this tart warm or cold.

Baked Alaska

Serves 6

1 cup sugar
½ cup Grand Marnier
2 tablespoons water
1 round sponge cake or pound
  cake, purchased or homemade
1 small block vanilla ice cream
4 egg whites

Dissolve 6 tablespoons of the sugar in 3 tablespoons of the Grand Marnier and the water. Cut the cake into three layers and brush each with the syrup. Place the bottom layer on a baking sheet. Top with the block of ice cream and wrap the remaining two cake layers around the ice cream to enclose it completely. Trim the cake to fit. Freeze until the cake and ice cream are firm.

Beat the egg whites into stiff peaks. Add the remaining sugar in two parts, whisking after each addition to form a meringue. About 10 minutes before serving take the ice cream cake out of the freezer. Cover it entirely with meringue, making a decorative pattern with a fork. Bake in a preheated 425° oven for a few minutes until lightly browned. While the meringue is cooking, heat the remainder of the Grand Marnier. Flame the warm liqueur, pour it over the cake and serve immediately.

Apple Cake

Serves 8

2 eggs
1 cup sugar
1¼ cups Crème Fraîche (page 398)
⅓ cup milk
2 cups self-rising flour
⅓ cup rum
5 large apples
2 tablespoons butter
1 quantity Basic Pie Pastry (page 431)

In a large bowl mix the eggs with the sugar, the crème fraîche and the milk. Add the flour and rum and mix everything together. The batter should not be too thick; if it is add a little milk. Peel the apples, remove the cores and cut them into fairly thin slices. Stir the fruit into the batter.

Butter an 8-inch quiche or tart pan or loose-bottomed cake pan and line it with the pastry. Pour in the apple mixture. Bake in a preheated 400° oven for 45–50 minutes. Unmold the cake and serve warm or cold.

Millefeuille

Serves 6

1½ lb frozen puff pastry, thawed
2 cups Confectioner's Custard
  (page 429)
3 tablespoons rum
¼ cup confectioners' sugar
½ cup chopped hazelnuts

Divide the pastry into 3 equal portions. Roll out each portion to a rectangle ⅛ inch thick. Leave to rest for 2 hours in the refrigerator. Prepare the Confectioner's Custard. Leave it to cool and mix in the rum. Prick each rectangle of pastry with a fork, lay these on baking sheets and bake in a preheated 425° oven for 20 minutes. Leave to cool. Put together the layers of puff pastry with Confectioner's Custard. Sprinkle the top of the millefeuille with confectioners' sugar and press the chopped hazelnuts along the sides.

Apple Fritters

Serves 4

½ package active dry yeast
1 cup lukewarm water
1 cup flour
pinch of salt
2 tablespoons oil plus oil for
    deep frying
1 lb apples
¼ cup sugar
½ cup rum
1 egg white

Dissolve the yeast in the lukewarm water. Leave in a warm place until frothy. Sift the flour and salt into a bowl. Make a well in the middle and add the oil and the yeast liquid. Gradually beat the flour into the liquid to make a thick batter. Leave to rise in a warm place for 1 hour.

Peel and core the apples and cut them into 1-inch thick slices. Leave them to macerate with the sugar and rum in a small bowl.

In a bowl, beat the egg white into stiff peaks. Fold it very lightly into the batter just before cooking the fritters.

Heat the oil for deep frying to 375°. Drain the apple slices before plunging them into the batter. When they are well coated, lower them one at a time into the hot oil. Cook until evenly browned and crisp. Drain the fritters on paper towels. Dust them with extra sugar and serve immediately.

Cream Puffs with Chocolate Sauce

Serves 6

⅔ cup water
¼ cup butter
½ cup + 2 tablespoons flour
2 eggs
FILLING
⅔ cup heavy cream
2 tablespoons confectioners'
    sugar
CHOCOLATE SAUCE
½ lb (8 squares) semisweet
    chocolate
¼ cup light corn syrup
¼ cup butter

Put the water and butter in a saucepan and heat gently until the butter melts, then bring quickly to a boil and tip in all the flour. Remove the pan from the heat. Beat well until the mixture forms a smooth paste which comes away from the sides of the pan. Leave to cool slightly.

Beat the eggs, then add them to the paste, beating all the time and continue to beat thoroughly until the paste is very smooth and glossy. Grease 2 large baking sheets and pipe or spoon small amounts of the paste well apart on them. Bake in a preheated 425° oven for 20 to 25 minutes, or until the puffs are well risen and golden.

Remove the puffs from the oven and split them open immediately – make a hole just large enough to fill the puffs with cream. Leave on a wire rack to cool.

Meanwhile, whip the cream with the confectioners' sugar. Melt the ingredients for the chocolate sauce together in a bowl over a saucepan of hot water. Fill the cooled buns with the cream and pile them on a serving plate or in individual dishes. Stir the sauce to combine all the ingredients thoroughly, then pour it over the cream puffs and serve at once.

Rice and Cherry Mold

Serves 6

1 quart milk
1 vanilla bean
½ cup sugar
1 cup short-grain rice
1 (16-oz) can cherries, drained

In a saucepan, boil the milk with the vanilla bean, split in half, and the sugar. Meanwhile, in another saucepan, cook the rice for 2 minutes in boiling water. Drain it, then add it to the boiling milk. Cover the saucepan and leave the rice to cook over a very gentle heat until it has absorbed the milk. Stir from time to time during cooking.

Remove the vanilla bean. Add the cherries to the rice and mix well. Pour the rice into a 1¾-quart mold. Press down lightly with a spoon, and leave to cool for 1 hour before putting in the refrigerator. Chill for several hours and unmold before serving.

Pear Cake

Serves 6

1¾ lb pears
2 eggs, separated
⅛ teaspoon salt
¾ cup sugar
1 teaspoon vanilla
1 teaspoon ground cinnamon
3 tablespoons warm water
1¼ cups self-rising flour
1¼ cups cornstarch

Butter an 8-inch loose-bottomed cake pan and line the bottom with parchment paper. Peel the pears and cut them in half. Remove the core. Arrange them in the bottom of the prepared pan. Set aside.

Beat the egg yolks with the salt, sugar, vanilla and cinnamon in a large bowl. Add the warm water and beat the mixture again. Sift together the flour and cornstarch. Fold carefully into the batter. Beat the egg whites until stiff and fold into the batter.

Pour the batter over the pears in the pan. Bake in a preheated 400° oven for 30 to 40 minutes or until risen and golden brown.

Allow the cake to cool for a few minutes in the pan, then unmold and cool on a wire rack. Serve cold.

Walnut Pudding

Serves 6

12 slices stale bread
½ cup sugar
2 cups milk
1½ cups walnut halves
3 pieces crystallized orange peel
2 eggs, separated
10 sugar cubes
1 tablespoon water

Cut the stale bread into pieces, sprinkle with the sugar and soak it for 30 minutes in the milk. Reserve a few walnut halves for decoration and chop the rest with the orange peel. When the bread is swollen, mash it with a fork and mix in the walnuts and peel. Add the egg yolks. Beat the egg whites into stiff peaks and fold them into the walnut mixture.

In a charlotte mold or 8-inch cake pan, dissolve the sugar cubes in the water over a moderate heat. As soon as the caramel turns golden, remove from the heat and tilt the mold to coat the sides evenly. Pour the pudding batter into the mold and place in a bain-marie. Bake in a preheated 425° oven for 1 hour. Leave the pudding to cool slightly before unmolding it. Decorate it with the reserved walnut halves before serving.

Chocolate Truffles

Makes 35 truffles

$\frac{3}{4}$ lb (12 squares) bittersweet or
   semisweet chocolate
$1\frac{1}{4}$ cups Crème Fraîche (page
   398)
3 tablespoons butter
2 tablespoons cocoa powder

Melt the chocolate in a bowl over a pan of simmering water. Meanwhile, bring the crème fraîche to a boil in a small saucepan. Leaving the bowl of chocolate over the hot water, pour in the cream and mix with the melted chocolate. Stir with a wooden spoon until the cream is completely absorbed by the chocolate. Add the butter in pieces and stir until the mixture is smooth and evenly blended. Leave the mixture to cool until it reaches a workable consistency.

Using a teaspoon, form balls the size of a walnut and roll them in the cocoa. Chill for at least 5 hours. These truffles must always be kept in a cold place, preferably a refrigerator.

Peach Soufflé

Serves 6

1 quart milk
1 vanilla bean
6 eggs
1½ cups sugar
¾ cup flour
2 lb peaches
½ cup water
pinch of salt
½ cup shredded almonds

Boil the milk with the split vanilla bean. Whisk 2 whole eggs and 4 yolks with ⅔ cup of the sugar until the mixture turns pale and creamy. Fold in the flour until smooth. Blend the strained hot milk with this mixture, a little at a time. Return to the pan and bring to a boil over a gentle heat, stirring continuously. Pour it into a buttered soufflé dish.

Peel the peaches. Cut them in half and take out the pits, then cut them into quarters. Poach the quarters in a syrup made with ½ cup of the sugar and the water. Leave the peaches in the syrup until lukewarm.

Beat the four egg whites with a pinch of salt into stiff peaks and gradually beat in the remaining sugar. Fold in the almonds. Tip the peaches into the soufflé dish and cover with the meringue. Bake in a preheated 325° oven for 10 to 15 minutes or until the meringue turns golden.

Lemon Tart

Serves 8

1 quantity Basic Pie Pastry
  (page 431)
$\frac{1}{2}$ cup butter
$\frac{1}{2}$ cup sugar
5 lemons
6 eggs, separated
pinch of salt

Roll out the pastry to a thickness of $\frac{1}{4}$ inch and use to line an 8-inch quiche or tart pan. Prick the bottom with a fork. Bake "blind" in a preheated 425° oven for 10 minutes. Set aside. Reduce the oven temperature to 350°.

In a heavy-bottomed saucepan, melt the butter and the sugar with the grated rind and juice of 4 of the lemons over a very gentle heat. Add the egg yolks, stirring continuously, and continue stirring until the mixture thickens. Do not allow to boil. Remove from the heat. Taste the mixture and add more sugar if necessary. Beat the egg whites with a pinch of salt into stiff peaks. Fold them gently into the lemon mixture.

Fill the pastry case with the mixture and bake the tart for 20 minutes. At the end of cooking, make sure that the filling is firm; if it is not, bake it a little longer. Serve the tart warm or cold, decorated with the remaining lemon cut into decorative slices.

Lemon Mousse

Serves 4

4 eggs
$\frac{3}{4}$ cup sugar
1 cup water
2 tablespoons cornstarch
juice of 3 lemons
1 egg white
$\frac{1}{2}$ cup heavy cream
thinly pared rind of 1 orange
(optional)

Beat the whole eggs with the sugar in a large bowl until pale and creamy. Heat the water in a saucepan. Meanwhile, dissolve the cornstarch in a little cold water. Add the hot water and lemon juice, return the mixture to the pan and bring to a boil. Cook for 2 minutes, stirring, then beat into the egg mixture. Pour back into the saucepan and cook over a gentle heat, stirring with a wooden spoon, until thickened. *Do not let the mixture boil.* Leave to cool, stirring it from time to time to prevent a skin forming.

Beat the egg white into stiff peaks. Whip the cream. Fold the cream gently into the mousse together with the beaten egg white. Divide the mixture between 4 individual glass dishes and chill for at least 1 hour before serving. Decorate with thinly pared orange rind if liked.

Rum Savarin

Serves 6

3 eggs
$\frac{3}{4}$ cup sugar
3 tablespoons butter, melted
$\frac{1}{2}$ cup milk
4 cups flour
1 package active dry yeast
1$\frac{1}{4}$ cups water
$\frac{1}{3}$ cup rum
DECORATION
1 cup heavy cream, whipped
a few crystallized fruits

In a large bowl, beat the eggs with $\frac{1}{2}$ cup of the sugar until the mixture turns pale and creamy. Add the melted butter, then the milk which you have warmed to blood heat. Sift the flour and mix it with the yeast. Fold it into the egg mixture, a little at a time.

Generously butter a savarin (ring) mold and flour it. Pour the batter into it and leave it to rise in a warm place until doubled in size.

Bake in a preheated 350° oven for 25–30 minutes. About 5 minutes before taking the savarin out of the oven, make the syrup: dissolve the rest of the sugar in the water. Add the rum. Leave the syrup to warm over a gentle heat without allowing it to boil. Take the savarin out of the oven, unmold it onto a serving dish and pour over the hot syrup. Serve the savarin cold, decorated with whipped cream and a few crystallized fruits such as angelica, orange peel and glacé cherries.

Rhubarb Pie

Serves 6

2 lb rhubarb
1½ quantities Basic Pie Pastry
  (page 431)
3 tablespoons ground almonds
⅔ cup sugar
1 egg yolk, beaten

Trim the rhubarb and cut into 1-inch pieces. Cook it in simmering water for 5 minutes, then drain well.

Divide the pastry into two unequal parts, one for the bottom crust and the other for the lid of the pie. Roll out the larger piece to ¼ inch thick and use to line a deep pie pan. Sprinkle with the ground almonds and half the sugar. Add the pieces of rhubarb and the rest of the sugar. Roll out the remaining pastry thinly and lay over the pie. Dampen the edges and press them together to seal. Flute the edges. Cut a slit in the lid to allow steam to escape. Using a pastry brush, glaze the top of the pie with egg yolk. Bake in a preheated 400° oven for 40 to 45 minutes or until golden brown.

Quince Paste

For 3 lb of paste

2 lb quinces
about 3 cups sugar
extra sugar for dusting

Wipe the quinces, cut them in half and cook them for 15 minutes in boiling water. Drain and pass them through a sieve. Measure the purée obtained and mix it in a saucepan with an equivalent quantity of sugar. Cook for 20 minutes over a moderate heat, stirring briskly and continuously with a wooden spoon. At the end of cooking, the mixture should be the color of light caramel.

Oil a dish or roasting pan and fill it with the quince mixture. Leave it to dry for 2 days in a dry place sheltered from dust. Cut the paste into little squares. Roll these in sugar so that they are well coated on all sides. Keep them in an airtight tin, separating each layer with wax paper or aluminum foil.

Christmas Log

Serves 8

4 eggs
1 cup sugar
1 cup flour
$\frac{1}{4}$ cup Grand Marnier
2 tablespoons water
1 (16-oz) can chestnut purée
$\frac{1}{4}$ lb (4 squares) semisweet
   chocolate

To make the Genoese sponge cake, warm the eggs and half the sugar in a bowl over a pan of simmering water. Beat until the mixture turns pale and creamy. Remove from the heat and fold in the flour.

Line the bottom of a jelly roll pan with parchment paper. Butter it with a brush. Pour the cake batter into the pan in a 1-inch layer. Bake in a preheated 450° oven for 5 to 10 minutes, or until well risen and golden. Unmold and leave it to cool.

In a saucepan, dissolve the remaining sugar in half of the Grand Marnier and the water. Bring to a boil over a gentle heat, stirring all the time. Brush this syrup over the cake.

Beat the chestnut purée with the rest of the Grand Marnier. Spread about three-quarters of this mixture over the cake. Roll it up and cover the ends with the rest of the chestnut mixture. Melt the chocolate in a bowl over a pan of simmering water. Spread it over the log and decorate it by scoring with a fork.

Surprise Melons

Serves 6

6 small melons (for example
  cantaloupes)
6 peaches
2 pints red currants
1 orange
$\frac{1}{2}$ bottle medium-dry
  champagne
6 tablespoons sugar

Cut off the top part of the melons and keep the lids.
Scoop out and discard the seeds. Using a grapefruit
knife, or small spoon, empty out some of the melon flesh.
Cut the flesh into dice and place in a bowl. Peel the
peaches, take out their pits, and cut them into little cubes
or balls. Wash the red currants and detach them from
the stalks. Squeeze the orange.

In a bowl, mix the champagne, the sugar and the
orange juice and pour over the mixed fruits. Fill the
melons with this fruit salad. Chill before serving.

Coffee Mousse

Serves 6

⅔ cup sugar
6 eggs, separated
1 quart milk
1 tablespoon instant coffee
   powder or granules
pinch of salt
small chocolate bar

Beat the sugar with the egg yolks until the mixture becomes foamy. Boil the milk and pour it gently into the eggs, mixing it carefully. Return the mixture to the saucepan and cook over a very gentle, heat stirring continuously and *without allowing it to boil*. When the custard coats the back of the spoon remove the saucepan from the heat. Add the instant coffee and mix well.

Beat the egg whites with a pinch of salt into stiff peaks. Fold them gently into the warm custard. Pour this mousse into individual glasses or into a large bowl and leave it to cool. When cool, chill for at least 1 hour. Decorate with chocolate curls, pared thinly from the chocolate bar.

Crystallized Fruit Cream

Serves 8

⅔ cup raisins
5 tablespoons Cointreau
1 quart milk
3 tablespoons ground rice
4 eggs
2 egg yolks
1 cup sugar
1 cup diced crystallized fruits
extra glacé cherries for
   decoration

Put the raisins in a bowl and sprinkle them with the Cointreau. Heat all but 5 tablespoons of the milk in a saucepan. Mix the ground rice with the reserved cold milk. Add to this the hot milk, return to the saucepan and bring to a boil. Simmer gently for 3 minutes, stirring all the time. Beat the whole eggs and the egg yolks with the sugar. Stir into the rice mixture and cook gently, *without boiling*, until thickened like a Confectioner's custard (see page 429).

Remove from the heat and stir in the crystallized fruits, the raisins and the Cointreau in which they have been soaked.

Pour the rice cream into a dampened mold and leave to cool. Chill for at least 3 hours before unmolding onto a serving dish. Decorate with glacé cherries.

Apricot Charlotte

Serves 6

2 cups Confectioner's Custard
  (page 429)
¼ cup rum
1 (2-lb) can apricots in syrup
12 thin slices of bread
6 tablespoons ground almonds
15 apricots preserved in liqueur
  or dried apricots soaked
  overnight in brandy or wine
1 cup whipped cream

Prepare the confectioner's custard, flavoring it with the rum. Drain the syrup from the apricots and reserve. Cut the apricots into fine slices.

Toast the slices of bread and cut into broad strips. Quickly dip the slices of toast in the apricot syrup and place them at the bottom and up the sides of a 1-quart charlotte mold. When your mold is completely lined with bread, cover the bottom with a layer of confectioner's custard, then add a layer of apricot slices and 2 tablespoons of ground almonds.

Add another layer of bread, again dipped in the apricot syrup. Repeat these layers twice more and finish with a layer of soaked bread. Place a plate and a weight on top of the charlotte. Chill for at least 12 hours. Unmold the charlotte onto a serving dish and decorate it with the apricots in liqueur and whipped cream.

ICED DESSERTS

Ice creams, sherbets and other frozen desserts are often the simplest to prepare. They can be made in advance (and need to be) ready for taking to the table at the last minute.

Throughout this chapter, the recipes suggest using an electric ice cream maker. These are the most time-saving gadgets to rely on, but the ices can be prepared just as successfully by hand. The important thing to remember is that if you want to make a very smooth ice cream, it will need to be whisked several times during freezing to break down the ice crystals which are formed. An ice cream maker does this for you by keeping the mixture stirred all the time it is freezing. If you do not have one, then take the mixture out of the freezer when it is half frozen and whisk it thoroughly. If you have a food processor, then it is ideal for this. Put the mixture back into the freezer, and repeat the whisking process at least once more or as often as possible. The more the mixture is whisked, then creamier the result will be.

Once you have achieved the texture required leave the mixture to freeze completely. Before serving, put the ice cream into the refrigerator for about 30 minutes, so that it will be soft enough to scoop. If the dessert is a molded one, dip the container briefly in hot water, dry it and unmold the dessert. This may need a short standing time in the refrigerator before it is soft enough to serve.

You will find some unusual and imaginative ideas for ways in which to serve iced desserts in this chapter. For example, the ices can be served in fruits, in the form of soufflés. Make or buy some light dessert cookies to accompany the ices because they will offer a contrast in texture. Some chopped toasted nuts, crushed macaroons or crushed caramel can also be sprinkled over the ice cream if you want to make it a bit different.

If you have never attempted to make your own ice creams before, then you will find plenty of inspiration in this chapter and if you are already a convert, then hopefully you will enjoy trying some of these ideas and add them to your repertoire. The key to success when making ice creams must lie in patience – allow plenty of time and keep whisking the mixture to ensure perfect results.

Orange Granita

Serves 6

¼ cup sugar
1 cup water
1 bottle good dessert wine such
   as Monbazillac or Sauternes
juice of 2 oranges
juice of 1 lemon
sprigs of fresh mint for garnish

You do not need an ice cream maker for this simple granita, but it must be made 6 hours in advance because the mixture takes a very long time to crystallize.

Dissolve the sugar in the water then bring to a boil. Pour the syrup into a large bowl and leave to cool. As soon as the syrup is cold, pour the white wine and the fruit juices into it. Mix with a whisk.

Transfer the mixture to an ice cube tray or trays or a plastic, freezerproof container and place in the freezer.

After 1 hour, stir and beat the liquid evenly with a fork, detaching the edges, which solidify first of all and mixing them into the still liquid part in the center. Carry on in this way until the mixture has completely crystallized into light flakes. You will need to repeat the operation three or four times before crystallization is finished.

Fill six sundae dishes with the granita and top each with a sprig of mint. Serve immediately. This granita also goes well with fresh or canned peaches.

Note: Granitas are a kind of water ice. They are very refreshing, and are made from a light sugar syrup base, flavored with the juice or pulp of various kinds of fruit, or else tea, coffee or chocolate. In order to arrive at their special texture – flaky and slightly granular – you must not use an ice cream maker. This, by stirring the mixture, would prevent the ice crystals from forming. When crystallization is complete, granita should be taken out of the freezer, otherwise it would turn into a block of ice. While waiting to serve it, put it into iced dishes for a few minutes, then place in the refrigerator. But be careful, granita cannot wait for very long.

Litchi Sherbet

Serves 6

1 lb canned litchis in syrup
grated rind and juice of 2 limes
6 tablespoons sugar
2 egg whites
1½ pints strawberries, washed
   and hulled
1 cup heavy cream

Drain the litchis, reserving the syrup. Mix the lime juice with the syrup from the litchis. Pour into a saucepan, add the sugar and dissolve over a low heat. Boil then cool.

Purée the litchis in a blender or food processor. Add the syrup to this purée. Beat the egg whites into stiff peaks and fold into the litchi purée. Pour into an ice cream maker. Place in the freezer and freeze until completely set (about 2½ hours). Alternatively, pour the litchi purée and syrup into a freezerproof container. Freeze until slushy, then whisk well to break up the crystals. Fold in the egg whites and freeze until firm.

Purèe the strawberries. Whip the cream in a very cold bowl. Fill a pastry bag with it.

Scoop the sherbet into dishes, add the whole strawberries. Decorate with cream piped into whirls. Serve with the strawberry purée, sweetened to taste.

Peach Ice Cream

Serves 6

4 ripe peaches
$\frac{3}{4}$ cup sugar
1 tablespoon kirsch
$1\frac{1}{4}$ cups plain yogurt
$\frac{2}{3}$ cup heavy cream
$1\frac{1}{2}$ pints raspberries
juice of 1 lemon

Scald the peaches for 1 minute, then peel them. Cut into pieces. Put $\frac{1}{2}$ cup sugar with $\frac{1}{2}$ cup water into a heavy-based saucepan. Dissolve over a low heat, then boil. Off the heat, cool slightly.

Purée the peach with the sugar syrup. Add the kirsch and yogurt. Mix well, then pour into a charlotte mold. Freeze until set around the edges; this will take about $1\frac{1}{2}$ hours. Whisk the mixture, loosening the frozen mixture from the mold. Lightly whip the cream and fold it into the mixture in the mold. Re-freeze. Leave to set for 1 hour or until slushy, then beat the ice cream with a fork. Do the same 1 hour later and then leave to set without disturbing it again.

Reserve a few raspberries for decoration. Purée the rest with the lemon juice and remaining sugar. Put in a cool place.

Just before serving, unmold the peach ice cream. Pour over the raspberry purée and decorate with the reserved raspberries.

457

Tea Ice Cream

Serves 4 to 6

1¾ cups milk
2 teaspoons Earl Grey tea leaves
1 strip of lemon rind
½ cup sugar
3 eggs, separated
⅔ cup heavy cream
FOR THE DECORATION
1 cup heavy cream
⅓ cup confectioners' sugar
  (optional)

Put the milk, tea and lemon rind into a heavy-based saucepan. Bring slowly to a boil, then cover and leave to infuse for 10 minutes. Strain the contents of the saucepan and reheat until it almost boils, then remove.

Put the sugar and the egg yolks in a bowl. Beat until the mixture becomes pale and creamy, then add the hot milk, little by little. Return the mixture to the saucepan and cook over a very low heat, stirring all the time, until the froth on top disappears. Pour into a bowl and leave to cool completely.

Whip the cream lightly, then fold it gradually into the cooled egg mixture. Pour the mixture into an ice cream maker and freeze. Alternatively pour into a freezerproof container and freeze, whisking two or three times during freezing to prevent ice crystals forming.

For the decoration, whip the cream. Fold in the confectioners' sugar, if using. Scoop the ice cream into little bowls. Decorate with whirls of cream.

Apricot and Almond Ice Cream

Serves 4

½ lb (about 1½ cups) dried apricots, soaked overnight in 1¼ cups warm water
2 strips lemon rind
½ cup ground almonds
3 drops almond extract
⅔ cup heavy cream, lightly whipped
8 fresh apricots
VANILLA CREAM
2 cups heavy cream
1 vanilla bean
3 egg yolks
½ cup sugar
PURÉE
1½ pints raspberries
3 tablespoons sugar

Put the apricots in a saucepan with the water they were soaking in. Add the lemon rind and heat gently. Cook for about 10 minutes. Remove the lemon rind and leave to cool a little then purée in a blender or food processor. Leave to cool completely.

For the vanilla cream, heat the cream with the vanilla bean in a saucepan. Put the egg yolks and the sugar into a bowl. Mix well, then add the hot cream, removing the vanilla bean. Cook for 2 to 3 minutes. Leave to cool.

Fold the apricot purée into the vanilla cream followed by the ground almonds and almond extract, then the whipped cream. Pour into an ice-cream maker and freeze. Alternatively, place in a freezerproof container freeze, whisking twice during the freezing process.

Purée the raspberries and sugar. Sieve to remove the seeds. Split the apricots and fill with a ball of ice cream. Arrange them on top of the raspberry purée. Decorate with the shelled apricot kernels, if liked.

Iced Rainbow Soufflé

Serves 8 to 10

8 egg yolks
1 cup sugar
1 teaspoon vanilla
$\frac{2}{3}$ cup heavy cream
$1\frac{1}{2}$ pints raspberries
$\frac{1}{2}$ cup finely chopped pistachio
    nuts
3 tablespoons ground hazelnuts
3 tablespoons ground almonds
1 teaspoon coffee flavoring
DECORATION
chocolate curls
a few sugar coffee beans

Prepare a bain-marie or bring some water to simmering point in a large saucepan. Put the egg yolks, sugar and vanilla into a large bowl.

Place the bowl in the bain-marie or over the hot water and beat the egg yolks with the sugar over a low heat for 10 minutes until the sugar has completely dissolved and the mixture is really smooth. The mixture should be thick enough to spread.

Take the bowl out of the bain-marie and place it inside another bowl containing ice cubes to stop the cooking process. Continue beating the mixture until it is so thick that it does not stick to the sides of the bowl.

Take the bowl out of the ice. Whip the cream in another bowl until thick and fold into the egg yolk mixture.

Purée the raspberries in a blender or food processor, then sieve to remove the seeds.

Divide the egg yolk mixture into four equal portions.

Mix the raspberry purée into one portion, the pistachios into another, the hazelnuts and almonds into the third and the coffee flavoring into the last. Put everything into the refrigerator still in separate bowls.

Wrap a collar of wax paper (double thickness) around the top of a soufflé dish, so that its height is increased by 3 to 4 inches. Fasten at the side with tape or a paper clip.

Pour in the first layer, then freeze for 30 minutes. Add the second layer and freeze. Continue the layering, freezing each before adding the next, until you have completed the layers.

Leave your soufflé in the freezer for 3 to 4 hours. Take it out and carefully remove the wax paper. Place the soufflé in the refrigerator for 10 minutes to soften it and bring out the flavors. Decorate with chocolate curls and sugar coffee beans.

Variations
You can of course make this iced soufflé with any other flavorings you like, as long as you take care with the mixtures and freezing the layers. The following alternative flavors are delicious, for example: coffee, pistachio, chocolate, hazelnut.

The secret of success with multi-flavored soufflés is making absolutely sure that each layer is given adequate time to set in the freezer.

Tropical Fruit Sherbet

Serves 4

½ cup granulated sugar
⅔ cup water
3 bananas
juice of 4 oranges
2 tablespoons white rum
1 egg white
¼ cup confectioners' sugar
1 small fresh pineapple

Melt the granulated sugar over a low heat in the water. Leave to cool.

Peel the bananas and mash finely. Mix with the orange juice. Add the sugar syrup and 1 tablespoon white rum to the fruit. Stir well and freeze in an ice cream maker or freezerproof container.

Beat the egg white to firm peaks and fold in the confectioners' sugar. After one hour, stop the ice cream maker. Mix in the beaten egg white. Continue freezing the sherbet for as long as necessary.

Slice the pineapple. Remove the hard central core and the skin. Cut four slices into small pieces. Macerate in a cool place in the remaining tablespoon of rum.

Just before serving, fill the sundae dishes with the sherbet, mixing in the pineapple pieces. You can hang half a pineapple slice over the edge of each dish.

Pineapple Surprise Cake

Serves 6 to 8

1 round deep sponge cake
ICE CREAM
1 pineapple (weighing about
   $1\frac{3}{4}$ lb)
$\frac{1}{2}$ cup confectioners' sugar
$1\frac{1}{4}$ cups plain yogurt
PURÉE
$1\frac{1}{2}$ pints raspberries
$\frac{1}{4}$ cup sugar
DECORATION
3 reserved slices pineapple
3 glacé cherries
a few pieces of candied angelica
a few pieces of orange rind

Peel the pineapple and remove the central core. Cut and reserve 3 slices. Cut the remaining flesh into small pieces and purée in a blender or food processor with the confectioners' sugar and the yogurt. Pour into an ice cream maker and freeze.

Turn the cake upside down on a pastry board and cut off a thin slice from the bottom. Then hollow out the cake, being careful not to make holes in the outside.

Take the ice cream out of the freezer and let it soften slightly. Fill the hollowed out sponge cake with the ice cream, pressing it down and smoothing it out. Then cover with the slice of cake that was cut off, to re-form the original cake shape. Turn the right way up on a plate.

Purée the raspberries in a blender or food processor with the sugar. Sieve this purée to remove the seeds.

Pour the purée over the cake. Decorate as shown and serve at once.

Stuffed Pineapple

Serves 6

1½–2 cups red or black soft fruit
   (e.g. black currants, red
   currants, raspberries,
   blackberries)
2 small apples
2 tablespoons water
juice of 1 lemon
2 tablespoons Calvados or
   applejack
1¼ cups heavy cream
½ cup sugar
½ cup crushed praline
¾ cup ground pistachios
1 medium-sized pineapple
DECORATION
½ kiwi fruit, peeled and sliced
few sprigs of mint

Trim the soft fruits, wash and drain them. Peel the apples and core them. Cut into pieces. Put all the fruit in a saucepan and cook over a gentle heat with the water and the lemon juice for 15 minutes. The fruit should be reduced to a pulp. Leave to cool. Add the Calvados. Mix well and sieve.

Whip the cream and divide into three portions. Mix the first portion with half the sugar and the fruit pulp. Pour into an ice cream maker and freeze.

Mix the praline and half the remaining sugar into the second portion of cream. Mix the pistachios with the remaining sugar and then with the third portion of cream. Pour these two mixtures into separate freezer-proof containers and freeze, whisking twice.

Cut the pineapple in half, including the leaves. Hollow it out, and fill with scoops of praline, pistachio and fruit ice cream. Decorate and serve at once.

Cream Hearts With Strawberries

Serves 4

3¼ cups heavy cream
2 egg whites
2½ pints strawberries
½ cup milk
¼ cup sugar

Whip 2 cups of the cream until thick. Beat the egg whites to firm peaks. Fold the egg whites carefully into the whipped cream.

Line one large or four small heart-shaped perforated molds (coeur-à-la-crème molds) with cheesecloth. Pour the mixture in. Fold the four corners of the cheesecloth back over the top and stand the molds on a plate. Put in the refrigerator for 3½ hours.

Just before serving, hull, wash and drain the strawberries. Put the remaining cream, the milk and the sugar in a bowl and whip until thick. Take the mold or molds out of the refrigerator. Carefully unfold the corners of the cheesecloth and unmold the cream hearts onto a plate. Cut the strawberries in half and arrange on top. Pipe the whipped cream around the edges. Serve well chilled.

Orange Parfait

Serves 6

1 cup heavy cream
2¼ cups milk
3 egg yolks
6 tablespoons granulated sugar
4 oranges
1¾ cups confectioners' sugar
1 tablespoon rum
1 egg white

Place a bowl containing the cream and ¼ cup of the milk in the refrigerator.

Make a custard by stirring the remaining milk, the egg yolks and the granulated sugar over a very low heat until it coats the back of a spoon. When the custard is ready, pour it into a deep bowl and beat for 5 minutes at a moderate speed. Chill the custard for 30 minutes so that it is the same temperature as the cream.

Thinly peel 3 of the oranges. Put the peel to one side. Remove the segments of orange from the membrane, discarding the white pith, and remove the seeds. Save the juice. Put the orange segments and juice into a blender or food processor and blend well. Add the confectioners' sugar and the rum. Mix and put aside in a cool place.

Take the bowl of cream out of the refrigerator. Whip until thick, taking care not to overbeat. Put to one side.

Take the custard out of the refrigerator. Beat the egg white to stiff peaks. Fold together the custard, whipped cream, orange purée and beaten egg white, little by little. Pour into an ice cream maker and freeze for 3 hours. Alternatively, place in a flameproof container and freeze, whisking twice during freezing to obtain a smooth texture.

Wash and scrub the remaining orange. Cut six slices from it. With a pastry cutter or sharp knife, cut decorative shapes out of the reserved orange peel, for decoration. Poach them for 3 minutes in a saucepan of boiling water. Drain and put to one side.

As soon as the ice cream is frozen, decorate the bottom of a fluted mold with the orange slices and the orange peel shapes. Fill with the ice cream, pressing down well. Put the mold back in the freezer for at least 1 hour.

Turn the parfait out of the mold and serve immediately with langues de chat cookies or wafers.

Grapefruit Sherbet

Serves 4

4 grapefruits
1 cup water
$\frac{2}{3}$ cup granulated sugar
1 orange
1 egg white
$\frac{1}{4}$ cup confectioners' sugar

Grate the rind of one of the grapefruits. Dissolve the granulated sugar in the water on a gentle heat. Add the grated rind and leave for about 10 minutes.

Add the squeezed juice from two of the grapefruits and the orange. Cool, strain and pour into an ice cream maker, reserving one tablespoonful. Freeze.

Beat the egg white to soft peaks. After $1\frac{1}{2}$ hours, add the reserved tablespoon of syrup, beaten egg white and confectioners' sugar. Put back in the freezer until completely frozen. Alternatively, pour the juice and syrup into a freezerproof container and freeze until mushy. Whisk well and fold in the egg white and confectioners' sugar. Freeze until firm.

Halve the remaining grapefruits. With a serrated knife, remove the grapefruit segments and then remove the membranes from the segments. Make tooth-shaped notches all around the edges of the grapefruit shells. Scoop the sherbet into balls. Place these in the grapefruit shells and decorate with grapefruit segments.

Lemon Granita

Serves 4

1¼ cups water
⅔ cup sugar
4 lemons
1 orange
lemon slices for decoration
½ cup vodka

Put the water and sugar in a saucepan. Heat gently to dissolve the sugar, then bring to a boil and remove from the heat. Grate the rinds of two of the lemons. Add to the warm sugar syrup and leave to cool.

Squeeze the juice from all four lemons and the orange. Add the fruit juice to the syrup. Strain through a fine sieve. Pour the mixture into ice cube trays or a freezerproof container and place in the freezer.

After about 1 hour, when the mixture is beginning to freeze around the edges, take the trays out of the freezer and stir the contents well with a wooden spatula, taking care to loosen the frozen edges. When the consistency is even, put the trays back in the freezer.

Freeze the granita for about 2 hours. It will then have formed large crystals of ice, but will not have solidified. Crush with the spatula to make small crystals.

Divide the granita between four sundae glasses. Put back in a cool place until ready to serve. Decorate with lemon slices and pour over some well-chilled vodka.

Pistachio Ice Cream in Pineapple Boats

Serves 4

8 egg yolks
1 cup granulated sugar
1 teaspoon vanilla
$\frac{2}{3}$ cup heavy cream, whipped
$1\frac{1}{4}$ cups finely ground pistachio nuts
3 tablespoons confectioners' sugar
2 tablespoons boiling water
TO SERVE
2 small pineapples
$\frac{2}{3}$ cup heavy cream, lightly whipped
2 oranges, cut into segments
$\frac{1}{2}$ cup flaked almonds, toasted
4 teaspoons chocolate sprinkles

Prepare a bain-marie or bring a large pan of water to simmering point. Put the egg yolks, granulated sugar and vanilla into a large bowl. Place the bowl in the bain-marie or over the pan of hot water and beat until the sugar has completely dissolved and the mixture is really smooth. It should be thick enough to spread. Take the bowl out of the bain-marie and put it on ice to stop the cooking process. Continue beating the mixture until it is thick enough not to stick to the sides of the bowl. Take the bowl off the ice. Fold in the cream.

Mix together the pistachios, confectioners' sugar and boiling water. Add this to the cream mixture. Pour into an ice cream maker and freeze.

Make 4 boat shapes out of the pineapples. Take the ice cream out of the freezer. Scoop out balls of the ice cream and arrange them in the pineapple boats. Decorate as shown and serve at once.

Iced Strawberry Fondant

Serves 6 to 8

3 pints strawberries
1 tablespoon lemon juice
3 cups confectioners' sugar
$2\frac{1}{2}$ cups heavy cream
3 cups milk
1 vanilla bean
6 egg yolks
$\frac{2}{3}$ cup granulated sugar

Wash the strawberries, drain and hull them. Purée them in a blender or food processor, reserving one for decoration. Sieve this purée, then add the lemon juice and the confectioners' sugar, a little at a time. Make sure the cream is very cold, then whip it, and fold carefully into the fruit purée. Pour the mixture into a fluted mold and freeze for 1 hour. Then beat the ice cream with a fork to break up the crystals. Freeze until firm.

Heat the milk with the vanilla bean, split lengthwise. Beat the egg yolks with the granulated sugar in a small bowl. Add the milk little by little (having discarded the vanilla bean). Cook over a gentle heat, stirring all the time until the foam on the surface disappears and the custard coats the back of the spoon. Cool.

Just before serving, unmold the strawberry ice cream onto a plate and pour a little custard sauce all around it. Decorate. Serve with the remaining custard sauce.

Yogurt and Cheese Ice Cream

Serves 4 to 6

1 (16-oz) can evaporated milk
$\frac{3}{4}$ cup confectioners' sugar
$1\frac{1}{4}$ cups plain yogurt
$\frac{1}{2}$ cup ricotta or small-curd cottage cheese
grated rind and juice of 2 lemons
lemon slices for decoration

Chill the evaporated milk in the refrigerator for 1 hour. Take it out and whip until it thickens. Then add the sugar, the yogurt and the cheese, still beating. Add the lemon rind and juice and mix well.

Pour the mixture into a charlotte mold or a deep cake pan. Put in the freezer and freeze for 1 hour. Then beat with a fork and freeze for another hour. Repeat the beating twice more, then leave to set.

Just before serving, plunge the mold for a few seconds into boiling water, then unmold the ice cream onto a serving dish. Decorate with slices of lemon.

Variations

You can serve this ice cream as an appetizer with a few scoops of tomato sherbet. Put 2 tablespoons sugar and $\frac{2}{3}$ cup water in a saucepan and dissolve the sugar over a gentle heat. Bring to a boil, then leave to cool. Add 2 tablespoons lemon juice, $1\frac{1}{4}$ cups tomato juice, 1 teaspoon of Worcestershire sauce, 6 drops of hot pepper sauce, 1 teaspoon of soy sauce and $\frac{1}{4}$ teaspoon of celery salt. Season with pepper and mix together well. Pour into an ice cream maker and freeze. Alternatively, freeze in a freezerproof container, whisking twice to obtain a smooth texture. To serve, halve a few tomatoes, remove the seeds, put in balls of sherbet and cover with the lids. Serve these stuffed tomatoes with the yogurt ice cream.

Alternatively, serve with cucumber sherbet. Squeeze $\frac{1}{2}$ lemon and add 1 teaspoon of unflavored gelatin. Put $\frac{1}{4}$ cup sugar and 1 cup water in a saucepan. Dissolve the sugar and bring to a boil; cool slightly, then pour in the lemon juice mixture. Mix together well. Peel a cucumber and cut into cubes, removing the seeds. Peel 2 very firm apples. Cut them into quarters, remove the core and cut the flesh into pieces. Put the cucumber, apples and the syrup into a blender or food processor and reduce to a purée. Add 1 teaspoon of dill, and some salt and pepper. Pour into an ice cream maker and freeze. Alternatively, freeze in a freezerproof container, whisking twice to obtain a smooth texture. Serve scooped into balls with the yogurt ice cream. Chop a sprig of fresh dill over each sherbet ball.

Iced Vanilla Bombe

Serves 8

6 tablespoons sugar
$\frac{1}{4}$ cup water
$1\frac{1}{2}$ cups strawberries
$\frac{2}{3}$ cup heavy cream
4 egg yolks
2 tablespoons orange liqueur
CUSTARD
3 cups milk
1 vanilla bean
6 egg yolks
$\frac{1}{2}$ cup sugar

Make the custard: heat the milk with the vanilla bean to boiling point. Leave to infuse. Beat the egg yolks with the sugar and pour over the strained hot milk. Return to the saucepan and cook over a very low heat until the custard coats the back of a spoon. Leave to cool. Pour the custard into an ice cream maker and freeze. Line the bottom and sides of a chilled mold with two-thirds of the ice cream. Re-freeze.

Dissolve the sugar in the water, boil, then cool. Hull and purée the strawberries. Whip the cream. Beat the 4 egg yolks in a bowl and add the sugar syrup, strawberry purée, whipped cream and orange liqueur.

Take the mold out of the freezer. Pour the strawberry mousse in, to within $\frac{1}{2}$ inch of the top. Finish with a layer of vanilla ice cream. Freeze for 12 hours.

Serve with a purée of red fruit, for example strawberries or raspberries.

Strawberry Vacherin

Serves 6

1 meringue case, bought or
   homemade
VANILLA ICE CREAM
2 cups milk
1 vanilla bean
4 egg yolks
$\frac{1}{2}$ cup granulated sugar
$\frac{2}{3}$ cup heavy cream
DECORATION
$1\frac{1}{2}$ pints strawberries
1 cup heavy cream
$\frac{1}{2}$ cup confectioners' sugar

Put the meringue case in the refrigerator.

Prepare the vanilla ice cream. Bring the milk to a boil with the split vanilla bean. Beat the egg yolks with the sugar until creamy. Pour over the hot milk, continuing to beat. Return the custard to the saucepan and cook over a very gentle heat, stirring constantly, until the custard coats the back of a spoon.

When the custard is ready, remove the vanilla bean and stir in the cream. Chill for about 30 minutes, stirring with a wooden spatula from time to time to prevent a skin from forming. Pour the mixture into an ice cream maker and freeze. Alternatively, freeze in a freezerproof container, whisking to obtain a smooth texture.

Take the meringue case out of the refrigerator. Fill with scoops of ice cream, then decorate with the strawberries and cream whipped with the confectioners' sugar.

Melon Ice Cream

Serves 4

3 small melons, including one
  weighing about 1½ lb
½ cup sugar
1 tablespoon orange juice
2 tablespoons lemon juice
1 cup heavy cream

Cut the largest melon in half. Remove the seeds, and then the flesh, using a small spoon and collecting the juice. Strain the juice and add enough water to make up to 1¼ cups. Purée the melon flesh in a blender or food processor. Put to one side. Pour the melon juice into a saucepan with a heavy base. Add the sugar and dissolve over a gentle heat. Then bring to a boil. Remove from the heat and cool slightly. Add the syrup to the melon purée, together with the orange and lemon juices.

Whip the cream and fold carefully into the melon mixture. Put in an ice cream maker and freeze. Alternatively, freeze in a freezerproof container, whisking twice during freezing to obtain a smooth texture. Just before serving, halve the other melons. Remove the seeds. Fill the melon halves with ice cream. Decorate with pieces of candied angelica and serve immediately.

Iced Strawberry Soup

Serves 5

2½ pints strawberries
2 lemons
2 cups milk
1 cup heavy cream
½ cup sugar
½ teaspoon vanilla
½ cup flaked almonds

Wash and hull the strawberries. Put them in a large bowl. Grate the rind of one lemon, then squeeze the juice from both lemons. Pour the juice over the strawberries and add the grated rind. Mix together well and macerate for 30 minutes in a cool place.

Put the milk in the freezer for 5–10 minutes. Put the cream in a very cold large bowl, add the sugar and the vanilla and whip until thick.

Toast the almonds in a skillet or under the broiler.

Take the milk out of the freezer, put it in a bowl and beat for 1 to 2 minutes until foamy. Pour the milk into a deep, very cold, serving bowl. Add about ten ice cubes, then the whipped cream, in spoonfuls. Then add the strawberries, halved. Sprinkle with the flaked almonds. Serve well chilled.

Iced Chocolate Mousse

Serves 6

¾ lb (12 squares) bittersweet or
   semisweet chocolate
⅔ cup water
⅔ cup sugar
2½ cups heavy cream
3 egg whites
a little grated chocolate for
   decoration

Break the chocolate into pieces and put in a saucepan with the water. Melt in a bain-marie. Alternatively place the chocolate and the water in a bowl above a pan of simmering water.

Add the sugar, mix well and cook for 10–15 minutes, stirring all the time. Allow to cool.

Whip the cream in a very cold bowl. Beat the egg whites to firm peaks in another bowl. Add the whipped cream to the chocolate. Then carefully fold in the egg whites, lifting the mixture as you blend in order not to lose the air beaten into the whites.

Wrap a strip of wax paper around a soufflé dish and keep in place with a rubber band or a piece of tape. Pour in the mixture up to the top of the paper. Freeze for 4 hours.

Just before serving, carefully remove the wax paper. Decorate the top of the soufflé with a little grated chocolate. Serve immediately.

Variations
As soon as the first red fruit such as strawberries, raspberries and red currants start appearing in the markets, you can make this iced mousse with it. Use 1½ pints fruit, all one type or mixed, to taste. Purée in a blender and then sieve. Mix the purée with ½ cup sugar. Allow the sugar to dissolve for 3 to 4 minutes so that it blends in well. Add the whipped cream and fold in the egg whites as described above. Pour into a soufflé dish and leave to freeze for 4 hours. Decorate with fresh mint leaves and a few pieces of reserved fruit.

You can also make these recipes in individual soufflé dishes, with wax paper wrapped around.

Serve the chocolate mousse with a hot coffee sauce. First make some very strong coffee. Mix ⅔ cup coffee with ⅔ cup sugar. Bring to a boil and simmer for 1 minute. Put to one side. Dissolve 1 tablespoon of cornstarch in 2 tablespoons cold water. Add to the coffee/sugar mixture and cook for 3 to 4 minutes until the sauce thickens slightly. Remove from the heat. Finally add 2 tablespoons coffee liqueur.

Melons with Liqueur Ice Cream

Serves 4

2 cups Crème fraîche (page 398)
$\frac{3}{4}$ cup sugar
$\frac{1}{4}$ teaspoon vanilla
3 egg yolks
6 tablespoons fruit liqueur (for example strawberry, pear etc.)
4 small melons (for example cantaloupe)
pieces of shredded chocolate for decoration

Heat the cream very slightly with $\frac{1}{4}$ cup sugar and the vanilla in a heavy-bottomed saucepan. Put the egg yolks and remaining sugar in another saucepan. Beat the mixture until pale and creamy. Add the warmed cream, little by little. Return to the pan, place over a very gentle heat and stir until the custard thickens. Remove from the heat and leave to cool.

When the custard is cold, add the liqueur and put in an ice cream maker. Freeze for about 4 hours. Alternatively, freeze in a freezerproof container, whisking gently twice to obtain a smooth texture.

About 30 minutes before serving, cut the top off the melons. Remove the seeds from the middle, and using a melon baller, or teaspoon, make little balls from the melon flesh; chill. Put the melon shells to one side.

Take the ice cream out of the freezer. Make some balls of the ice cream. Fill the melon shells with the ice cream balls and the melon balls. Decorate with a few pieces of shredded chocolate. Serve on a bed of crushed ice.

Pear Sherbet

Serves 4 to 6

2 lb Comice pears
$\frac{1}{2}$ cup sugar
$\frac{2}{3}$ cup water
2 lemons
2 tablespoons Poire William
(pear eau-de-vie) or brandy

Peel $1\frac{1}{2}$ lb of the pears. Cut them into quarters, and remove the core and seeds. Put the sugar and water into a saucepan. Bring slowly to a boil, then add the pieces of pear. Simmer for 8 to 10 minutes and leave to cool. Squeeze one of the lemons. Put the pears and the syrup into a blender or food processor with the lemon juice and pear brandy. Blend well together until smooth. Pour the mixture into an ice cream maker and freeze.

Chill a sufficient number of sundae dishes for your guests in the refrigerator. About 1 hour before serving, peel the rest of the pears. Cut them into quarters, remove the core and seeds, and cut into small pieces. Pour over the juice of the second lemon. Leave to macerate.

Just before serving, take the sherbet out of the freezer. Make balls of the sherbet and put one or two in each dish. Decorate with the pieces of pear. You can pour on some extra pear brandy if you like. Serve immediately.

Chocolate and Chestnut Ice Cream

Serves 5

1 cup milk
1 vanilla bean
3 egg yolks
6 tablespoons sugar
3 oz (3 squares) semisweet
  chocolate
8 oz canned chestnut purée
⅔ cup heavy cream
DECORATION
1 cup heavy cream
¼ cup sugar
chocolate coffee beans (optional)

First make a custard. Bring the milk to a boil with the split vanilla bean and leave to infuse. Beat the egg yolks with the sugar and pour in the hot strained milk, beating continuously. Return to the saucepan and cook over a very gentle heat, stirring constantly, until the custard coats the back of a spoon. Leave to cool completely.

Break the chocolate into a heavy-bottomed saucepan and melt in a bain-marie. Or melt in a bowl placed over a pan of simmering water. Leave to cool slightly, then stir into the custard. Add the chestnut purée. Whip the cream and fold in. Freeze in an ice cream maker.

Chill some sundae dishes. For the decoration whip the cream with the sugar.

Take the ice cream out of the freezer. Divide between the chilled dishes. Pipe the whipped cream on top. Decorate with chocolate coffee beans, if obtainable.

Champagne Ice Cream

Serves 4

1¼ cups water
1 cup sugar
2 cups brut champagne
3 tablespoons orange juice
1 tablespoon brandy
1¼ cups heavy cream
1½ pints strawberries

Put the water into a saucepan. Add the sugar and dissolve over a gentle heat, then bring to a boil. Leave to cool slightly. Add the champagne, orange juice and brandy to the syrup. Whip half the cream and add to the mixture. Pour into an ice cream maker and freeze. Alternatively, freeze in a freezerproof container, whisking twice during freezing to obtain a smooth texture.

Wash and hull the strawberries. Then cut in half. Take the ice cream out of the freezer. Fill chilled sundae dishes with the ice cream. Add the strawberry halves and then pour a little of the remaining cream into each dish. Decorate with the rest of the strawberries and the remaining cream, whipped and piped into whirls.

The cream, part of which is reserved until the last moment, adds lightness to the ice cream, making the whole dessert much smoother.

Red Currant and Raspberry Granita

Serves 6

1½ pints red currants
1 pint raspberries
3 tablespoons framboise
   (raspberry eau-de-vie) or
   kirsch
1 cup sugar
juice of 1 lemon
DECORATION
small bunches of red currants
sprigs of fresh mint

Wash the red currants and strip them from the stalks. Put them in a large bowl with the raspberries. Pour over the framboise and macerate for 30 minutes. At the end of this period, put the fruit and liqueur into a blender or food processor with the sugar and the lemon juice. Blend to a purée, then sieve this purée to remove the seeds.

Pour the mixture into an ice cube tray or other freezerproof container and freeze for several hours. Stir and beat the mixture regularly with a fork, pulling away the edges as soon as they freeze.

As soon as the granita has completely crystallized, fill some sundae dishes with balls of the granita. Decorate with a few bunches of red currants and a few fresh mint leaves.

Cook's tips
Out of season you can, of course, use frozen fruit.

To make a granita really smooth, do not stint on the sugar, otherwise it will become dry and solid pieces of ice will form. The smoothness depends on the sugar, which helps to emulsify the mixture.

You can make other granitas from red fruit using this recipe for example: blackberries and alpine strawberries with red currants; strawberries and raspberries; raspberries and lemons; strawberries and oranges; red currants and black currants.

You can serve a red fruit granita with homemade egg custard sauce, raspberry sauce or homemade red currant syrup. To make this, wash 3 pints red currants, drain them and strip them from the stalks. Purée in a blender or food processor, then push this purée through a fine sieve. Pour into a saucepan, add ⅔ cup sugar and mix over a gentle heat. When the sugar has dissolved, turn the heat up and allow the syrup to boil for a few minutes. Plunge a slotted spoon into the syrup – blow through the holes, and bubbles should form. Leave to cool, then pour into bottles. This syrup can be kept in a cool place for up to 12 days.

Apricot Sherbet

Serves 4 to 6

2 lb apricots
⅔ cup sugar
1 cup water
slices of apricot for decoration
SAUCE
½ lb apricots
⅔ cup water
¼ cup sugar
1 teaspoon lemon juice

Wipe the apricots. Halve them and remove the pits. Put the sugar and water into a saucepan and dissolve the sugar over a gentle heat, then bring to a boil. Add the apricots, cover and poach over a gentle heat for 10 minutes. Leave to cool. Purée the apricots with their syrup in a blender or food processor.

Pour the mixture into a fluted mold and freeze for 1 hour. Beat the fruit pulp with a fork. Put back in the freezer. Repeat twice, then freeze completely.

Meanwhile, make the sauce. Wipe the apricots, halve them and remove the pits. Put the apricot halves into a saucepan with the water and the sugar and cook for about 10 minutes over a gentle heat until the apricots are soft. Remove from the heat and leave to cool. Purée the apricots in the blender or food procesor, then push through a sieve. Add the lemon juice.

Unmold the sherbet onto a serving dish. Decorate with slices of apricot and serve immediately with the sauce handed separately.

Summer Pudding

Serves 6

2½–3 pints mixed soft fruit (for
    example raspberries, cherries,
    red currants, black currants,
    blackberries)
¾ cup sugar
10 slices stale bread, crusts
    removed
1 cup heavy cream

Trim the fruit, remove the stalks and pits and wash as
necessary. Put the black currants and the sugar into a
saucepan. Cook over a gentle heat for about 5 minutes
until the juice runs. Add the raspberries, cherries, red
currants and blackberries. Simmer for another 5
minutes.

Line the bottom and sides of a mold with the slices of
bread. Using a slotted spoon, fill the mold with the fruit
to half the depth. Put a layer of bread on top, then the
rest of the fruit. Finish with another layer of bread. Pour
over the rest of the fruit juice so that it soaks into the
bread. Put a plate on top of the mold and place a weight
such as a heavy can on top. Chill in the refrigerator
overnight.

Just before serving, whip the cream. Remove the
weight and the plate. Carefully slide a knife blade
around the edge of the cake. Unmold onto a serving dish.
Decorate the top and around the base with piped
whipped cream.

Red Currant and Raspberry Sherbet

Serves 6

½ cup sugar
1½ cups water
1 pint red currants
1½ cups raspberries
2 teaspoons lemon juice
1 cup heavy cream

Make a syrup with the sugar and 1¼ cups water. Bring to a boil, then leave to cool completely.

Wash the red currants and drain them. Reserve a few small bunches for decoration and strip the remainder off the stalks. Put the red currants and raspberries into a saucepan. Add the remaining water and cook over a gentle heat until they become mushy. Push through a sieve and put to one side.

When the sugar syrup is cold, stir it into the fruit purée, together with the lemon juice. Pour into a charlotte mold. Freeze for 1 hour, then beat the sherbet with a fork. Re-freeze and repeat the beating twice.

Whip the cream. Use to fill a pastry bag. Unmold the sherbet onto a serving dish. Decorate with piped whipped cream and the reserved bunches of red currants. Serve immediately. You can also make this sherbet with a mixture of red currants and black currants, strawberries and raspberries, or red currants and blackberries.

Multicolor Sundaes

Serves 6

1 lb bananas
1 tablespoon lemon juice
2 tablespoons white rum
$\frac{1}{3}$ cup brown sugar
$2\frac{1}{2}$ cups heavy cream
2 oz (2 squares) semisweet
  chocolate
1 (16-oz) can evaporated milk,
  chilled overnight in the
  refrigerator
$1\frac{1}{2}$ cups confectioners' sugar
1 tablespoon brandy
1 cup crushed macaroons
$\frac{1}{2}$ cup sherry
$\frac{1}{4}$ cup shelled hazelnuts
DECORATION
chocolate coffee beans
langues de chat cookies

Banana ice cream Peel the bananas and purée them in a blender or food processor, adding the lemon juice, rum and sugar. Whip half the cream, then fold into the banana purée. Pour into an ice cream maker and freeze.
Chocolate and brandy ice cream Grate the chocolate into little shavings. Beat the evaporated milk until it is thick and frothy. Add half of the confectioners' sugar, little by little, beating all the time. Fold in the grated chocolate and brandy. Pour into an ice cream maker and freeze.
Macaroon ice cream Put the macaroons in a bowl and pour over the sherry. Leave them to soak up the alcohol for 20 minutes. Chop the hazelnuts. Whip the remaining cream. Fold in the remaining confectioners' sugar, then add the macaroons and the hazelnuts. Pour into an ice cream maker and freeze.

Chill the dishes and put scoops of banana, chocolate and macaroon ice cream in them. (You may add other flavors if you like.) Decorate with chocolate coffee beans and langues de chat cookies.

Honey Ice Cream

Serves 4

1 cup milk
$\frac{1}{3}$ cup good quality honey (for
   example acacia or heather)
2 egg yolks
$\frac{2}{3}$ cup heavy cream

Boil the milk in a saucepan. As soon as it starts to rise up the pan, add the honey. Mix well, stirring briskly with a small whisk. Bring to a boil again. Put the egg yolks into a small bowl and beat with a whisk. Add the cream. Mix together, still stirring with the whisk. Add the milk little by little, then strain the mixture through a fine sieve into another bowl. Leave to cool.

Pour the mixture into an ice cream maker and freeze. Alternatively, freeeze in a freezerproof container, whisking twice during freezing to obtain a smooth texture. Make balls of the ice cream and serve in chilled sundae dishes.

Cook's tips

This creamy, straw-colored ice cream can be used as an unusual substitute for vanilla ice cream.

A sauce made from red fruit such as strawberries and raspberries can be served with it. Purée with confectioners' sugar to taste.

You can fill miniature cream puffs with this ice cream. Cut them carefully in half with a serrated knife. Fill with a teaspoon of honey ice cream. Put the halves back together and arrange on a plate or serving dish.

You can also serve the ice cream with pears in syrup, with a hot chocolate sauce poured over. Briskly heat $\frac{1}{3}$ cup cocoa powder, $\frac{3}{4}$ cup sugar and 1 cup water in a saucepan, stirring until you have a smooth even paste. Bring to a boil and simmer for 3 minutes. Then add 2 tablespoons butter. Cook for 4 minutes longer, beating all the time to prevent sticking. Keep the sauce warm in a bain-marie and pour over just before serving. You can keep this sauce in a plastic tub, well sealed, for one or two weeks in the refrigerator. It just needs to be heated in a bain-marie, beating it, with a teaspoon of cold water to make it smooth.

Iced Lemon Soufflé

Serves 6

2 lemons
1 orange
$\frac{1}{2}$ cup sugar
2 tablespoons water
3 egg whites
$\frac{2}{3}$ cup heavy cream, whipped

DECORATION

10 ladyfingers
1 glacé cherry
2 tablespoons confectioners'
  sugar (optional)

Scrub the lemons carefully and dry. Grate the lemon rinds finely, then squeeze the lemons and the orange. Make a syrup with the sugar, water, fruit juice and grated rind. Bring to a boil and boil for 5 minutes.

Beat the egg whites to firm peaks. Gradually add the boiling syrup, beating constantly until cold.

Wrap a strip of wax paper around a soufflé dish so that it rises about 1 inch above the rim. Keep in place with a rubber band or a piece of tape. Whip the cream in a very cold bowl. Carefully fold together the egg white mixture and the whipped cream. Fill the soufflé dish up to the top of the paper collar and place in the freezer.

After 3 hours, carefully remove the paper collar.

Decorate the top of the soufflé with ladyfingers trimmed to make flower petals around a glacé cherry. Sprinkle with confectioners' sugar. Serve immediately.

Frosted Oranges and Lemons

Serves 5

ORANGES
5 large, thick-skinned oranges
$\frac{1}{4}$ cup sugar (approximately)
LEMONS
5 thick-skinned lemons
$\frac{1}{4}$ cup sugar (approximately)
DECORATION (OPTIONAL)
10 glacé cherries
10 sugar roses
$\frac{2}{3}$ cup heavy cream, whipped

Wash and wipe the oranges. Halve without cutting right through. Hollow them out with a sharp-edged spoon, without going through the rind, then chill. Hollow out the lemons in the same way.

Put the orange and lemon flesh separately through a food mill using a fine cutting disk. Measure the juice collected and add $\frac{1}{4}$ cup sugar per 1 cup juice. Mix well with a whisk and pour the mixtures into two ice cream makers or one which has two compartments. Freeze.

When the sherbet is frozen, use it to fill the fruit shells. Decorate as shown. You can serve the frosted fruit on a bed of crushed ice or a plinth of ice with flowers.

Coconut Sherbet

Serves 8

1 cup sugar
$\frac{1}{2}$ cup water
1 quart coconut milk, *or* 2$\frac{1}{3}$ cups
   shredded coconut, soaked in
   1 quart water and strained
$\frac{1}{8}$ teaspoon vanilla
1 (8-oz) can cherries in syrup
1 lemon, sliced, for decoration

Put the sugar and water in a saucepan. Heat gently until the sugar dissolves, then bring to a boil and leave to cool. Mix the coconut milk, the vanilla and the sugar syrup in a bowl. Pour into an ice cream maker and freeze. Alternatively, freeze in a freezerproof container, whisking several times during freezing to obtain a smooth texture. Drain the cherries, retaining the juice, then pit them.

As soon as the sherbet has frozen, transfer it to a fluted mold, folding in half the cherries. Press down well and put back in the freezer for 1 hour.

Just before serving, unmold the sherbet onto a serving dish. Surround with the rest of the cherries. Add a little syrup and decorate with lemon slices. Serve immediately.

Strawberry Yogurt Mold

Serves 6

$\frac{1}{2}$ cup sugar
$\frac{1}{2}$ cup water
$1\frac{1}{2}$ pints strawberries
$1\frac{1}{4}$ cups plain yogurt
2 tablespoons kirsch
$\frac{2}{3}$ cup heavy cream

Put the sugar and water into a saucepan. Heat gently until the sugar has dissolved, then bring the syrup to a boil. Leave to cool. Hull the strawberries, then wash and drain them. Reserve a few for decoration. Purée the rest in a blender or food processor. Fold the yogurt, sugar syrup and kirsch into this purée.

Pour the mixture into a fluted mold. Freeze for $1\frac{1}{2}$ hours, by which time the mixture should be frozen around the edges. At the end of this time, whip the cream. Fold it into the strawberry mixture. Put back in the freezer and freeze for another hour. Beat the mixture with a fork to get rid of any crystals. Leave to freeze for another hour. Repeat the operation once more, then leave in the freezer until the ice cream is completely frozen.

Just before serving, dip the mold very briefly in hot water and unmold the ice cream onto a serving dish. Cut the remaining strawberries in half and use to decorate the top of the ice cream and around the dish.

Melons Filled with Black Currant Sherbet

Serves 6

1 cup sugar
1¼ cups water
2 pints black currants
juice of 1 lemon
2 tablespoons crème de cassis
  (black currant liqueur)
DECORATION
3 small melons
1 cup heavy cream
1½ cups raspberries

Put the sugar and 1 cup water in a heavy-based saucepan. Dissolve the sugar and then bring to a boil. Remove from the heat and leave to cool completely.

Meanwhile, trim and wash the black currants. Put the currants in a saucepan with the remaining water. Cook over a gentle heat until they become mushy. Push them through a sieve. Put to one side.

When the syrup is cold, fold it into the black currant purée, together with the lemon juice and the liqueur. Pour into an ice cream maker and freeze. Alternatively, freeze in a freezerproof container, whisking twice during freezing to obtain a smooth texture.

Just before serving, cut the melons in half. Carefully remove the seeds. Keep the melons in a cool place. Whip the cream.

Take the sherbet out of the freezer. Make some balls with an ice cream scoop and put two in each melon half. Add a few fresh raspberries. Fill a pastry bag with the whipped cream and decorate each melon half with whirls of whipped cream. Serve immediately.

Variation
Replace the black currant sherbet by a cherry one. Drain 1 (16-oz) can cherries in syrup, reserving the syrup. Add enough water to it to obtain 2½ cups liquid. Heat this liquid with ½ cup sugar. Bring to a boil and leave to cool. Pit the cherries and purée them in a blender or food processor, then push them through a sieve. Add some cherry brandy. Freeze as for the black currant sherbet. Serve this sherbet on large slices of watermelon.

Cook's tip
Sherbet always takes longer to freeze when a small glass of alcohol is added to enhance the flavor so allow for this when planning the meal.

Iced Praline Soufflé

Serves 5 to 6

3 egg yolks
1 cup sugar
1 cup milk
1 cup water
1 cup blanched almonds
1¼ cups heavy cream
DECORATION
¼ cup liquid caramel
16 small meringues (optional)

Beat the egg yolks with half the sugar. Bring the milk to a boil and pour over the egg mixture, beating continuously. Pour the mixture back into the saucepan and heat very gently, stirring, until thickened.

Dissolve the rest of the sugar over a gentle heat in the water, then add the almonds. Bring to a boil and cook for 10 minutes or until you have a light caramel. Grease a metal baking sheet and pour the caramel over it. Leave to harden. When this praline is hard, grind it in a blender to reduce it to tiny pieces. Add to the custard. Whip the cream and fold it into the custard.

Surround a soufflé dish with a strip of wax paper (rising about 1 inch above the rim). Keep in place with a piece of tape. Pour in the mixture and place in the freezer. Carefully beat the mixture every 2 hours. Freeze completely. Serve as shown.

Iced Coffee with Vanilla Ice Cream

Serves 4

2 cups milk
1 vanilla bean
4 egg yolks
1 cup granulated sugar
2 cups very strong coffee
1 cup heavy cream
½ cup confectioners' sugar

First make a custard. Bring the milk to a boil with the vanilla bean. Leave to infuse. Beat the egg yolks with 6 tablespoons of the granulated sugar, then pour in the hot milk, continuing to whisk. Return to the saucepan and stir over a very low heat until the custard thickens. Leave to cool. Remove the vanilla bean and place the custard in an ice cream maker. Freeze for 3 hours.

About 1 hour before serving, dissolve the remaining granulated sugar in the coffee. Leave to cool, then chill in the freezer. Whip the cream and sweeten with the confectioners' sugar. Keep in a cool place.

Chill some glass sundae dishes in the refrigerator. Take the ice cream out of the freezer, together with the iced coffee. Pour 2 tablespoons of the coffee into the bottom of each dish. Make balls of the vanilla ice cream and put 2 in each dish on top of the coffee. Cover with the whipped cream and serve immediately.

Iced Zabaglione

Serves 4

5 egg yolks
$\frac{1}{2}$ cup sugar
$1\frac{1}{4}$ cups Marsala or dry sherry
TO SERVE
1 pineapple
$\frac{2}{3}$ cup glacé cherries

Place the egg yolks in a bowl. Add the sugar and beat vigorously until the mixture becomes pale and creamy. Add the Marsala or sherry. Prepare a bain-marie. Place the bowl in it and place over a gentle heat. Continue stirring the mixture; the water in the bain-marie should not boil, but barely simmer. After 15 minutes you will have a smooth, frothy cream with a good consistency. The zabaglione can also be cooked in a bowl over a pan of simmering water. Pour the zabaglione into another container and leave to cool, then freeze for 1 hour.

Slice the pineapple. Remove the hard core in the center. Cut each slice in half. Arrange the pineapple slices on a serving dish. Decorate with glacé cherries. Serve with the zabaglione.

You can also serve this zabaglione with other kinds of fruit – kiwi fruit, poached pears, peaches, strawberries, raspberries etc.

Grapefruit and Mint Ice Cream

Serves 6

3 grapefruits
½ cup sugar
1 tablespoon chopped fresh
  mint
1¼ cups plain yogurt
⅔ cup heavy cream
DECORATION
1 orange, peeled and segmented
1 kiwi fruit, peeled and sliced

Remove the peel and pith from the grapefruits over a bowl in order to collect the juice. Divide them into segments and take off the skin around each segment. Cut the flesh into little pieces. Put to one side.

Pour the grapefruit juice into a measuring cup and add enough water to make it up to 1 cup. Pour this liquid into a saucepan, add the sugar and dissolve over a gentle heat. Bring to a boil and leave to cool. Stir the grapefruit pieces, the finely chopped mint and the yogurt into the sugar syrup. Whip the cream and fold carefully into the syrup.

Pour the mixture into a mold and freeze for 1 hour. At the end of this time, beat the mixture with a fork and put back in the freezer. Repeat the beating twice. Leave to freeze.

Unmold the ice cream onto a serving dish. Decorate with the orange segments and the slices of kiwi fruit.

Coffee Granita

Serves 4 to 6

$\frac{3}{4}$ cup sugar
2 cups water
2 cups strong coffee
2 tablespoons rum or brandy *or*
  $\frac{1}{2}$ teaspoon vanilla
1$\frac{1}{4}$ cups Crème Fraîche (page
  398)
$\frac{2}{3}$ cup light cream

Put the sugar and water into a heavy-based saucepan. Mix well and melt over a gentle heat. Dip a brush into the hot water and wipe the sides of the pan with it. But do not stop stirring. When all the sugar has melted and the syrup is clear, stop stirring. Turn up the heat and bring the syrup to a boil. Boil for 1 minute, then take the saucepan off the heat.

Flavor the coffee with rum, brandy or vanilla, according to taste. Pour the coffee into the saucepan containing the syrup. Stir the mixture well and leave to cool. Pour the coffee mixture into some ice cube trays and leave to cool completely, then freeze.

When the coffee granita starts freezing around the edges, about 1 hour later, take the trays out of the freezer and mix the contents well with a wooden spatula. When the consistency is perfectly even, put the trays back in the freezer. Leave the granita to freeze for another 2 hours, approximately, when it will take the form of large ice crystals, without being solidified. Crush with the spatula to break it down to small crystals. Keep the granita cold until ready to serve.

Whip the crème fraîche and use to fill a pastry bag. Put a little light cream in the bottom of some very cold sundae dishes, then spoon out the granita into the dishes. Decorate with whipped cream. Serve chilled.

Cook's tip
To make good coffee, the beans should be ground at the last moment – that way their flavor will be more intense. The amount of coffee to use depends on how strong you like your coffee and how finely the coffee is ground; the finer the coffee is ground, the more flavor it will have.

Good coffee is made with cold water, freshly drawn. To get the best possible flavor, never pour boiling water onto the coffee, as this would release the bitter and astringent substances contained in the beans. Let the water barely come to a boil and then cool for 10 seconds before using it.

Ginger Ice Cream

Serves 6

2 cups milk
1 teaspoon ground ginger
4 egg yolks
6 tablespoons sugar
⅔ cup heavy cream, whipped
½ cup coarsely chopped
   crystallized ginger *or* ginger
   preserved in syrup
CHOCOLATE SAUCE
2 oz (2 squares) semisweet
   chocolate
½ cup sugar
1 tablespoon cocoa powder
5 tablespoons boiling water
2 tablespoons butter
1 tablespoon cold water

Heat the milk with the ground ginger in a heavy-based saucepan. Beat the egg yolks with the sugar and pour in the hot milk, stirring all the time. Return the mixture to the saucepan and heat very gently, stirring constantly, until the custard coats the back of a spoon. Whip the cream. Add the ginger and the cream.

Pour the mixture into a mold. Freeze for 1 hour. Beat the ice cream, then return to the freezer. Repeat the operation twice, then freeze completely.

Prepare the sauce. Break the chocolate into small pieces and place in a heavy-based saucepan. Add the sugar, cocoa powder and boiling water. Cook over a gentle heat until the chocolate has melted. Off the heat, add the butter, little by little, and the cold water.

Unmold the ginger ice cream onto a serving dish. Decorate with pieces of crystallized ginger. Serve immediately with the hot chocolate sauce.

Peach Melba

Serves 4

1 cup milk
1 vanilla bean
3 egg yolks
½ cup granulated sugar
⅔ cup Crème Fraîche (page 398)
4 just ripe peaches
½ cup flaked almonds
1½ pints raspberries
½ cup confectioners' sugar
juice of 1 lemon
⅔ cup heavy cream, lightly
   whipped

Bring the milk to a boil with the vanilla bean and leave to infuse. Beat the egg yolks with the granulated sugar, then pour in the hot strained milk. Return the mixture to the saucepan and heat very gently, stirring constantly, until the custard coats the back of a spoon. Cool. As soon as the custard is cold, add the crème fraîche to it. Mix together well. Pour into an ice cream maker and freeze.

Peel the peaches, having scalded them for 1 minute. Cut in half and remove the pits. Brown the almonds in a skillet or under the broiler. Put the raspberries, confectioners' sugar and lemon juice into a blender or food processor and blend well together, then sieve.

Make balls of the vanilla ice cream. Place a half peach in each dish, then one or two scoops of ice cream, then the other half of the peach. Spoon over a little whipped cream, sprinkle with toasted almonds and then pour over the raspberry sauce. Serve immediately.

Viennese Coffee

Serves 5

⅓ cup coffee beans, coarsely
   ground
1 cup milk
⅔ cup granulated sugar
3 egg yolks
⅔ cup Crème Fraîche (page 398)
1¼ cups heavy cream
1 tablespoon confectioners'
   sugar

Add the coffee beans to the milk, sweetened with 6 tablespoons of the granulated sugar. Boil, then set aside for 10 minutes. Strain the milk through a fine sieve and reheat gently. Beat the egg yolks with the remaining granulated sugar. Pour in the hot milk, continuing to beat. Return the mixture to the saucepan and heat gently, stirring constantly, until the custard coats the back of a spoon. Add the Crème fraîche and leave to cool for 30 minutes, stirring from time to time. Pour into an ice cream maker and freeze.

A few minutes before serving whip the heavy cream with the confectioners' sugar. Use to fill a pastry bag.

Pipe a layer of whipped cream into the bottom of chilled dessert glasses, then add a layer of coffee ice cream. To complete the dish, pipe whirls of whipped cream around the edges of the glasses. Serve immediately.

Mandarin Delights

Serves 4

1½ lb mandarins
¾ cup confectioners' sugar, sifted
1¼ cups plain yogurt
½ cup light cream
4 mandarins for decoration
1 (12-oz) can litchis in syrup

Wash the mandarins, wipe them and grate the rind coarsely. Cut the mandarins in half and squeeze to obtain the juice (about 1¼ cups). Add the grated rind and leave to macerate for 1 hour.

Add the sugar to this juice, beating with a whisk. Then blend in the yogurt, little by little, followed by the cream. Pour into an ice cream maker and place in the freezer. Freeze until the mixture has set.

Remove peel and pith from the four reserved mandarins, then cut out the segments, leaving the membrane behind. Drain the litchis. Chill four sundae dishes in the refrigerator for a few minutes.

Take the ice cream out of the freezer and the dishes from the refrigerator. Scoop out balls of the ice cream and arrange them in the dishes with the litchis. Decorate with the mandarin segments. Serve immediately.

INDEX